"This book is unmissable, because it gives sense to trauma reactions. On reading it, you suddenly understand the logic behind panic, OCD, dissociation …"

Olga Castanyer, clinical psychologist, writer, and director of the "Serendipity" Collection for publisher Desclee de Brouwer. Bilbao

"I wholeheartedly recommend *Attachment and Psychopathology: Anxiety and Its Origin* by Manuel Hernández Pacheco. This book brilliantly bridges attachment theory, neurobiology, and clinical practice through the groundbreaking PARCUVE model, offering a powerful lens to understand and treat anxiety disorders rooted in trauma. Its evidence-based insights and practical case studies have enriched my work with patients, providing a clear roadmap to address attachment wounds that amplify traumatic stress. For trauma professionals seeking innovative, actionable strategies to elevate their practice, this book is an essential resource. Read it – you'll find transformative tools to better serve your clients."

Oscar Joe Rivas, PhD., executive director of Instituto Newman, México.

"The author's erudite knowledge about biology, psychology, trauma, and attachment is intertwined with his profound life experience, spanning hundreds of peoples and cultures around the world, to present us with this extraordinary work written by Manuel Hernández, which is a must-read for all those seeking to expand their understanding and transform their approach to the fundamental issues this book addresses."

Esteban Gómez Muzzio, Ph.D., executive director of Fundación América por la Infancia, Chile.

Attachment and Psychopathology

This English translation of the Spanish bestseller *Apego y psicopatología* is an interdisciplinary study on how the early years of our lives can influence the way we view ourselves and others.

The book is split into two parts, the first exploring the theoretical foundations of the PARCUVE model created by the author, which describes the importance of the early years of our lives on the origin of many psychological pathologies. The second addresses the treatment of emotions, feeling, and behaviors associated with psychological disorders from a body–mind–brain integrative approach, as well as through different therapeutic approaches that have proven their efficacy in the past. It provides readers with tools to intervene with patients from different angles, and thus attack psychological pathologies at the root, beyond the symptoms.

Enriched with real-life examples to assist in readers' understanding of the neurobiological and emotional processes, *Attachment and Psychopathology* is an ideal resource for psychologists and psychology students, psychiatrists and psychiatry students, and social workers.

Manuel Hernández Pacheco is a licensed psychologist and biologist with expertise in both areas to explain psychopathology and deep-rooted trauma. He is also the president of the Spanish Trauma Association and travels worldwide sharing and teaching his therapeutic model, PARCUVE. He has written several books, including *Why Do the People I Love Hurt Me?; Attachment, Dissociation, and Trauma; Obsessive-Compulsive Disorder: An Addiction to Thought; Emotional Dependence and Toxic Relationships;* and *Identity and Psychopathology.*

Attachment and Psychopathology

Anxiety and its Origin

Manuel Hernández Pacheco

Translated by Victoria Rodríguez Rincón and Miriam Ramos Morrison

NEW YORK AND LONDON

Designed cover image: Getty Images

First published in English 2026
by Routledge
605 Third Avenue, New York, NY 10158

and by Routledge
4 Park Square, Milton Park, Abingdon, Oxon, OX14 4RN

Routledge is an imprint of the Taylor & Francis Group, an informa business

Published in Spanish by Editorial Desclée De Brouwer 2017

ISBN: 9781041086444 (hbk)
ISBN: 9781041086437 (pbk)
ISBN: 9781003646341 (ebk)

DOI: 10.4324/9781003646341

Typeset in Times New Roman
by Deanta Global Publishing Services, Chennai, India

**This book is dedicated to the two women of my life:
Laura and Cristina**

Contents

List of Figures

List of Tables

Acknowledgments

This book could not have existed without the trust my clients have placed in me during my years of experience as a therapist. Behind this book is a lot of reading, but above all there is my experience of connecting with other human beings who have opened their hearts and abandoned their fears so that I could give them the confidence to face their pain and fears.

Lucía Martínez has been present since the day I started writing this book. I was continually asking for constructive criticism, and I always got the same answer: “Keep on going, you are doing very well.”

José Ángel Castillo was also critical with the initial drafts, and I want to thank him for his trust in me when this book was just a project.

Miriam Ramos has been instrumental in the editing of the initial chapters and an immense support in helping me improve aspects of editing this book.

Finally, I want to thank Arun Mansukhani, my friend and teacher, for having sparked my interest in attachment; his supervision and classes are always a masterclass. The UNED (National Distance Learning University) Master’s Degree in Eye Movement Desensitization and Reprocessing (EMDR) and Psychopathology was largely the beginning of this book, and its faculty members were of much help for me to learn and develop many concepts. I cannot but highlight the teachings of, among others, Anabel Gonzalez, who guided my master’s degree; Dolores Mosquera; and Natalia Seíjo.

Francisca Guerrero has been the foundation on which the EMDR Association in Spain has been built. Both her teachings and the different training programs she constantly brings to our country have allowed for much of the learning that was necessary for my clinical skills to develop and for writing this book. I wanted it to start with her prologue.

My friends and classmates and many teachers who have helped me lay down the bricks to further delve into the study of biology and psychology can see flashes of their immaterial presence in this book. Thank you all.

Prologue

It is with great satisfaction that I write the prologue for this book. I have seen the author grow as both a human being and therapist over the last few years after his solid training in the Eye Movement Desensitization and Reprocessing (EMDR) therapeutic approach, and I have seen him mature after finishing a Master's Degree in Psychotherapy with EMDR.

This is a book that consolidates his years of learning as a psychotherapist, starting with hypnosis, mindfulness, and other psychotherapy approaches, and gradually learning how to superbly integrate these to help his patients in the clinical setting through the use of EMDR therapy. This book is the result of both his clinical and research experience. In addition to involving many hours of consultation and study, there is no doubt that this book delves into two areas which, for me, are crucial in the field of psychotherapy: attachment and emotions. He approaches them from a neurobiological perspective without forgetting the way in which we perceive and are affected by our first years of life: our beliefs.

The PARCUVE model is the foundation on which the treatment with his patients will be subsequently substantiated. Different approaches will be used to work with emotions, trauma, case comprehension, patient preparation, dissociation, resources to stabilize the person before working with parts, defenses, and phobias, which may emerge when addressing the problems. All of this is presented without forgetting the importance of working with the body as a reflection of what goes on in our present lives.

In the section dedicated to treatment, he focuses on and describes the Adaptive Information Processing (AIP) model, the construct which underpins EMDR, with clear and didactic examples obtained from his patients in his work as a clinician.

In my opinion, this is a highly recommended book for professionals whom it might help to understand the problems of their patients from a more integrative approach, as well as for the general public, whom it might help to see the origin of their fears, anxiety, blame, shame, and so on. Throughout their lives, patients may feel these emotions without being aware of their neurological and social origin.

It is important to highlight the author's training, first as a biologist and later on as a psychologist, which makes this read highly interesting and practical for professionals working in the mental health field. The book is accessible to every kind of public in general and to psychotherapists in particular. I hope all of you, therapists and readers, will find it useful.

Francisca García Guerrero
President of the EMDR Spanish Association EMDR Europe
Accredited Senior Trainer

Introduction

I do not remember my childhood as a happy one. I felt the loneliness I so often see in my patients. Perhaps to calm down this feeling, I developed an insatiable curiosity and dedicated hours and hours to reading, almost obsessively: novels, mythology, and books on biology or chess. I now believe that the thirst for knowledge helped me find a haven in reading, a refuge from the things I did not like about my surroundings.

Studying biology was something that happened irremediably; it combined my thirst for knowledge and my love of nature. Studying psychology, instead, was an accident, something that happened almost by chance. But the random combination of these factors conformed for me that the sciences of the mind and biology were merged into one.

When I started working with Eye Movement Desensitization and Reprocessing (EMDR) three years ago, a whole new world opened up to me both personally and professionally. I discovered many aspects of myself that I did not know about and that helped me understand and assist my patients.

Studying the workings of the mind lead me to investigate everything related to attachment and the importance of the first years of our life on the rest of our existence. From there, studying the relationship between biology and trauma was only a step away.

This book is the ensemble of a multitude of readings on different aspects of the workings of the brain and the influence it has on our mind and our relationships with others. I have written the book I would have liked to have found a few years ago when I started gathering information about all these topics. I have presented it as a journey in which I start with our emotions and relationships with others during the first years of our life; it is a journey that shapes the way our mind works.

I have divided the volume into two parts. In the first one I describe the theoretical foundations of the model I have created to describe the importance of the early years of our lives on the origin of many psychological pathologies. In Chapter 1, I explain the close relationship that exists between our body and our brain and how it influences the realm of psychology: the mind.

In Chapter 2, I speak about the more primitive and relevant emotions for survival: fear. When fear appears, all emotional systems lose their importance, for the priority becomes survival. The objective of Chapter 3 is twofold: 1) seeking for the figures that can provide protection and 2) explaining how the cerebral areas we share with all other mammals regulate our emotional development in connection with our caregivers.

If there was no protection and security during childhood, the child will have to find strategies so it can still relate to its caregivers, trying to make the relationship as stable as possible. These adaptations in the personality of the child due to the behavior of the caregivers will be covered in Chapter 4. Different strategies for achieving comfort in childhood will give rise to different attachment styles.

Chapter 5 explains how the regulatory mechanisms that are developed to obtain a sense of control may become pathological when they cease to become adaptive. They become unconscious due to repetition. When repetition takes place unwillingly, it becomes a disease. Learning when, how, and why it was necessary to act that way allows us to know the individuals behind the symptoms so we can help them understand themselves and mentalize, thus regaining control of their life.

The PARCUVE model that I develop in Chapter 6 describes how the rupture in the emotional relationship with the attachment figures leads to the emergence of unconscious emotions such as fear, anger, blame, and shame that turn out to be toxic for the person. The thoughts and behaviors necessary to manage these emotions and their associated anxiety are what lead to pathology.

In the second part, I describe the treatment for these emotions, feelings, and behaviors associated with psychological disorders from a body–mind–brain integrative approach, as well as through different therapeutic approaches that have proven their efficacy in the past.

Chapter 7 describes the elements common to all therapeutic approaches. These are cross-disciplinary matters which we find in every patient. The therapeutic alliance, the requests our clients bring to the session, and the emotions that we have looked at in the previous chapters constitute the elements of this chapter.

In Chapter 8, I explain the different treatments that work with the various aspects of the mind. I believe that taking the best of each helps apply a multidisciplinary treatment, therefore becoming much more effective.

Trauma and memories that have been imprinted in the mind constitute a source of pain and suffering for our patients. I believe EMDR is the most effective therapy that currently exists for the treatment of trauma. Chapter 9 is dedicated entirely to this therapy that has been such a help in my professional career.

Chapter 10 explains how crucial it is to perform proper data gathering to be able to better know the patients and learn about the circumstances that have led to their current situation. Alongside this stage, the foundation is laid for what will be the therapeutic process by explaining to the patient the different aspects of human psychology that will help them regain a sense of control. This is discussed in Chapter 11.

The dissociation of the personality is another element that every therapist interested in the field of trauma has to know in depth, theoretically as well as in practice, in order to work with the different aspects that characterize it. Chapter 12 explains why it happens and how to resolve it.

Chapter 13 explains how important it is to have professionals who can provide stabilization resources to their patients. These resources include mindfulness and hypnosis techniques.

Chapter 14 explains how the body stores memory of past experiences and how it is completely linked to what happens in the brain. Working with bodily sensations is a very powerful tool to stabilize and heal our patients.

Chapter 15 talks about how psychological defenses that were created unconsciously in the patient can be obstacles that have to be overcome during therapy in order to access the mental content that caused the pathology.

The end of any therapy comes with coping with situations, thoughts, behaviors, or emotions that have been avoided throughout the patient's illness (sometimes almost all of their life). Facing the fears, whatever they may be, is the goal to achieve a healthy mental balance.

The last chapter is devoted to explaining how the type of attachment of the patient influences the focus of the therapy and how the symptoms and personality disorders are the tip of the iceberg of pathological elements which caused the disease and which should be the goal of therapy.

Throughout the book, I have used the words *individual*, *patient*, or *person* indistinctly to lighten the text as is the case with the words *caregivers* or *parents*; I have used them as

Part 1

Theoretical Approach

1 Brain, Body, and Mind

Emotions and Cognition

Both our anatomy and physiology are the result of millions of years of evolution; a process that has been adding nerve structures that proved useful to those species that precede us at a phylogenetical level. The brain has continued to develop, maintaining structures and functions that proved useful for survival, and reaching ever more complex levels. For human beings, this has meant the development of cerebral structures that perform specific tasks, which have allowed, among other things, the emergence of language. This opened the possibility of establishing complex communications with other beings, of building tools, and of being able to adapt to various different ecosystems. This is what we understand as cognition, and it is a characteristic we do not share with any other animal species.

We also share many brain structures and functions with the beings that preceded us on the evolutionary scale. We have brain areas that regulate fear, reproduction, and feeding – regions that reptiles also have. With mammals, we also share the presence of "emotions," which help us nurture our offspring, be social animals, and modulate, with more or less success, our actions.

I do not exaggerate when I say that, on a psychological level, the implications of the previous sentence are huge. Human beings have to process information on two different levels: a cognitive one – through thought – and an emotional one. No other animal species can drive a car or conduct an orchestra, but they can feel emotions such as anger, fear, and attachment to their offspring. Emotions regulate a big part of our behavior and our thoughts, and often contradict what we know to be logical. As a human being, I am not alienated from this paradox. Like everyone else – and many times during the course of my life – I have done things I knew I would probably regret, yet was unable to stop myself.

The word emotion comes from the Latin word *emotio, emotionis,* which in turn derives from the verb *emovere*, meaning "movement or impulse," "that which moves towards something." Therefore, the etymology indicates that emotion is what makes us act or feel in accordance with certain internal (interoceptives) or external (exteroceptives) stimuli that we cannot voluntarily control. Emotions are unconscious and, unlike cognitions, cannot willingly be evoked.

DOI: 10.4324/9781003646341-2

They arise spontaneously according to different stimuli or – as we shall see later on – are mediated by our thoughts.

During my university years, incredible as it may seem, I never heard anyone speak in depth about emotions nor of the role they represent in our lives. In those days, the dominant paradigm was the cognitive school of thought, to which some notes on psychoanalysis were added. Afterwards, during my first years of post-graduate studies, I did not find anyone who talked about the importance of emotions, as if they were not relevant in therapy, even though they were present. Later on, I discovered that there are many authors who are currently studying emotions from a biological point of view and highlighting the dominant role they play in our lives and which they should play in the field of therapy.

One of the contemporary authors who most insists on the importance of emotions in psychological processes is Siegel (2002). He asserts that "*emotions represent dynamic processes created within the socially influenced, value-appraising process of the brain*" (p. 184). Emotions are vital for survival and all its implications, such as fear, searching for a mate, raising children, etc. They allow us to evaluate, in a conscious or unconscious way, the opportunities and risks that surround us in relation to ourselves and others.

Siegel (2002) indicates that emotions are the result of the subjective assessment of certain stimuli, which can be internal or external. Through emotions, therefore, we assess consciously or unconsciously whether a situation is more or less favorable for our survival or for that of our descendants. Porges (2009, 2011) developed the concept of *neuroception* to highlight the unconscious neural process that distinguishes whether the external (and internal) stimuli are safe, dangerous, or life-threatening. But this mechanism – as we have all experimented and seen in our daily lives and our practice – is not exact and can sometimes fail. We may feel an emotion (and the added sensation) that wrongly assesses the danger to which we are exposed. Danger can be overestimated and an excessive reaction may be produced towards an innocuous stimulus, such as happens, for instance, in the case of phobias. Moreover, said stimulus may be ignored because a more intense emotion is present, as is the case of the abused woman who maintains a relationship with her abuser because the fear of rejection overcomes the fear of suffering physical injuries.

Emotions are unconscious in the sense that we cannot control their emergence; they will involuntarily dominate a great part of our mind and body. We can control the expression of the emotion – smiling, for instance – when we are angry, but we cannot have any control over the emotion itself (Ramos et al., 2009). Humans, unlike other animals, can experience emotions without the intervention of thought, such as when something or someone elicits fear from us. However, there can be no cognition without emotion. If we think about the holidays that we are going to enjoy in the next few days, we will be thrilled in a positive way. However, when we imagine cockroaches in our kitchen, we might feel disgust or even fear. Emotions, in turn, help to modulate thinking and decide what actions we are going to take.

I remember when, as a child, I lost a tooth and kept it under my pillow hoping that in the morning the tooth fairy would have brought me a gift. I felt excitement and diverse emotions and, as with the great majority of children, I never questioned the fact that a fairy would come during the night looking for one of my teeth and, in return, leave some money. Now I know that I had not yet developed many of my cerebral regions and, therefore, could not analyze what was going on around me as I can now with the knowledge I have today. The regions related to logical thinking form and mature later until we reach the point where we begin to abandon childhood and to see the world with more logic and less innocence.

In humans, thought-related brain circuits begin to mature after 2–3 years of age and do not develop until we are about 25–27 years old. On the other hand, emotional circuits develop –as we will see in the next chapters – during the first months of gestation in the maternal womb and most are already operative from birth. As we grow, we can feel emotions and make rational decisions in terms of maturational development and environmental circumstances. Often, the emotional circuit will be predominant in the behavior either because the cerebral circuit relative to thought has not yet developed due to age or because the emotion is so intense (e.g., fear due to danger) that it does not allow any cognitive valuation.

Emotion can also function as a filter or a shortcut, reducing the amount of information needed to respond to familiar stimuli. Thus, the responses that allow us to adapt to different situations in the shortest possible time are optimized and, consequently, expend the lowest possible amount of energy (Palmero, 1996). This would explain why we often act instinctively and correctly without having to think about what we do, although this "instinct" can also be a source of problems if we act impulsively in situations that merit reflection.

In my clinical experience, most people who come for help do so because there is a struggle between what they *know* they have to do (cognition) and what they *can* do (emotion). In situations that are perceived as generating anxiety or alertness, emotions will, on the one hand, make thinking become very difficult or impossible and, on the other hand, make it possible to act impulsively, which may even become pathological at times.

Emotions are either positive or negative unconscious dispositions originating from significant stimuli and occurring in different brain systems. They may be studied according to the following factors (Aguado, 2010):

- *Subjective experience*: Internal and unconscious emotions;
- *Cognitive appreciation*: Consciously felt emotions that can be explained verbally;

- *Behavioral experience*: The action performed because of an internal or external stimulus;
- *Physiological activation*: Hormonal and somatic responses of the autonomic nervous system and the central nervous system.

This can be graphically observed in Figure 1.1.

From a psychological perspective, anything that happens to us can be explained within the field of neurobiology, the science of our brain's physiology and anatomy. Many brain organs are involved in thoughts and emotions. I shall highlight two of them: the prefrontal cortex, which plays a fundamental role in decision-making; and the amygdala, an essential emotional structure (LeDoux, 1994) in the process of assessing danger. The junction between the ventromedial prefrontal cortex (neocortex) and the amygdala forms a neurobiological circuit that explains the role of emotions in decision-making. This circuit could be considered the neuroanatomic structure involved in the connection between emotion and cognition (Palmero, 1996).

Homeostasis and Pathology

My experience as a biologist has provided me with a global perspective on the functioning of living creatures both at microscopic levels, studying bacteria and cells, and macroscopic levels, analyzing ecosystems with multiple animal and vegetable species. Human beings do not function differently from ecosystems: internal organs are interrelated as well as related to the outside world.

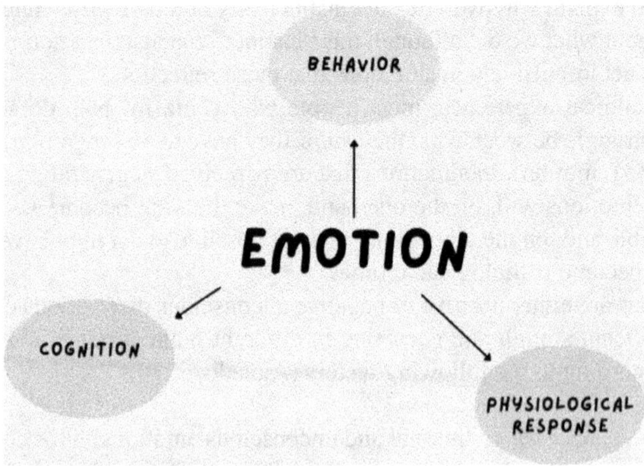

Figure 1.1 Emotion is interconnected with thought, cognition, and physiological responses. We cannot understand one without the others.

Systems Theory affirms that all living beings are systems that have a relationship with both the outside world (several systems constitute a suprasystem) and their internal organs (subsystems). All subsystems, in turn, can be divided into smaller systems. Based on this network of relationships, a model may be developed in which our mind is connected to our body and to the environment. A person is a system made up of other subsystems such as the brain and the body which, in turn, are composed of organs (subsystems). This person has siblings and parents which would make up the family suprasystem. All systems are open systems, which are in a continuous relationship influencing one another.

The capacity to maintain a balance between all systems is known as homeostasis. Achieving homeostasis implies a great deal of effort. Thanks to the science of physics, we know that every open system – each human being is one – tends to have the maximum entropy or disorder (the second law of thermodynamics), and reducing this disorder to a minimum entails a great expense of energy. Therefore, living organisms tend to use energy in the most cost-effective way possible.

In our daily life, we try to maintain the balance between our personal life and our work life; we try to have time for leisure and for taking care of our loved ones. This involves an effort as well as an expense of physical, financial, and/or time resources. We can also spend energy trying to keep at bay people who are toxic for us, as well as thoughts and feelings that affect us in a negative way.

When said balance or homeostasis is broken in the relationship we have with ourselves and/or with others, we speak of disease or pathology. As far as psychology is concerned, breaking the balance leads to the suffering of individuals and/or that of their environments. We speak of integration when homeostasis between all internal and external systems results in coordinated, effective, and healthy actions.

As we have seen, emotions function as decision-making short-cuts with the highest speed and the least expenditure of energy possible. In most cases, this is very useful and effective. Yet, sometimes, these short-cuts lead to pathology. If something is experienced as useful by our emotional brain, we will tend to repeat it, although the response in the present (maybe many years later) could be pathological.

Many pathological behaviors are maintained in time because certain strategies proved useful; they helped us feel well or, at least, alleviate discomfort. Our emotional brain stores a memory of the event and tends to repeat the behavior when a stimulus appears resembling the original one. For this reason, psychologists always ask about the first time the person felt a sense of well-being associated with the problem.

At 20 years of age, Peter routinely used marijuana. When I asked him when he started smoking, he told me he started at 15. He felt his life was chaotic at the time and, once he smoked drugs, he discovered that his problems disappeared.

Needless to say, his current coping strategy is smoking pot and not thinking about what worries him.

As we will see in the following chapters, pathologies include thoughts, emotions, or behaviors that seem inevitable, even though we may be aware they are currently inadequate and pathological. At the time, they served to achieve homeostasis internally, externally, or both, but continuing to think, feel, and act in the same way at the present time might generate a pathology.

According to Siegel (2009), there are three fundamental systems in psychology to maintain balance or homeostasis:

- The *nervous system* refers to the functioning of the central and autonomic nervous system. It interacts with everything that is organic and physiological;
- The *mind* refers to our interpretation of what we feel inside and around us. For example, a person may feel a stomach pain and think he may have cancer, which will lead him to worry excessively. He may not be able to stop worrying, even though he has no medical evidence of the illness;
- *Interpersonal relationships* refer to how we interact with other human beings from cradle to grave. Humans are social animals, and emotions play a vital role in our way of relating to others. Our childhood will create the foundation for our relationships throughout our lives.

Figure 1.2 reflects the dynamic balance between what happens in our brain, the way in which this impacts our mind (how we interpret the world), and our relationships with others. When this dynamic balance is broken, a pathology arises.

Damasio (1994), one of today's most prestigious neurobiologists, argues that human beings cannot be conceived of without an integrated perspective of the mind and the brain. When these systems are not integrated, we find states of stiffness, chaos, or both. For health to exist, there must be a dynamic balance between these elements. When the balance is disrupted, such as by problems in the family environment, we will try and find a new, satisfactory balance.

Fear and Attachment

For millions of years, evolution has been creating biological systems containing multiple emotions related to survival and reproduction. These systems need, in turn, multiple organs for their operation. Throughout this book we will focus mainly on two systems:

- *Defense system*: a basic mechanism used to know what things to avoid, what things may harm us, or who we should fear. This system includes all aspects concerning fear in situations related to traumatic experiences.

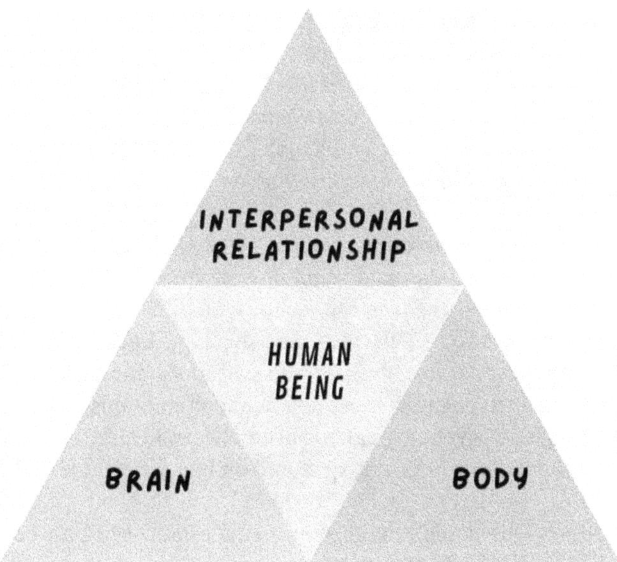

Figure 1.2 Mutual relationship between the three vital human systems in order to maintain a healthy psychological balance (Siegel, 2002)

- *Attachment system*: vital for survival during the early years of life and, later on, for reproduction and the conservation of the human being as a species. This system will modify itself with age.

During childhood, the foundation of the personality will be built through the relationship with the caregivers. In adolescence, with the onset of sexuality, there will be an emotional rupture with the parents and the choice of a partner (in all species the rupture will be physical; in humans, for cultural reasons, it is usually only emotional). Finally, in adulthood, a family will be formed, children will be born, and the cycle will be perpetuated.

Each stage has its own objectives. For a child, the most important thing will be to have physical and emotional contact with the caregivers; in adolescence, to be accepted by peers and to find a partner; and in adulthood, to be able to take care of the offspring. In each period, there will be different threats that will vary as we grow, as will the resources.

Anomalies in either of these two systems will cause a rupture in the psychological balance, and the mind must look for different elements to restore homeostasis. These will be arranged in a gradient from *extremely rigid* (e.g., "I avoid everything related to something that is scary.") to *chaotic* (e.g., "I have a lot of sex, so I can find love.").

Fear-related emotions are mainly shame, guilt, anger, or disgust, and the associated feelings are pain and anxiety. The emotions involved in attachment include everything related to loved ones in childhood and the search for like-minded people as well as love in adolescence and adulthood. We might conclude that the emotions we feel in relation to fear are negative and those related to attachment are positive, but things are much more complex. In many cases, it is the people who love each other the most who do the most damage and elicit the most fear.

Every time we feel an emotion, our body keeps a memory of it (Damasio, 1994; Scaer, 2014). Our body and mind always store memories of what happened so as to remember them in the future with either a positive (search) or negative (avoidance) affect. This idea was shocking both in my professional career and in my personal life: noticing the sensations and making the patients notice them helps us to be much more aware of our emotions.

In order to achieve psychological balance between healthy search and avoidance, we have to integrate information stored on two different levels.

- *Vertical level*: This is the relationship that is established between our body and our mind. These two parts are connected through the autonomic nervous system. Our body continuously sends information about different sensations to the brain and vice versa. This constant exchange of information between the two parts makes it possible to assess the most appropriate avoidance or approach responses. As we have seen, this information can often be ignored or overrated, which can lead to pathology.
- *Horizontal level*: This is the relationship that is established between cognition (cortical level) and emotion (subcortical level), and, therefore, exists only in humans. Our brain is lateralized and there are differences between both hemispheres: the right hemisphere is related to emotions and the left hemisphere to language and logic. These aspects differentiate us from all living beings, since the human being is the only animal that has language and cognition.

During childhood, we learn how to relate to ourselves and others, and these learnings accompany us for the rest of our lives. In Figure 1.3 we can observe that the quality of the affection we receive in our early years and the predictability (cognition) of parental behavior will result in different attachment styles (Crittenden, 2005). These emotional learnings determine much of the behavior in our interactions with other human beings in adulthood (see Chapter 4).

People who experienced lack of affection (avoidant attachment) will give more importance to cognitions (mind), while those who were unable to foresee the actions of their parents and developed an anxious attachment will give priority to bodily sensations over cognitions. Individuals who, during childhood, had a balance between cognitions and feelings (safe attachment) will be more balanced in adulthood and more capable of acting in a much more successful way.

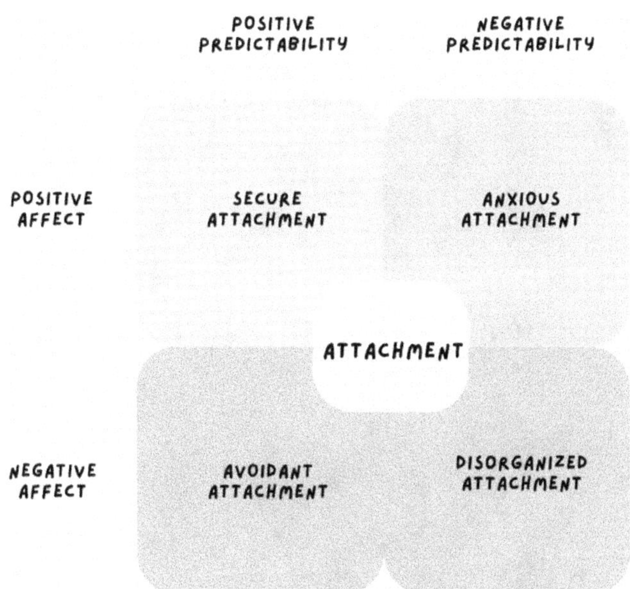

Figure 1.3 According to Crittenden (2015), the quality of the parents' affect and the predictability of their behavior make it possible for there to be a balance between the cortical (cognitive) and subcortical (emotional) areas. According to the balance that is produced, different types of attachment will be developed.

We can also create a horizontal division between mind and body, as well as between cognition and emotion. These four aspects are constantly interacting and influencing each other. Figure 1.4 illustrates the relationships between the different aspects that will determine the psychology of each individual.

Those who have not been able to find a healthy balance in their childhood regarding the relationships with themselves and others will try to find homeostasis either through external factors that make them not feel the sensations of discomfort (e.g., food, drugs, other people) or through internal factors (thoughts or feelings).

Psychopathology and Anxiety

The DSM-5 (APA, 2013) classifies psychological disorders according to symptoms. The disorders are described on the basis of the type of regulation that is unconsciously chosen to regain homeostasis and a feeling of well-being. They are:

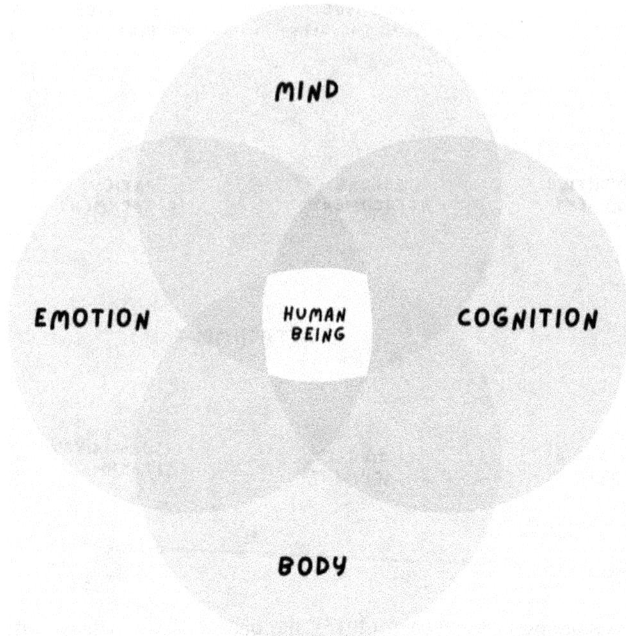

Figure 1.4 In human beings, there is an interrelation between different elements that constitute the singularity of our psychology. They all influence each other; health would consist of a healthy balance or homeostasis between them.

- *Cognitive*: In this type of disorder there will be a predisposition to overuse cognitive areas and everything related to thinking and control. Examples of such disorders may be obsessions or obsessive-compulsive disorders;
- *Emotional*: This type includes all disorders related to fear. Fear can either be real, such as phobias, or imaginary. They include social phobias and panic attacks;
- *Somatic*: In this group of disorders it is the body that suffers the greatest damage. They include eating, conversion, or psychosomatic disorders;
- *Interpersonal*: These are personality disorders that affect relationships with others such as borderline personality disorder or narcissistic personality disorder. In this group, we can also include emotional dependence;
- *Addictive*: This type includes behaviors that try to avoid confrontation with the associated pain of some memory or of a current situation. They include substance addiction, gambling, and risky behaviors;
- *Organic*: These disorders have a biological basis and require medication for their treatment; they can be bipolar disorders or schizophrenia, among others.

In these cases, the origin is obviously not an emotional regulation mechanism but something totally organic.

Throughout this book, we will talk about a division between the conscious and unconscious elements of the mind, which Ginot (2015) described as:

- *Conscious mind*: It refers to everything that has to do with our will, what we do consciously. This learning is stored in our explicit memory. Learning starts at the onset of language but it will not be fully developed until the end of adolescence;
- *Unconscious mind*: It is related to what is emotional and somatic, that is, not under our control. It is stored in our implicit memory and has to do with what we learn in the early years of our lives since it is the only learning that our brain allows at that stage.

My consultation experience has made me see that the vast majority of people who come for help do so because of a struggle between these two levels. Individuals know what they must not do, but they cannot help doing it. People who cannot stop thinking or who feel that their behavior has escaped their control have the same element in common: emotions and thoughts that they cannot handle and that dominate their behavior.

Anxiety is triggered by the negative sensations we feel in our body when our brain activates alarm signals. These can be internal (bodily sensations) or external elements, such as any stimulus that causes fear or problems in interpersonal relationships. In most cases, anxiety manifests itself recurrently without the individual being able to know its origin or how to placate it. Anxiety can be manifested by something that happened long ago and has been stored as a traumatic memory for fear of something bad happening in the future or because of feelings of loneliness, among other reasons. In all cases, it is an ancestral alarm mechanism indicating that there is a rupture of the psychological balance.

Most psychological therapies are based on only one aspect of what has been covered so far. Cognitive behavioral therapy is based on cognition; the psychoanalytic and Gestalt therapies on emotion; medical therapies on the biology of the brain; and somatic therapies on the body. The focus of this book is to provide an integrative model between the three parts that make up the psychology of the human being: cognition, emotions, and the body.

Conclusions

Emotions are a basic element of the psychological functioning of human beings. These are shared with all mammals. Human beings also have cognition, the ability to think and reason. Emotions play a regulatory function in thinking and behavior.

The body reflects emotions through sensations and our mind uses these, in turn, to assess safety or danger in the environment. Fear and attachment constitute two basic emotional systems, among others, for the survival of the individual and the species.

Early experiences with caregivers determine the emotional traits children will have throughout their lives. These will be stored as unconscious (implicit) memory and will be repeated involuntarily in relation to other individuals throughout their lives.

In the event of a rupture of the internal balance or in relation to others, the mind will tend to find regulatory mechanisms so as not to feel discomfort. These mechanisms, which may have been useful initially, can become pathological over time, making the individual feel that emotions, cognitions, and behaviors are beyond their control.

The bodily sensations of discomfort are known as anxiety and, originally, they are an alert mechanism that activates the brain to search for a new balance. However, the mechanisms used to prevent it often create a new pathology and may cause more damage than the one they intended to avoid.

References

Aguado, L. (2010) *Emoción, afecto y motivación*. Ed. Alianza.

American Psychiatric Association. (2013). *Diagnostic and statistical manual of mental disorders* (5th ed.). APA.

Crittenden, P. (2005). Attachment theory, psychopathology, and psychotherapy: The dynamic-maturational approach. Teoria dell'attaccamento, psicopatologia e psicoterapia: L'approccio dinamico maturativo. *Psicoterapia*, *30*, 171–182.

Crittenden, P. (2015). *Raising parents: Attachment, representation, and treatment*. Ed. Routledge.

Damasio, A. R. (1994). *Descartes' error: Emotion, reason, and the human brain*. G.P. Putnam's Sons.

Ginot, E. (2015). *The neuropsychology of the unconscious*. Ed. Norton.

LeDoux, J. (1994). *The emotional brain*. Ed. Phoenix (2004).

Palmero, F. (1996). Aproximación biológica al estudio de la emoción. *Anales de psicología*, *12*(1), 61–86.

Porges, S. (2009). Reciprocal influences between body and brain in the perception and expression of affect. A polyvagal perspective. In D. Fosha, D. J. Siegel, & M. F. Solomon (Eds.), *The healing power of emotion* (pp. 27–55). Ed. Norton.

Porges, S. (2011). *The polyvagal theory.Neurophysiological foundations of emotions*. Ed. Norton.

Ramos, V., Piqueras, J. A., Martínez, A., & Oblitas, L. (2009). Terapia psicológica. *Sociedad Chilena de Psicología Clínica*, *27*(2), 227–237.

Scaer, R. (2014). *The body bears the burden: Trauma, dissociation, and disease*. Ed. Routledge.

Siegel, D. J. (2002). *The developing mind: How relationships and the brain interact to shape who we are*. Guilford Press.

Siegel, D. (2009). *Emotion as integration: A possible answer to the question, what is emotion?* In D. Fosha, D. J. Siegel, & M. F. Solomon (Eds.), *The healing power of emotion affective neuroscience, development & clinical practice*. W. W. Norton & Company.

2 The Neurobiology of Fear

Who has not felt fear at some point in life? In childhood, fear of doing something that our parents disapprove of; in adolescence, fear of falling in love with someone and not being reciprocated; in adulthood, fear of not being able to financially support oneself. The examples are innumerable. We have all gone through situations where we have been afraid for believing that we will not live up to the circumstances, feeling rejected, or seeing our life or that of someone close at risk.

Fear is an emotion that we share with all animals that have a nervous system, however rudimentary, and is directly related to our survival and that of the people close to us. Undoubtedly, most of the pathologies we see in our practices have their origin in fear. All therapists are forced, at some point, to help patients deal with their fears. In order to be able to perform suitable therapeutic work, it is essential to know, in depth, the ins and outs of fear and anxiety.

Alert and defense action systems, as well as the associated emotions – fear and panic – are characteristic of all mammals, including humans (Barg, 2010). We differentiate ourselves from the rest of the species by having highly developed cortical structures (neocortex) that facilitate language and allow for reflection and thought. As we will see throughout the chapter, unlike other species, we may be afraid of situations that are not real but imaginary and, more importantly, many of the situations that provoke alert and fear are based on relationships with other people.

> *The first time Michael came to my office, I was struck by the difference between his public image as a successful person in his work and personal life, and the misery with which he lived in his intimacy. He was afraid of blushing in public, which led to avoiding all types of social situations for fear of making a fool of himself. The discrepancy between what I saw and what he told me is something I will never forget; this person who was so successful in life lived with a constantly paralyzing fear. There was no real danger but, since childhood, his feeling of unworthiness had made him live in fear.*

During my first year as a student at the School of Biology, the professor told us about McLean's theory (1990). This author described that ontogenesis collects phylogenesis; that is, throughout development – from the time we are a fetus

DOI: 10.4324/9781003646341-3

up to adulthood – our brain develops in stages throughout life: the same ones that our evolution has been going through as a species. At that time, I could not imagine the implications that this would have in my professional life over the years. This relationship between our human part and the most primitive and emotional part has helped me understand why we are afraid of things or situations that would never really pose a vital threat. No animal is afraid of not paying their debts or not feeling loved; they can only feel fear when their life or that of someone close to them is in danger.

During the first months of intrauterine life, the brain areas that we share with reptiles are formed: the brainstem or reptilian brain. During the following months of pregnancy and the first two years of life, the limbic system or mammalian brain develops. This is what McLean called the brain area that includes the organs which he believed were related to emotions. At present, we know that there are more organs involved than he initially supposed, but we will use this term to refer to the brain areas that regulate emotions. The most recent developmental area – the one that sets us apart from other living things – is the neocortex or human brain, which appears around 2–3 years of age and does not form completely until after adolescence.

I describe these brain areas in more detail here:

1. *Brainstem* (reptilian brain): Located at the base of the skull on top of the spine, this regulates the physiological aspects that are essential for survival such as breathing, temperature, or digestion, as well as the most basic attachment reflexes for bonding with caregivers in the first months of life. The most representative organ of this area is the hypothalamus, which plays a crucial role in the endocrine system and the autonomic nervous system (ANS). The latter, in turn, is divided into two branches: the sympathetic branch that causes activation and the parasympathetic branch that causes deactivation.
2. *Lymbic system* (mammalian brain): This is the area of the brain that allows us to feel emotions like hatred or love, and that makes us social and empathic animals, regulating non-verbal communication. The limbic system determines our emotional self (Wallin, 2007). The organs that form it will be very important in our therapeutic work. Most of the time, our patients will feel that they cannot handle their emotions and thoughts. In my experience, when we inform the patients in a pedagogical way how their brain works, they begin to understand the origin of their problems and regain a sense of control over what happens to them. The limbic system contains many nuclei, but in relation to anxiety and fear, we are interested primarily in the amygdala, hippocampus, insula, locus coeruleus, and nucleus accumbens:

1 The *amygdala* assesses and records non-conscious or emotional (implicit) memories. It is the most important organ related to fear and attachment,

and is fully formed at birth. It is divided into three distinct areas: one connects with the orbitofrontal cortex and is related to interpersonal relationships, another connects with the frontal cortex responsible for cognition and thought, and a third one with the hypothalamus, which in turn regulates bodily functions (Purves et al., 1996). It constitutes a mediating and regulating organ of all stimuli perceived both externally and internally. Its function is to remember everything that has been dangerous in the past so as to be able to cope more appropriately with threats in the future. The problem occurs when it is activated in situations that were dangerous in the past, but which have now ceased to be dangerous, such as in cases of phobias or situations that cause pathological shame (LeDoux, 2004). Studying the functioning of this organ has helped me improve in many situations that I previously avoided or used to block me, and help my patients understand how something that happened in the past can affect them so negatively in the present.

2 *The hippocampus* modulates the reaction of the amygdala, avoiding indiscriminate, uncontrollable, or irascible reactions, and regulating its activity. It is related to conscious or explicit memory (Siegel, 2002). It does not appear until approximately 2 years of age. The amygdala has no filter and directly activates the sympathetic system; in contrast, the hippocampus filters the information it receives and activates the parasympathetic system. The function of the hippocampus is to remember the contextual variables in which the event occurred (the place, the time when it occurred, what triggered it, etc.,) but if stimulation is excessive – for example, because the situation was very dangerous – it will not activate or regulate the amygdala (LeDoux, 2004). In these cases, trauma would be generated, with all the characteristics that accompany it: emotional activation, phobias, or amnesia.

3 The *insula* facilitates introspection and allows us to evaluate our bodily states and the emotional states of others. This organ is connected to the amygdala and the orbitofrontal cortex, causing pleasant or unpleasant sensations before different stimuli. According to Damasio (2003), our emotions are based on our bodily sensations, which is why the insula is vital when it comes to evaluating how we perceive others and how we feel about their reactions. At a conference in Rome, attending a lecture by Vittorio Gallese, I discovered that when this organ is damaged, individuals cannot empathize with other people's emotions. Since they feel nothing, they are not able to interpret what the other person feels (Ammaniti & Gallese, 2014). This information corroborates the importance of sensations over emotions.

The *locus coeruleus* (located in the brainstem) is the nuclei that regulates the synthesis of noradrenaline in the brain. This neurotransmitter causes activation reactions in the brain, stimulating both the amygdala to recall danger and the hippocampus to recall all contextual variables related to the threat.

4 The *nucleus accumbens* is a key brain region involved in the reward circuit. It plays a crucial role in the processing of pleasure, reinforcement, and motivation, often associated with the release of dopamine. This area is linked to behaviors related to addiction, enjoyment, and emotional responses.

5 3. *Neocortex* (human brain): This is the part of the brain that is evolutionarily more recent and we share with primates, although it is much more developed in humans. It is related to language, culture, art, music, and so on, and allows you, for example, to read this text (the limbic system will be in charge of you enjoying it). It interprets our experiences in a cognitive way: it represents the reflexive self. To work normally, it is necessary that the amygdala not be very activated. In the face of a threat, the amygdala prevents us from thinking clearly and making lucid and thoughtful decisions. Needless to say, it is the part of the brain that develops later and, therefore, will not be functional in the early years of life. As a consequence, during this stage, all learning will be emotional, that is, unconscious.

The neocortex is divided into different areas with specific functions. For our purpose, we will emphasize the frontal and prefrontal cortex:

The *frontal cortex* is the executive brain. It enables planning, memory, and conscious action (Cozolino, 2016). It is where semantic and episodic memory is stored, that is, the explicit memory.

The *prefrontal cortex* (PFC) is the cortical region that is most developed in primates. The PFC is a collection of neocortical areas that sends and receives projections from all sensory and motor cortical systems, and from various subcortical structures. It is the most relevant brain region for therapy and is divided into two parts: the dorsolateral zone (connected to the hippocampus and the left hemisphere, and oriented towards language) and the middle prefrontal cortex (connected to the amygdala and right hemisphere, and related to emotions) (Siegel, 2010).

The *middle prefrontal cortex* is an integrative area that connects the body (through the brainstem and the ANS), the limbic system, and other cortical structures. It is related to attachment behaviors (Schore, 2001; Siegel, 2002). In this book, we are interested mainly in two parts of this area:

The *orbitofrontal region* is part of the PFC and regulates affections and attachment bonds. Although, anatomically, it belongs to the cortical regions, it acts physiologically in coordination with the limbic system. It is connected to the amygdala and is responsible for inhibitory control, so it is critical for emotional self-regulation. In the next chapter, we will see in detail that, when a severe breakdown occurs in the attachment relationship, this area activates the amygdala, which causes fear reactions that prevent the child from learning to regulate him or herself emotionally.

The *prefrontal region* receives many nerve responses from the hippocampus. It is involved in social situations and emotional communication, for example through voice modulation.

Figure 2.1 illustrates the division of the brain into three layers according to their developmental features.

Some areas in the human brain regulate emotion, and others regulate cognition and thought. They will not always work towards the same goal or have the same priorities (Ginot, 2015). In consultation, I have met many patients who are attending because they wanted to quit smoking and explained to me the many reasons why they had to quit: financial, family, health, and so on. They all had something in common: they were not able to quit on their own. One part of the mind acts by what it believes to be logical and suitable, and another part, by contrast, can do so by impulses or emotions. There may be discrepancies between what we know to be logical and what our emotions and feelings dictate.

Clearly, we feel fear when something happens that puts our life in danger, but often we can feel fear and anxiety without knowing the cause of the discomfort.

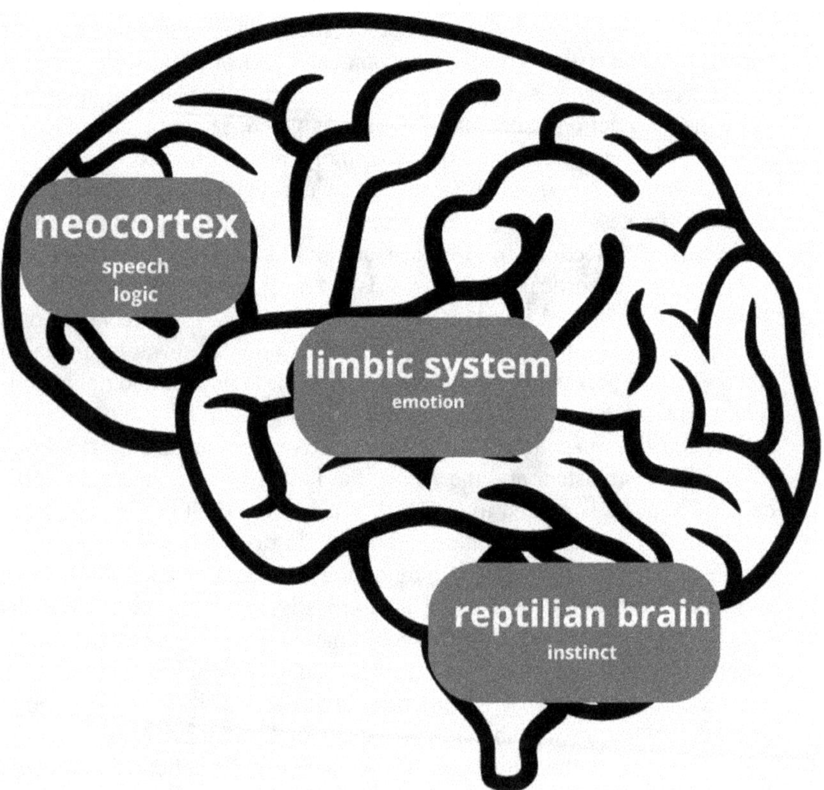

Figure 2.1 The brain is composed of numerous organs, each with a different function, but related to each other. The division of the brain into three layers helps to better understand the differences between the conscious (human) and the unconscious (animal).

However, in both cases, we will feel unable to control unpleasant sensations or catastrophic thoughts. The activation of defense-related subcortical areas acts impulsively and autonomously, independently of the cortical areas that govern rational criteria. With therapeutic work, we help patients learn how to manage those fears by controlling their thoughts and their emotions, or by modifying harmful behaviors. We help cortical areas modify the activation of subcortical areas. We teach our patients to regulate themselves emotionally and to do it in attunement with others.

The Fear Circuit

Nearly all existing research on the brain has been performed using animals such as octopuses, worms, rats, or monkeys, among others, as experimental subjects. Individuals with brain lesions have also been studied. When certain organs were damaged or when these did not function correctly, researchers were allowed to observe *in vivo* their emotional or cognitive deficits.

Studies on fear-related brain circuits have mainly been obtained by using electric shocks in subcortical areas which we share with other mammals (these experiments are usually performed on rats). When these discharges occurred, fear responses were observed in the animals even though there was no real stimulus that caused them. Simply activating the amygdala to trigger an alert response is enough; this could explain why us humans can be afraid of situations that only exist in our imagination.

LeDoux (1994, 2004) – at present the greatest scholar on fear – argues that there are two independent circuits related to alertness. Both involve the amygdala and play different roles in situations of stress, fear, or panic (see Figure 2.2):

- *Rapid system*: This is instantaneous and sends information from the sensory organs (eyes, ears, skin) to the thalamus, which in turn forwards it to the amygdala. Smell, evolutionarily more primitive, does not pass through the thalamus. The amygdala immediately transfers information to the body through the ANS to evaluate whether a search for help or a fight-flight response is more appropriate.
- *Slow system*: This circuit is slower than the previous one because it incorporates more organs in its processing (hippocampus, thalamus, and amygdala). When there is a stimulus that causes an alert that is not excessive, the information reaches the hippocampus, is compared with previous situations, and is sent to the cortical areas for a conscious evaluation of the danger. This information is passed on to the thalamus and then to the amygdala, which activates the body response based on the information received. In humans, this slower circuit may be influenced by feelings or thoughts that cause fear but which do not present real danger.

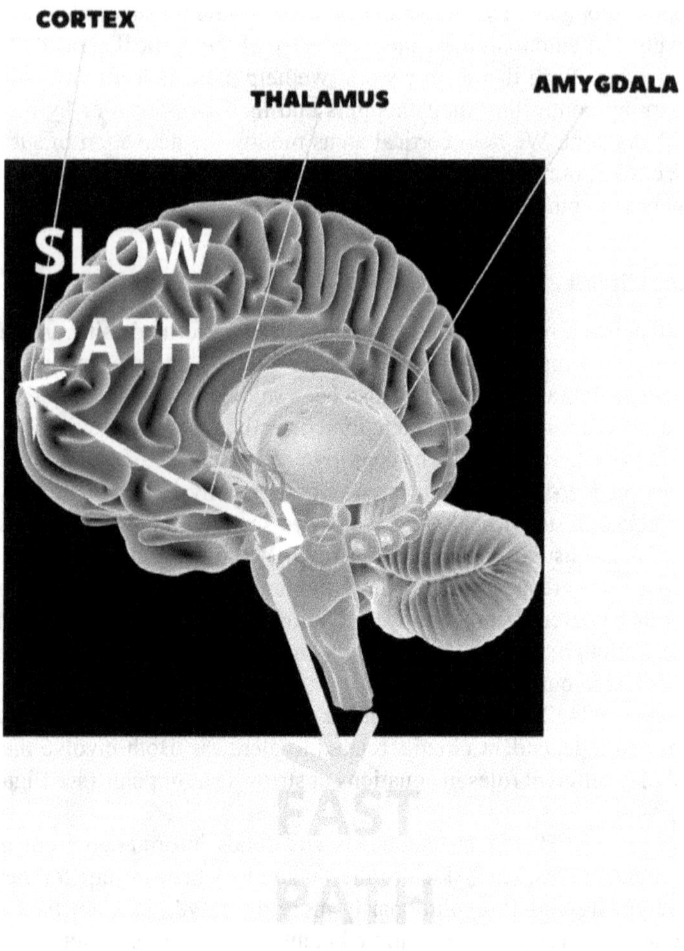

Figure 2.2 The amygdala can be activated immediately by a stimulus causing fear or after thinking of something that causes alarm. In both cases, the brain activates the circuits of fear, and anxiety is felt.

Susana is a 26-year-old patient who has finished her university studies. She suffers from constant anxiety that does not let her sleep, so she self-soothes by bingeing. During the first interview, it is obvious from the onset that she does not see herself as capable of finding a job and developing a career related to what she has studied. In addition to this, there is the guilt of feeling she has let her parents down because of the effort they have made to pay for her university studies.

In the case of this patient there is no situation that can put her life at risk, yet her mind and body react with the same symptoms as if she were facing a serious danger. In this case, the fear of failure and the guilt of not living up to her own expectations create the same physiological effects as if her life were in danger. It is her own thinking, her assessment of the circumstances, which triggers the activation of the fear circuits.

Something that sets us radically apart from other species is that human beings can fear situations that do not exist in reality and only exist in our imagination (reflective capacity) – situations that have not happened or that we anticipate. Our subcortical areas cannot differentiate a real fear from an imaginary one, and the physiological responses (anxiety, sweating, dizziness, tachycardia) will be the same whether there is a serious threat to our physical integrity or when we anticipate experiencing a stressful situation, for example, being rejected or making a fool of oneself. The unpleasant bodily sensations that occur in the face of a real or imagined threat are what we call *anxiety*.

In extreme cases, such as panic attacks, the feeling of imminent death and lack of control will be remembered as one of life's worst experiences. In the words of Cozolino (2002), "With the expansion of the cerebral cortex and the appearance of imagination, we have become capable of feeling anxious about potential outcomes and situations that can never exist" (p. 237).

Fear of an object or situation is what we know as *phobia*. Since these phobias are associated with increased alertness and anxiety, we tend to avoid everything related to the cause of our fear. Phobias are innumerable: syringes, bridges, night, spiders, snakes, heights, tunnels, and so on. I use the term *tangible phobias* to refer to the fear of physical things.

Humans can also fear things that are not real (in the sense of not being something physical or tangible), which will cause the same physiological reactions by activating the same brain circuits related to fear. These *intangible phobias* are related to activities involving interpersonal situations, such as the fear of speaking in public, not being loved, or not being worthy.

> *Daives is a 32-year-old patient with a thyroid disease that forces him to periodically be tested. His phobia of needles (belenophobia) prevents him from getting the pertinent tests done, which causes a very significant deterioration of his health. His fear of needles wins over the deterioration of his health.*

We know from attachment studies (Holmes, 2001; Bowlby, 1993; Wallin, 2007) that many intangible phobias are conditioned by our early experiences with our caregivers. In adulthood, fear of being rejected, not being loved, or making a fool of oneself in certain social situations may cause a lot of fear and anxiety depending on what the attachment relationships in childhood were like. The brain remembers how traumatic those experiences were, and the natural tendency in adulthood will be to avoid similar situations.

A real danger, or the prospect of it (anticipatory anxiety), causes physiological reactions identical to those that occur when our actual life is in danger (Panksepp & Biven, 2012). In abused and abandoned children, there is a chronic activation of the amygdala which could impair the development of the prefrontal cortex. This could lead to alterations in the acquisition of appropriate behaviors and emotions in adulthood, including impulse control (Mesa-Gresa et al., 2011). Both self-regulation and interpersonal skills may deteriorate. People with a hyperactivated fear system in infancy cannot handle their internal states nor correctly interpret the gestures and emotions of others (Ammaniti & Gallese, 2014).

Imagine these three situations:

- We see that a child is going to cross the street and a car is coming his way. We react immediately without thinking; we do it impulsively. In this case, the "fast track" is activated. The eyes receive the stimulus and send the information to the thalamus which immediately activates the amygdala. Through the sympathetic system, this will activate the fight-flight mode.
- We are walking on the street at night. We see a shady-looking person coming towards us and we think that he may rob us. We decide to take a taxi. In this case, we have seen a potential danger, reflected on the most appropriate behavior, and decided to avoid danger. These decisions may take a few seconds. In this example, the amygdala will hardly be activated, but if the person runs after us when he sees that we are escaping, the amygdala would become much more activated. This "slow path" is usually activated in almost all social phobias and panic attacks. By assessing the situation and perceiving discomfort, our amygdala becomes more activated, which causes positive feedback.
- We get home and start thinking that the next time we go out, we may run into someone who wants to rob us. We begin to feel anxious when we imagine what could have happened if we had not taken the taxi. In this case, there is no real stimulus that causes fear, but the amygdala becomes activated through thought, generating the same reactions as if the danger were real.

Response habits, if they occur repeatedly, may become embedded implicitly in the brain (for example, in the somatosensory cortex, the hippocampus, or in the amygdala). This is known as *kindling*. Feelings of discomfort may be felt without any stimulus to cause them (see Chapter 14). The brain assesses that we are not safe in the here and now, which will cause the activation of the fear circuits without there being any real danger. This phenomenon is very common in hypochondriac people or those with panic attacks who are afraid of their own sensations. Anticipatory anxiety (i.e., fear of fear) is what sustains the pathology.

The nervous system is divided into two major components: the central nervous system (CNS), which includes what is commonly known as the brain; and the autonomic nervous system (ANS), which connects the brain to the body. The

ANS is divided into two subsystems: the sympathetic, which acts as an activator, and the parasympathetic, which acts as an inhibitor of activation and anxiety.

In the event that the brain should perceive danger (real or imaginary), the hypothalamic-pituitary-adrenal axis (HPA) is activated which, in turn, activates the sympathetic branch of the ANS and causes the adrenal glands (adrenaline, noradrenaline, and, if stress is maintained, cortisol) to secrete stress hormones.

Porges' Polyvagal Theory

If we hear a loud noise, our brain generates a warning signal. This activates the sympathetic branch of the nervous system, which causes an alarm signal in the body. If the threat is perceived as harmless, the parasympathetic branch is activated, bringing back a sense of calm. However, if the threat is perceived as real and the amygdala remains activated (and the hippocampus does not modulate that activation), the HPA axis activates the sympathetic nervous system (SNS), with the following symptoms (see Figure 2.3) (Yanes, 2012):

- *Visual hyperactivity*: scanning with the eyes for sources of danger, escape routes, and so on;
- *Auditory hyperactivity*: the same as above but applied to our ears;
- *Muscular contraction*: the body gets ready to defend itself by fleeing or fighting;
- *Increased respiratory and heart rates*: this causes an increase of nutrients and oxygen in the muscles;
- *Perspiration*: this process cools the body down because of the increase in temperature due to hyperactivation.

A relationship exists between what the senses perceive, how the brain interprets the stimuli, and how the body reacts. This information does not act one way in a top-down manner. The information for soothing or activation can also be transmitted from the gut to the brain in a bottom-up way.

Porges (2009, 2011) has developed Polyvagal Theory, leading to a broader vision of the ANS, and studied how it intervenes in the regulation of viscera, social interaction, attachment, and emotions. Porges argues that the parasympathetic nervous system consists, for the most part, of the vagus nerve, the main element in the regulation of the ANS.

The vagus nerve is a cranial nerve of the parasympathetic branch and consists of motor and sensory fibers. It innervates the posterior tongue, pharynx, larynx, esophagus, stomach, heart, lungs, and intestine. Motor fibers go downward, thus carrying the stimulation from the brain to the viscera; sensory fibers carry visceral sensory impressions from the bottom upwards. The descending current regulates the viscera from the brain, while the ascending function informs the brain of the sensations of the lower organs. The limbic system can receive

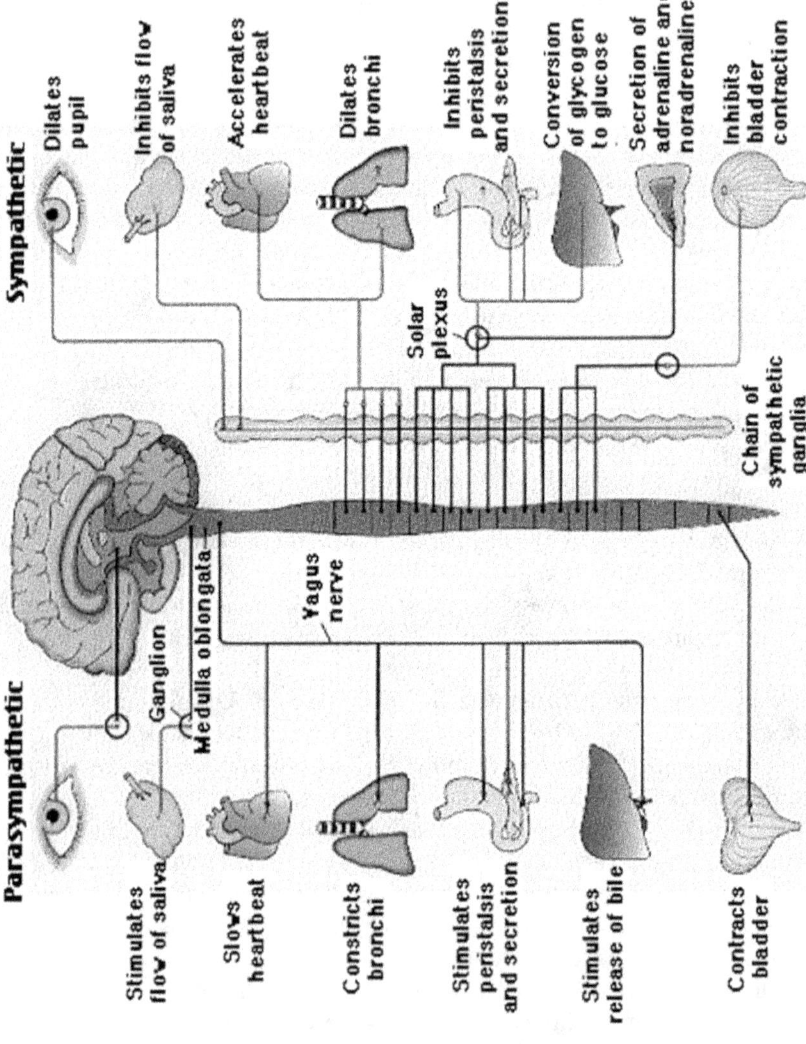

Figure 2.3 The sympathetic system acts as ANS activator while the parasympathetic system intervenes by calming the body down. Both are a means of a two-way communication between the brain and the viscera.

constant information from the distant viscera of the brain (as we will see, this is fundamental for understanding anxiety) and is capable of influencing them by slowing down the heart and digestion.

The two branches of the vagus nerve have an inhibitory capacity, which is why they are opposed to the sympathetic one that stimulates the production of catecholamines (adrenaline and norepinephrine), with the subsequent activation of the organism.

> *Laura, 35, told me how hard the week had been, because on Sunday she had suffered paralysis in her legs and arms that left her exhausted for the rest of the day. She was paralyzed for a long time, and it caused stiffness in her hands and feet – as if they were bent and she could not move them. No physician had found an organic cause that could explain the paralysis. Exploring what had happened during the week, she told me that she had an argument with her father – with whom she works – on Friday. He did not pay attention to any of her suggestions, dismissing them as if they were childish, and she recognized feeling very frustrated with her father's attitude. Explaining what it was like, she arched her hands back and I asked, "Is that how your hands get when you become paralyzed?" She confirmed this, and told me that she now realized that the paralysis always appeared after a discussion with her father.*
>
> *It is very likely that the paralysis was provoked by an excess of stress and anxiety that the patient could not handle. These occurred in an almost automatic fashion.*

Porges' Polyvagal Theory holds crucial value for psychologists because it allows us to understand why, in the face of a situation that causes a lot of stress or fear, paralysis occurs and, at a mental level, causes the traumatic dissociation of the personality. It allows us to understand the importance of the sense of security of children with their caregivers or of patients with their therapist. If there is no safety, effective therapy cannot be performed.

Throughout evolution, we have developed two branches of the vagus nerve:

- *Ventral vagus*: Evolutionarily more recent and myelinated. We have this in common with mammals. It is related to social behavior and interpersonal communication; it activates the sensation of calm when the danger has passed and regulates cardiac tone, viscera, and facial signs when there is tranquility.
- *Dorsal vagus*: Phylogenetically more primitive and non-myelinated. We have this in common with reptiles and, when activated, it causes immobilization.

Throughout evolution, nature has been creating three neural systems that regulate behavioral and physiological adaptation to social situations, threatening situations, and moments when life is in danger. The three phylogenetic states are:

- *The non-myelinated and evolutionarily more primitive branch of the vagus nerve*: This is related to behaviors of immobilization, dissociation, and collapse. It is activated in situations where a threat is perceived that exceeds the person's resources or threatens their life. The situation of immobilization is optimal for reptiles because it helps them stay without breathing for a long time and be still to regulate their temperature. However, its activation is extremely traumatic for mammals.
- *The sympathetic branch of the SNA*: This is related to the activation of the viscera (e.g., acceleration of breathing and heart rate). It is activated in fight-flight situations.
- *The myelinated branch of the vagus nerve*: This is related to social communication. It allows non-traumatic immobilization because the person feels relaxed and calm (e.g., during sex or sleep). It promotes the physiological regulation of a calm state after the activation of the sympathetic branch.

When the brain senses danger, the amygdala is activated, which sends a signal to the body through the ANS (see Figure 2.4). First, the parasympathetic branch is activated, trying not to activate the sympathetic one, which is much more energetically costly. The steps the ANS takes regarding danger go in the opposite direction of the evolutionary acquisition:

- *Social response*: The first response is searching for help; social support is sought. In the case of infants and children, physical and emotional contact with caregivers is sought.
- *Fight-flight mobilization*: If help does not appear or is not enough, there is an activation of the sympathetic system. It supports motor and metabolic defense activity. If this does not solve the perception of lack of safety either, then the dorsovagal circuits are activated.
- *Immobilization*: If it is impossible to fight nor to escape, the dorsovagal branch is activated, which causes an immobilization and apnea response (asphyxia) with bradycardia (the heart beats slower). In adults, it is activated when they feel that their life is in danger. In infants and children, it is activated when the threat is perceived as excessive and there are no cognitive or emotional resources to deal with it. The younger the children's age, and therefore the scarcer their resources, the more easily the activation of the dorsovagal branch will occur.

When emotional ties of trust exist, either with caregivers at an early age or with other adults at a later age, immobilization is not traumatic. If the immobilization is caused by someone who generates safety, the ventrovagal branch is activated, promoting emotional connection and relaxation.

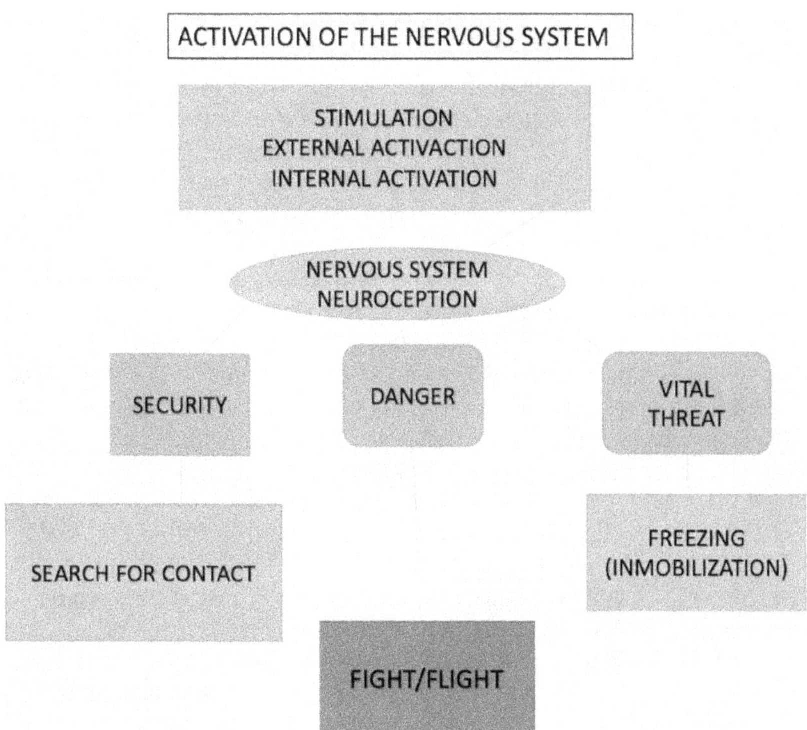

Figure 2.4 The activation of the nervous system by danger will lead to the sequential activation of strategies to deal with it. First, seeking help; afterwards, fight/flight attitudes; and, if these are not possible, immobilization. In extremely traumatized people, the immobilization can appear immediately without going through the previous states.

In mammals, activation of the dorsovagal branch seeks immobilization as a way to escape potential predators and not waste resources. However, it is extremely traumatic in humans. A baby or child who perceives a danger that proves too big for their coping skills may be immobilized by fear, causing a very characteristic stupor in extremely frightened or abandoned children (Bowlby, 1993).

With the activation of the dorsovagal branch, traumatic dissociation of the personality (Van der Hart et al., 2006) and somatoform dissociation (Scaer, 2014; Nijenhuis, 2000) are triggered at the mental level. As we will see in the next chapter, if the activation of the dorsovagal branch is frequently activated during infancy, there is a permanent sensitization that precludes the emotional development of the child in adulthood.

The activation and brake impulses are adaptive, but if the brake is defective because it has not been activated in childhood (e.g., there was no mother to calm the child) or the alert has been activated (e.g., because there was a lot of screaming and fighting in the house or an excess of control that caused fear in the child), the dorsovagal branch becomes easily activated, as we saw in the previous case example. Due to the kindling effect (Morrell, 1990), the fear circuit tends to be activated every time with less intense stimuli which leads to an excessive response of fear to any stimulus – however bland – that can lead to immobilization.

Some authors (Panksepp, 2012; Panksepp & Biven, 2012) argue that there is an attachment-related brain circuit that, if altered in childhood, causes hyperactivation of the alert system and the dorsovagal nerve becomes easily activated. A childhood in which there has been abuse or mistreatment, parental neglect, or parentification (reversal of parent–child roles) will cause an alteration of the physiology and cerebral anatomy (Sapolsky, 2004) that will, in turn, cause the occurrence of emotional disorders in adulthood.

The Panic Circuit

Panksepp (2004, 2009) and Panksepp and Biven (2012) describe seven human brain circuits that we share with other mammals: search (exploration), fear, anger, sexuality (reproduction), care (attachment), panic/separation, and play.

If a zebra, a gazelle, or any other mammal lost contact with its mother when it was 3 months old it would be dead in a matter of minutes or hours. It will be a life-or-death imperative to re-establish contact with a caregiver as soon as possible in order to survive. The energy of the animal will focus on seeking the protection of its attachment figure while experiencing those minutes or hours in true panic. In order to recover the bond with the caregivers, the animals use what is known as the *attachment cry*, which allows the pup to catch the mother's attention and recover the bond. This cry is innate in both humans and other mammals (Purves et al., 1996).

The brain circuit of panic or separation is also present in humans; in infants or children it can be activated not only in the absence of a real mother but also due to lack of emotional connection (e.g., a negligent or anxious mother). If attachment figures that take care of the child are also a source of threat – as in cases of physical, psychological, or sexual abuse or neglect of care – the panic circuit will be overactivated. (Schore, 2001; Tronick, 2007; Bowlby, 1993; Siegel, 2010). According to Schore (2010):

> The emotion-processing limbic circuits of the infant's developing right brain, which are dominant for the emotional sense of self, are influenced by implicit intersubjective affective transactions embedded in the attachment relationship with the mother … facial expressions, posture, and tone of voice …

> the implicit dyadic processing of these non-verbal communications are the product of the operations of the infant's right hemisphere interacting with the mother's right hemisphere (p. 34).

There is a classic study by Tronick (2007) called the Still Face Experiment (it can be watched on the Internet at https://www.youtube.com/watch?v=apzXGEbZht0), in which a mother plays with a 1-year-old child. Suddenly, the mother becomes expressionless for 2 minutes and the experimenters observe the reaction of the child. At first, he tries to maintain the connection with the mother through gaze and game and after a short time – seeing he cannot get it back – he begins to avoid the mother's gaze and later starts crying, suffering considerably. When the mother reestablishes emotional contact, the lost connection is recovered. The child's reaction is different in each experiment depending on the attachment relationship with his mother.

These situations of emotional disconnection can be extremely traumatic for children if they occur repeatedly and/or are sustained over time. No obvious physical or psychological abuse is required to trigger the panic/separation circuit. Anything that causes an emotional disconnection between the adult and the child may activate it. Some examples may be a hospitalization of the child or the mother, a mother's depression, or a child feeling responsible for the welfare of the parents.

The lack of synchronization on an emotional level with the attachment figures will cause the child to seek regulatory strategies that are extraneous to the caregivers to help them self-regulate. At later stages in life, such as adolescence or adulthood, these strategies may become pathological (see Chapter 5).

The brain of a child dealing with neglect or abuse by caregivers will simultaneously activate the brain circuits of attachment (search for physical and emotional connection) and fear (feelings of withdrawal and alertness). It is important to emphasize that short breaks in attachment bonds are healthy because they allow the child to develop autonomy and emotional growth. However, they are traumatic if they are very intense or long-lasting (Schore, 2001; Tronick, 2007).

The child's sensation of alertness or danger results in the activation of the amygdala. If there are no caregivers available, or if these are the source of the threat, the panic circuit and other less evolved survival-related mechanisms such as the fear circuit (with the consequent activation of the fight-flight mode), the pain circuit, or the rage circuit (Panksepp & Biven, 2012) (see Figure 2.5) become activated.

The activation of the amygdala and associated physiological mechanisms increases stress hormone levels and the activation of the sympathetic branch of the ANS. As we have seen, this causes seeking for help (in the case of infants and children, seeking for attachment figures). If fight-flight is impossible, either because the necessary resources do not exist, the threat is excessive, or the

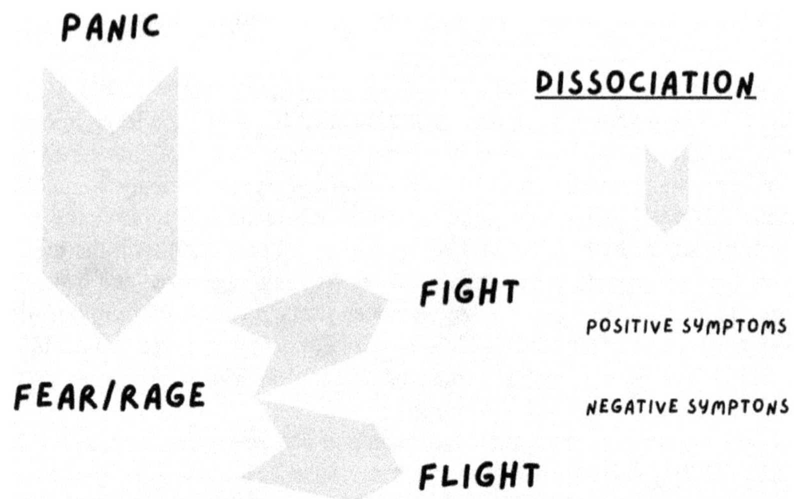

Figure 2.5 The activation of the panic circuit causes the activation of the circuits related to fear and rage. If the threat persists, and neither fight nor defense is possible, dissociative states occur.

source of the threat is one of the attachment figures, the dorsovagal nerve can cause immobilization and consequent dissociation (see Figure 2.6).

Based on observations from orphanages, Bowlby (1993) points out that children who feel abandoned have a continuous cry that after a few hours – or a couple of days at most – gives way to a very characteristic stupor that, although it can be confused with an apparent calmness of the child, we now know is an activation of the immobilization system. It is believed that this system is reinforced in mammals to prevent the young from being located by other predators before the mother finds them.

According to Panksepp and Biven (2012),

> *The warm affective feelings of security that arise from loving attachments – the primary mechanisms of the "secure base" – are gradually transported to higher forms of consciousness around 2 to 3 years of age. Throughout the first six years of childhood, early social loss – excessive separation distress/GRIEF – sensitizes the child to chronic anxiety and insecurity, often heralding depression later in life. Loving social attachments, on the other hand, strengthen the positive affective powers of the brain, promoting healthy actions of PLAY (see the next chapter), which are fundamental psychological forces that helped make humans, indeed all mammals, the sophisticated social creatures that we are. We respond intensely to uncaring emotional*

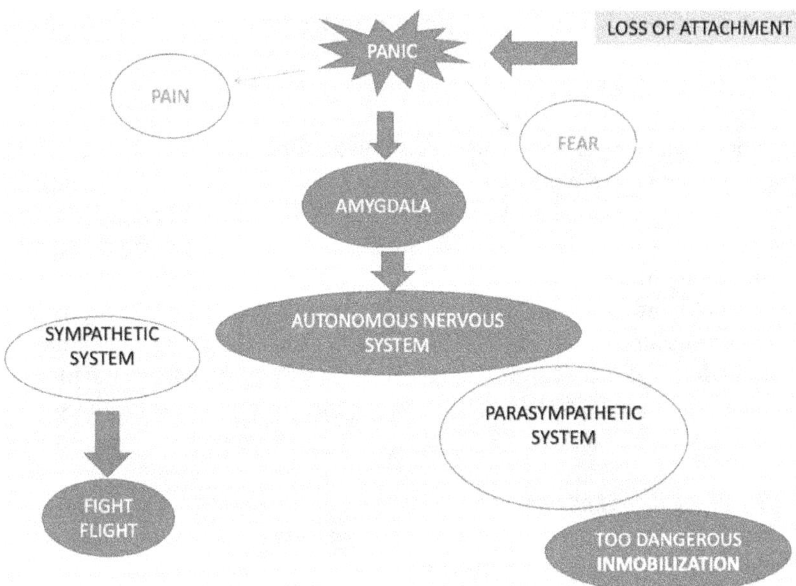

Figure 2.6 An event that causes a rupture in the attachment relationship with the caregivers causes the activation of the brain circuit related to panic/separation. This will, in turn, activate the circuits related to fear and pain by stimulating the amygdala. When this occurs, physical and emotional closeness with the attachment figures is sought first, and then the possibility of fight/flight is assessed, and if these options are not possible, immobilization and consequent dissociation occur.

> *gestures directed towards us; anything that hints at shunning or even milder forms of social exclusion is experienced as psychologically painful.*
>
> (p. 192)

Patients with panic attacks in adulthood – and even more so when these occur at an early age – have lived in insecure attachment relationships with problems of inattention and/or abuse. People with childhoods where there has been no safe attachment have a predisposition to strong anxiety levels and even panic attacks if, in the future, stressful events come about that go beyond their coping strategies.

The brain circuitry for panic has emerged evolutionarily in mammals from previous circuits that were related to physical pain (Panksepp, 2004). If any event reactivates these circuits in adulthood, the implicit memory will cause a similar reaction in similar situations. This will generate ruminating thoughts, depression, feeling of emptiness, and emotional hyper- or hypoactivation. In other cases, it can lead to severe anxiety, social phobias, eating disorders, or panic attacks.

According to Panksepp and Biven (2012):

> As noted earlier, we formerly called this the PANIC system because when young animals are abandoned, they experience a special form of alarmed anxiety – an agitated panicky state. We favored this term because there were good reasons to suspect that panic attacks stemmed, in part, from excessive arousability of this primary emotional system. However, many readers found the label confusing, probably because when older people are deprived of companionship, they tend to feel lonely and sad rather than panicky like little children. Of course, this only reflects the tertiary-process ruminations of adults, who have a lifetime of ways to cognitively adjust to social loss.
>
> (p. 193)

As we will see in the next chapter, if there have been negative experiences during childhood, the brain circuits related to anxiety and fear may become overactive, which would hinder the natural process of maturation and emotion regulation for the rest of the person's life.

Conclusions

We share fear-related brain structures with other living beings but, unlike them, humans can confuse real and imagined fears, which cause cognitive and emotional behavioral reactions that are identical.

The relationships of children with their caregivers during their first years of life are literally vital, so any break in attachment – whether through abuse or neglect – will cause alert and fear reactions in the child's brain, which, in most cases, will be compensated by the behaviors of the caregivers. In this way, the capacity for self-regulation in the child develops more and more.

The younger the child's age, and the more intense and lasting these ruptures of attachment are, the greater the deficits that occur in the child's emotional development. This leads to overactivation of the amygdala, low discrimination of non-dangerous stimuli in the hippocampus, and overactivation of the dorsovagal nerve, which causes any state of alert, especially in social situations, to generate unbearable anxiety and discomfort.

People with these attachment systems damaged during childhood are much more likely to suffer from different pathologies related to bodily and/or anxiety disorders in adulthood, such as hypochondria, somatization, permanent anxiety, and, of course, panic attacks.

Through therapy, in a healthy relational environment between the therapist and the patient, they can learn to self-regulate and allow all those maladaptive childhood learnings to be replaced, creating increasingly adaptive reactions to adverse stimuli.

References

Ammaniti, M., & Gallese, V. (2014). *The birth of intersubjectivity*. Ed. Norton.

Barg, G. (2010). Bases neurobiológicas del apego. *Revisión temática. Ciencias Psicológicas*, *V*(1), 69–81.

Bowlby, J. (1993). *Attachment and loss: Volume I. Attachment*. Basic Books.

Cozolino, L. (2016). *Why therapy works. Using our minds to change our brains*. Ed. Norton.

Damasio, A. R. (2003). *Looking for Spinoza: Joy, sorrow, and the feeling brain*. Harcourt.

Holmes, J. (2001). *Attachment theory and therapy: Seeking a secure base*. Whurr Publishers.

Ginot, E. (2015). *The neuropsychology of the unconscious*. Ed. Norton.

LeDoux, J. (1994). *The emotional brain*. Ed. Phoenix (2004).

MacLean, P. (1990). *The triune brain in evolution*. Plenum Press.

Mesa-Gresa, P., & Moya-Albiol, L. (2011). Neurobiología del maltrato infantil: el "ciclo de la violencia". *Revista de neurología*, *52*(8), 489–503.

Morrell, F. (1990). *Kindling and synaptic plasticity: The legacy of Graham Goddard*. Ed. Birkhauser.

Nijenhuis, E. (2000). Somatoform dissociation: Major symptoms of dissociative disorders. *Journal of Trauma & Dissociation*, *1*(4), 33–66.

Panksepp, J. (2004). *Affective neuroscience. The foundations of human and animal emotions*. Oxford University Press.

Panksepp, J. (2009). Brain emotional systems and qualities of mental life: From animals models of affect implications for psychoterapeutics. In D. Fosha, D. J. Siegel, & M. F. Solomon (Eds.), *The healing power of emotion* (pp. 1–26). Norton.

Panksepp, J., & Biven, L. (2012). *The archeology of mind. Neuroevolutionary origins of humans emotions*. Norton.

Porges, S. (2009). Reciprocal influences between body and brain in the perception and expression of affect. A polyvagal perspective. In D. Fosha, D. J. Siegel, & M. F. Solomon (Eds.), *The healing power of emotion* (pp. 27–55). Norton.

Porges, S. (2011). *The polyvagal theory. Neurophysiological foundations of emotions*. Norton.

Purves, D., Augustine, G. J., Fitzpatrick, D., Hall, W. C., & Lamantia, A.-S. (1996). *Neuroscience*. Sinauer Associates.

Sapolsky, R. M. (2004). *Why zebras don't get ulcers: The acclaimed guide to stress, stress-related diseases, and coping*. Holt Paperback.

Scaer, R. (2014). *The body bears the burden: Trauma, dissociation, and disease*. Ed. Routledge.

Schore, A. (2001). The effects of a secure attachment relationship on right brain development, affect regulation & infant mental health. *Infant Mental Health Journal*, 22, 7–66.

Schore, A. (2010). Relational trauma and the developing right brain. In T. Baradon (Ed.), *The neurobiology of broken attachment bonds. Psychoanalytic, attachment and neuropschological contributions to parent-infan psychotherapy*. Ed. Routledge.

Siegel, D. J. (2002). *The developing mind: How relationships and the brain interact to shape who we are*. Guilford Press.

Siegel, D. J. (2010). *Mindsight: The new science of personal transformation*. Bantam Books.

Tronick, E. (2007). *The neurobehavioral and social-emotional development of infants and children*. Norton.

Van der Hart, O., Nijenhuis, E. R. S., & Steele, K. (2006). *The haunted self: Structural dissociation and the treatment of chronic traumatization*. Norton & Company.

Wallin, D. J. (2007). *Attachment in psychotherapy*. Guilford Press.

Yanes, J. (2012). *El control del estrés y el mecanismo del miedo*. Ed. Edaf.

3 The Neurobiology of Attachment

In his book *The Search for the Perfect Language*, Umberto Eco (2013) tells of a legend that deeply impressed me. In the thirteenth century, the Emperor Frederick II of the Hohenstaufen dynasty wanted to know what language humans spoke before the fall of the Tower of Babel. The scholars of the time made scholarly disquisitions about what was the original language of humanity, predominating those who defended either Greek or Hebrew. In order to avoid doubt, the emperor ordered that a newborn child be locked up in a room in solitude. All his needs for food, hygiene, and clothing were to be met, but the people who looked after him were totally forbidden to speak to him or touch him. They assumed that the child, when he spontaneously spoke, would do so in the primordial language, uncontaminated by the one spoken in the area. Unfortunately, the experiment failed because the child died around age three. It is believed to be of sorrow.

Until the first half of the twentieth century – and I think that many people, and even many professionals, still believe it today – it was thought that children loved their caregivers because they fed, cleaned, and protected them from heat or cold. Studies by Harlow, Spitz, and Bowlby in the 1960s began to scientifically demonstrate that attachment bonds went beyond physical care and included emotional bonds between the baby and his caregivers.

I remember the birth of my first daughter as if it were yesterday, as well as the feeling of protection and care that bred inside me when I saw how helpless she was. Like many first-time parents, I was afraid of picking her up, dropping her, or hurting her if I made any sudden movement. My instincts of protection were present from the first moment I saw her. I now know that she began to activate attachments as well. Our babies, like all mammals, are born totally defenseless and without any possibility of survival if they do not have the presence and care of their parents. For this reason, they need the protection of attachment figures that feed them and take care of them for many years, until they can fend for themselves.

During their first years of life, the priority of the young is survival, linked to the preservation of a physical and emotional relationship with their caregivers. Subsequently, in puberty, hormonal changes will cause the appearance of sexuality, and the priority will change towards the search for new social bonds.

DOI: 10.4324/9781003646341-4

In adulthood, our hormones drive us towards reproduction in order to have offspring.

We are all born with innate biological schemes that are necessary for survival. In this book, we will mainly highlight two: the defense system (fear) and the attachment system (Van der Hart et al., 2006; Crittenden, 2015).

In the previous chapter, aspects of neurobiology related to defense – such as anxiety, fear, panic and, in extreme cases, traumatic dissociation – were described. In this chapter, we will look at aspects related to attachment bonding, that is, the creation of the baby's attachment bonds to the mother in the first months of life and to the other caregivers and people close to him over the next few years.

The Importance of Attachment

During childhood, as I mentioned earlier, the priority will be to preserve the attachment bond at any cost. If it is broken, the child will have to develop strategies (most of the time unconsciously) in order to find a balance that allows for emotional regulation in relation to the caregivers. With the advent of puberty and the appearance of sex hormones, the priority will not only be to preserve the bond with the caregivers, but also to look for like-minded friends and to choose intimate partners (Crittenden, 2015). While in most species there is a physical separation from the caregivers during this stage, in our species, children usually stay much longer in physical and emotional contact with their caregivers; this requires the search for a new equilibrium in order to maintain a level of emotion regulation within the family as well as with people outside of it. As we will see, it will be during this step from childhood to adolescence when many pathologies appear.

Vickie is a 14-year-old teenager who was brought to therapy by her mother because of hyperactivity problems, academic failure, and starting to use soft drugs. When I met her for the first time, I saw a girl who had already ceased to be a girl, but who had not yet begun to be a woman. She was extremely angry at her parents for the frequent fights they had in front of her and her brother (he was younger, and she felt she had to protect him). The environmental tension she felt at home prevented her from concentrating in class and her friends did not help because they too lived very difficult family situations. As with most adolescents, her main complaint was that nobody understood her.

For Bowlby (1985), attachment is "any form of behavior that results in a person attaining or retaining the proximity of another differentiated and preferred individual, usually conceived as stronger and/or wiser" (p. 203). Attachment figures are the people who will allow the child to obtain feelings of worth and safety.

The basic functions of attachment figures (see Figure 3.1) are:

A secure base: a person with whom to explore the world. It is important that caregivers do not feel afraid, because the child will learn to regulate himself through them. If the parents do not regulate the child well, he or she will not feel safe whilst exploring and learning.

The secure base has the following characteristics (Vargas & Chaskel, 2007):

- *Empathy*: understanding the child. The child should be and feel *seen*. (This is going to have a lot of impact in therapy. We often encounter patients who did not feel *seen* during childhood.);
- *Sensitivity*: correctly interpreting the needs of the child;
- *Responsiveness*: the capacity to adequately respond to the needs of the child;
- *Availability*: providing the child with the assurance that the mother will be present physically and/or emotionally when the child needs her;
- *Emotional validation*: the ability to emotionally support and also punish the child when necessary. Used in the extreme, both could become pathological.

A safe haven: These are the people to go to for protection in case of danger or threat. If the parents are a source of threat or do not help the child to regulate himself, he will have to look for alternative attachment figures or create avoidance mechanisms that allow him to survive without trusting caregivers.

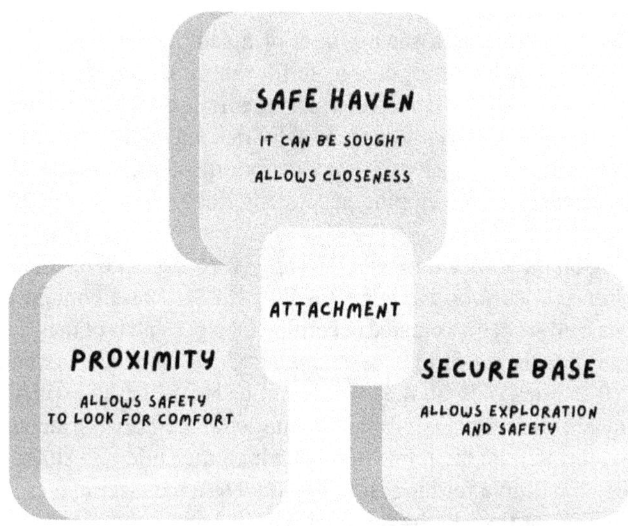

Figure 3.1 The role of caregivers with children in relation to attachment is to enable the child to feel secure, both to be able to explore-play, thus developing their self-esteem and sense of worth, and to be able to feel well-being when the child is close to the attachment figures.

In therapy, I usually ask: "During your childhood, who was the person you felt safe with?" This helps us to quickly see what the attachment relationships were like within the family. Normally, they tell us it was their mother or father. If they tell us it was a grandmother, an aunt, or a neighbor, we may suspect that the parents did not constitute a safe haven.

The function of a safe haven is to allow the child to gradually explore and move away from the caregivers, knowing that these will always be available. Exploration and play allow for the creation of important resources for emotional and physical autonomy, starting at puberty. If there is any threat or fear, there can be no exploration or play; they are two incompatible biological systems.

The child's alert circuit can be activated from the first day of life if the necessary conditions for safety by the caregivers are not provided. If the parents act as emotional regulators (as a secure basis and safe haven) the ventrovagal branch of the ANS is activated, generating a sense of peace and calmness. These sensations will allow healthy emotional development.

All parents know from experience that it is good for children to become accustomed to tolerating a degree of frustration, because it helps them develop resources to self-regulate and become stronger in the face of future threats. However, if the level of discomfort is excessive, the sympathetic branch of the ANS will be pathologically activated and, in more severe cases, so too will the dorsovagal nerve of the parasympathetic branch, leading to the possibility of collapse and dissociation.

If parents do not act as a secure basis or a safe haven, the child will tend to look for other attachment figures to fulfill that function. If he does not find them, he will have to look for alternative emotion-regulation mechanisms, such as other people, material things, or activities that help with self-regulation (Hilburn-Cobb, 2004). An excessive activation of the alert neural circuits will increase the chances of developing severe emotional disorders in adolescence and adulthood.

Depending on the interaction with the caregivers, the child develops what are known as *internal working models* (Bowlby, 1985). These contain memories, beliefs, goals, and strategies created according to experiences of the past (Botella, 2005). These models are formed at an age at which language has not yet been developed (0–3 years old), so they would not be stored in the explicit memory. Instead, they are stored in the implicit or emotional memory (Crittenden, 2005).

These models will be the foundation on which the child will shape the building in which he will live for the rest of his life – as a teenager and as an adult. If these foundations are weak, the building will not withstand difficult situations. If, for example, the parents have been very strict regarding their child's studies, he will expect everyone to be very demanding about everything he does once he is an adult; he might feel that nothing he does is ever enough.

Sean comes in suffering from irritable bowel syndrome for which doctors find no organic cause. He works as a doctor in a hospital in Malaga and recalls his final exam with horror. He spent much time vomiting, due to anxiety, due to fear of not getting good enough grades to enter medical school. This is what his father, who was also a doctor, wanted. From then on, university became an ordeal; vomiting before every exam.

T: What was it like for you to hear your father's keys opening the front door when you were young?

C: The keys? I recognized his car engine. I could hear it from afar, and I'd get up out of bed or stopped whatever I was doing, so when my father arrived, he'd find me studying.

It is important to highlight that, oftentimes, the sympathetic system in children is not necessarily activated by mistreatment, fights between the parents, or violence, but by not perceiving safety and affection from their parents. This will increase the likelihood of feeling scared or anxious in social or intimate relationships in adulthood.

The internal working models may vary from caregiver to caregiver: a child may feel a strong attachment to his mother and a lot of fear towards his father. Working models that relate to secondary caregivers, such as other family members or teachers, may also exist. These can also vary throughout life. A very good relationship may be established with a parent in childhood, yet in adolescence may become very bad, and then return to being good in adulthood (Marrone, 2009). That is to say, the internal models are not rigid and inflexible, but can change depending on the attachment figure and the person's history.

Attachment and the Brain

Hill (2015) argues that there are three important phases in neural development during the first 3 or 4 years of life:

- A neural growth that begins during the prenatal stage and continues until 16–18 months of age. During this time, the structures of the limbic system appear sequentially and are organized in a hierarchical way. The cortical structures begin to inhibit the subcortical ones; the child learns to regulate himself in a very incipient way. During this period, the circuits that connect the limbic system to the sympathetic system are developed. In addition, the child has a functional emotional system that regulates the body–mind connection.
- From 16–18 months on, the child begins to walk, and the limbic circuits that regulate the parasympathetic nervous system are innervated. The mother–child relationship continues to act as affect regulator, but the child is

increasingly able to do this in a more autonomous fashion. The orbitofrontal cortex joins the limbic system, which will allow the regulation of bodily sensations. The child can now learn to self-regulate.

- From 18 months on, the mother goes from playing 90% of the time with the child to prohibiting something every 7 minutes (Schore, 2001). This means that caregivers begin to inhibit those activities that may be inconvenient or dangerous to the child. It is at this stage when shame, the feeling of not doing what the caregivers expect, is consolidated. This stage, up until 4 years of age, is vital for the social learning that will be unconsciously coded in implicit memory.

Parents act as mirrors in which children see themselves reflected. This allows them to learn to self-regulate emotionally, since children have immature mental structures that will be developed in tune with the parents' mental structures, emotions, and behaviors. Let's see how this happens at a neurobiological level and what the repercussions are if this process is not produced optimally.

The human brain is lateralized, that is, anatomically and functionally divided into two hemispheres. These, in turn, are connected to each other by fibers called the corpus callosum. The right hemisphere matures first and is responsible for the emotional aspects; the left matures later and is related to cognitions. It has been observed that crying as a reaction to separation tends to occur more frequently in children showing a right activation pattern than in those in which the left hemisphere predominates (Aguado, 2010). Some authors argue that differences in attachment patterns in different individuals could be explained depending on which hemisphere is predominant (Crittenden, 2015).

One of the organs operative from birth is the amygdala, which, as we have seen, performs a mediating function to determine if something is dangerous or attractive. In all mammals, the first recognition factor between mother and child is smell; this is also true for human beings. Our babies, despite the poor development of this sense in our species, establish a bond with the mother through smell because the olfactory bulb sends the stimulus to the amygdala, which will store a memory of this as something pleasant. Several studies show that babies have a preference for breasts that smell like those of their mother(Panksepp & Biven, 2012).

This olfactory bonding is reinforced in a few days by positive stimuli, given that the brain of the child produces oxytocin and opiates that generate a sensation of pleasure through physical contact and caresses from the mother. This causes a virtuous cycle of pleasure and well-being in both mother and child, which guarantees the care and survival of the child. As can be seen in Figure 3.2, each hemisphere is specialized in different tasks. It is the emotional connection of the mother's and the child's right hemispheres that causes emotional attachment (Montgomery, 2013).

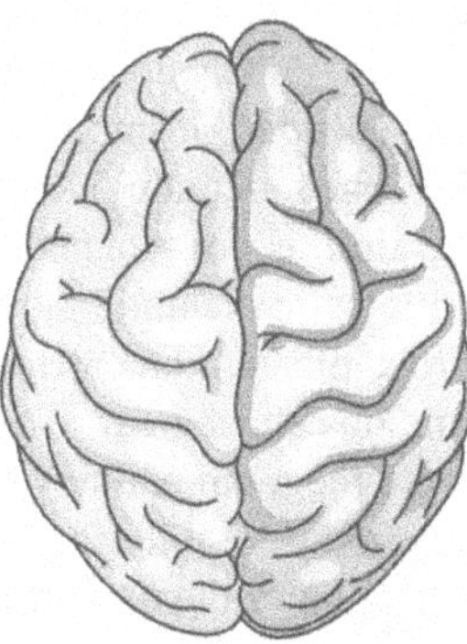

Figure 3.2 The interhemispheric division into two parts: left and right. Each hemisphere fulfills a function. The right will be more strongly related to the emotional and the abstract, while the left works with language, logic and reasoning (Source: https://www.blogdebiologia.com/lateralizacion-hemisferica.html).

After a few months, the relationship involves other bodily senses such as sight and hearing, which come to occupy the place of smell and have a shared importance with touch. Schore (2010) defines it as follows:

> The attuned mother synchronizes the spatiotemporal patterning of her exogenous sensory stimulation with the infant's spontaneous expressions of his or her endogenous organismic rhythms. Via this contingent responsivity, the mother appraises the nonverbal expressions of the infant's internal arousal and affective states, regulates them, and communicates them back to the infant. To accomplish this regulation, the mother must successfully modulate non-optimal high *or* non-optimal low levels of stimulation that would induce supra-heightened or extremely low levels of arousal in the infant. Secure attachment depends upon the mother's psychobiological attunement with the infant's internal states of arousal.
>
> (p. 299)

The mother–child relationship during the first years of life will mainly be an emotional one established through the senses, which causes synchronization in both of their respective right hemispheres (Schore, 2010). The sensations will help produce a healthy development in the child.

Let us take a look at the role of each of the senses in detail:

- The skin is the largest organ of the human body and the one through which we communicate with the outside world. It has millions of receptors that allow us to feel synchronized with the outside world. Skin contact with closely related figures generates, as we have seen, endogenous opiates and causes the child to have feelings of well-being encoded in implicit memory. These will be fundamental later on in adolescence and adulthood when the search for an intimate partner begins. If the child is not touched, kissed, or hugged when young, the body will store a traumatic memory and the adult will tend either not to feel the body, leading to avoidant attachment, or to have an excessive need for contact, leading to anxious attachment.
- The inner ear and the mouth are the main endings of the vagus nerve in the head (Porges, 2009). Its stimulation is vital for the neurological development of the child; that is why vocalization of the mother and of the caregivers are so important. Rhythmic sounds are vital for a healthy growth of the brain areas. Primates only use the maternal breast for feeding 20% of the time; the other 80% is used as a form of relaxation (Bowlby, 1985), one of the reasons why we humans give our children pacifiers. When the child sees the mother smile or move her lips, or when she uses her voice, he tends to repeat those movements, which stimulate brain areas responsible for emotions.
- Sight is another crucial sense for the mother–child attunement. We now know that the visual-facial relationship determines much of the attachment relationship (Schore, 2010). The development of the ability to recognize faces when we are adults (the ability to relate to others) depends fully on the right hemisphere.

I would like to recommend watching the video "Still Face Experiment" on YouTube (Tronick, 2007), in which a mother interacts with her son. At a certain point, her facial expression changes and turns serious and flat for 2 minutes, in order to observe the child's reaction. The child's face shows terror when he sees his mom does not react; he loses emotional attunement. In early attachment relationships, nonverbal behaviors are most important; these include gestures, vocal prosody, and touch, representing the emotional activation of the child. Attachment is not simply psychological; it is primarily a biological phenomenon.

I remember one day while I was driving the car, with my ex-wife in the passenger's seat and my one-year-old daughter sitting in the back in her safety seat. My daughter began to cry inconsolably and her mother tried to calm her down by smiling and caressing her, without being able to move from her seat. My daughter would not stop crying, much to our despair. I suggested my ex-wife take her sunglasses off and try again, which had a magical and immediate effect. I think that her eyes looking directly at the girl helped calm her down; she could not recognize her mother's gaze through the sunglasses.

Schore (2010) has created a model of the development of the right hemisphere and the regulation of emotions as detailed below (Table 3.1):

During the first 2 years of life, very rapid neuronal growth takes place, which is critical for the maturation and development of the child's brain for the rest

Table 3.1 The table shows, in detail, how the child and the mother act, and how both interact when different sensory organs are stimulated. Table adapted from the affect regulation model (Schore, 2010).

Child Context	*Maternal Context*	*Interaction*
Visual/Face		
Regulated response Oriented, explores. Stares at the mother and others. Uses a wide spectrum of expressions. Expressions of well-being.	**Regulated response** Responds to the child with a wide repertoire of facial expressions (eye contact, smiles, facial expressions).	**Regulated response** Stress regulation through eyesight. Emotional connection in the gaze. Emotional connection promotes states of well-being in both.
Stress response Eye contact is avoided. There is no exploration.	**Stress response** Still faces, incongruous or fearful expressions, such as laughing when the child is scared.	**Stress response** One of them breaks eye contact. No gaze synchronization. Absence or avoidance of eye contact.
Vocal Tone		
Regulated response Turns towards the mother's voice. Uses play language (babble, laughter).	**Regulated response** Gives varied responses of pitch and rhythm. Adjusts the tone and rhythm to the child.	**Regulated response** Synchronized hearing. Both imitate each other's tones and rhythms.
Stress response When there is stress, avoids the mother's voice. Uses crying in response to the absence of reciprocity.	**Stress response** Does not speak to the child or, if she does, does so in a way that responds to the child's emotions. Does not vocalize or yell at the child.	**Stress response** One uses a discordant tone while the other is silent or both use a discordant tone. No attunement between each other's states.
Postures/Gestures		
Regulated response Relaxed postures. Moves the body and limbs fluidly.	**Regulated response** Approaches the child gently and affectionately. Responds to the child's movements.	**Regulated response** Bodies are coordinated and there are intimate contacts. From the first year on, movements become intentionally coordinated.
Stress response Moves limbs chaotically. Moves the head, arches the body, or avoids contact with the mother.	**Stress response** Approaches the child abruptly. Touches or manipulates the child abruptly. Does not take the child's gestures into account or does not respond to his initiatives.	**Stress response** The child is uncoordinated or avoids contact with the mother. The mother accentuates abrupt gestures towards the child. The dyad fails to calm each other down.

of his life. A large part of the neuronal increase and associated synapses occurs in the prefrontal cortex which, as we have seen, is responsible for affect and self-regulation. This area, immature at birth, develops in accordance with the relationship with the mother (Coan, 2008). The internal models that regulate the relationship with oneself and others through different organs such as the amygdala, hippocampus, and prefrontal cortex depend on this development.

If everything occurs normally and the parents are able to self-regulate, they can calm and activate the child whenever necessary, allowing him to gain safety and autonomy until he reaches adolescence. By this time, he will have to start looking for like-minded people to establish relationships, and move away, emotionally and physically, from his parents. If the relationship with the mother, and later with the father, is not adequate in the first 2 years of life, the effects can last throughout the person's life and affect the choice of a suitable partner in adulthood (Crittenden, 2015). If attachment relationships are unsatisfactory or dangerous, the child is subject to painful feelings that are stored in procedural memory. In the future, his body will remember this discomfort, which will be reflected in situations when he is emotionally connected to other people. In many cases, the result will be to feel nothing at all, neither positive nor negative; not feeling is a strategy so as not to suffer.

According to Bowlby (1985), during childhood, the attachment system seeks to strike a balance between the pursuit of closeness to caregivers on the one hand and exploration on the other. If the attachment figure is close by and the environment is safe, the child will be comfortable and confident, and the exploratory behaviors (activation of the ventrovagal branch of the ANS) will be activated. On the contrary, if the child finds himself in a strange or threatening situation, behaviors of seeking the protection of attachment figures (activation of the sympathetic system of the ANS) will be activated. There are three types of situations that can trigger alertness or fear:

- *Environmental conditions*: circumstances that cause alarm or fear in adults or children. In an extreme case, if the caregiver is always anxious or scared, the child will find it impossible to explore;
- *Caregiver's conditions*: illness, absence, or loss of attachment figures;
- *Physiological conditions of the child*: hunger, thirst, cold, or illness, among others.

Luisa is a 19-year-old girl who dropped out of school and is currently unemployed. She comes to consultation because she has a severe problem with her body; she does not like her legs and is ashamed of other people seeing them. This prevents her from wearing anything other than pants, going to the beach, or getting undressed in front of her boyfriend. While gathering the clinical history, she tells me that her mother is bipolar and, ever since she was a little girl, she had to be in charge of calling the doctors when her mother entered a manic or depressive phase. She remembers her mother telling her that it was too bad she had such ugly legs; "wire legs" were the words used by her mother.

Luisa associated the discomfort caused by her mother's crises and the lack of emotional attunement to something that was defective in her own person, in this case, her legs. It is as if she placed all the discomfort she felt because of her belief of being defective or unworthy due to the relationship with her mother in one part of her body. It is what we know as body dysmorphic disorder, which we so often see in eating disorders.

> *Cristina is a 36-year-old woman who, as she describes it, has never had any luck in her relationships. Now she has found someone with whom she has stability, but is unable to convince herself that everything is going well. She is still afraid that, at any moment, things will go wrong and her partner will abandon her. When we went over her clinical history, she told me that she was the third of three siblings. She had one more sister, but she died at 3 years of age of meningitis and so they decided to have another child (Cristina) as a way to overcome the pain and the grief. They even gave her the same name as her deceased sister: Cristina.*
>
> *T:* How did you feel as a child? How did it feel to replace that child who had left?
>
> *C:* It was a constant sensation of feeling that everything I did was wrong. I was constantly compared to her: Your sister didn't cry, your sister was very good, your sister finished her meals … It was as if I was constantly competing with someone so perfect it was impossible to live up to. Maybe it would have been better if I had not been born; that way I would not have been a burden to my parents.

In humans, unlike in other animals, ruptures in the dyadic mother–child relationship can be real or imaginary:

- *Real ruptures in attachment*: the death of the mother or the father; abandonment by the father (and, although they are scarcer, abandonment by the mother may also exist); hospitalization of the mother or the child; long absence of the mother because she takes care of other people, works long hours, or travels frequently.
- Imaginary ruptures of attachment: postpartum depression; unwanted children; replacement children; death of someone close to the mother; personality disorders; avoidant, anxious, or disorganized attachment of the mother, the father, or both.

Healthy attachment allows for the healthy maturation of the nervous system. When the baby feels stress or fear, the right hemisphere is activated, increasing the activity of the sympathetic branch of the ANS, accelerating the heart rate and increasing catecholamines in the bloodstream and hypothalamus; the same happens when the environment is perceived as dangerous (Schore, 2001).

The emotional connection between mother and child is vital during the first 2 years of the child's life. The limbic system, responsible for the emotions, is myelinated in the first year of a human being's life. The right hemisphere, which ideally connects to this system, develops long before the left one. Therefore, authors such as Schore (1994) postulate that an attachment experience would be the attunement between the right hemisphere of the child and that of the mother, specifically the orbitofrontal cortex.

In threatening or fearful situations, if the caregivers do not regulate the child (i.e., do not provide safety for the child) and the sympathetic nervous system is activated for too long, the dorsovagal branch will cause a traumatic dissociation both on a mental (van der Hart et al., 2006) and physical level (Nijenhuis, 2000; Scaer, 2014). In this state of dissociative numbness, the endogenous opioids are extremely high and the brainstem, through the dorsovagal branch, will cause a drop in arterial or blood pressure, metabolic activity, and heart rate, which, in turn, causes the circulation of more adrenaline in the blood. This activation of the parasympathetic system (hypoactivation) is a way of counteracting the hyperactivation of the sympathetic system, which, paradoxically, is extremely traumatic (Schore, 2010) (see Chapter 2).

At an early age, when the hippocampus has not yet reached maturity, all memory will be emotional, and trauma will be stored in procedural memory (Scaer, 2014). It has been observed that chronic stress favors the acquisition of basic emotional learning related to the amygdala (fear), but prevents the acquisition of more complex learning dependent on the hippocampus (Aguado, 2010).

Figure 3.3 details the sequence before the risk of a threat. It is the same as that produced in an adult brain, but in infants it is extremely dangerous and pathological due to the fragility and immaturity of the system.

This dysregulation does not only occur in the baby when the mother is not present; it may also occur in the face of other types of threats. If this process is repeated frequently, dysregulation will become chronic and cause constant states of hypo- and hyperactivation in adolescence and adulthood. This biological process is the origin of disorganized attachment. Damage to the right hemisphere, hippocampus, and other organs of the brain will prevent the person from emotionally regulating himself in adulthood when faced with stressful events, such as having children, which will transmit the pathology to the offspring.

This emotion regulation or mentalization in humans is vital for achieving three goals at a biological level (Trevarthen, 2009):

- Subjective regulation: learning to self-regulate within healthy boundaries;
- Inter-subjective regulation: learning to relate to others;
- Next-generation regulation: adequately regulating offspring.

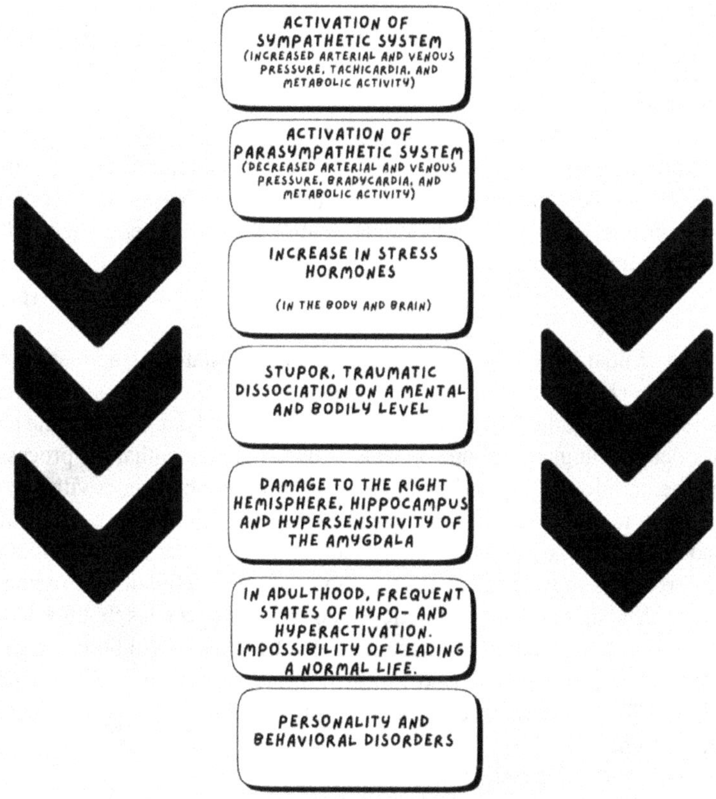

Figure 3.3 In this diagram, we can see the different phases that the nervous system goes through in case of an alarm, which might range from a slight activation to traumatic dissociation depending on the level of danger and the resources available to face it.

According to Schore (2001):

> A number of functions located within the right hemisphere work together to aid the monitoring of a baby. As well as emotion and face processing, the right hemisphere is also specialized in auditory perception, the perception of intonation, attention, and tactile information. Social experiences thus facilitate the experience-dependent critical period maturation of right brain systems that process visual-facial, auditory-prosodic, and tactile-gestural affective communications. From infancy through all later stages of life, the right hemisphere is the dominant one for non-conscious reception, expression,

> and communication of emotion, as well as for the cognitive and physiological components of emotional processing.
>
> (p. 301)

Trevarthen (2009) highlights:

> The emotional expression of a person and the sympathetic response to them elicited in another individual are associated with increased activity in the same brain regions in both individuals, with activated systems that include subcortical, limbic areas, and neocortical elements.
>
> (p. 59)

The mother–child relationship regulates the internal states of activation and calmness in the child. If there is sympathetic hyperactivation without emotional stabilization on the mother's part, or if she is causing the dysregulation, the child will suffer deep feelings of discomfort. It is important to know that the process of rupturing the emotional connection and subsequent reconnecting is vital, so the child can learn to self-regulate without the presence of the mother. These ruptures become pathological if they are frequent, long lasting, or either too intense.

Good caregivers regulate extreme situations of hyperactivation or hypoactivation in the child that may be traumatic. Cozolino (2016) argues that the activation occurring in a situation of fear, as we saw in Chapter 2, will be internalized by babies as "I am not loved" and "I am rejected," because of its traumatic impact. Later, these internalized sensations cause feelings of shame, rejection, and abandonment in adulthood.

Once again, following Schore (2010):

> The mother may lay the foundation for the child for a lifelong tendency towards propagation of anxiety or other emotions. By forcing the child to distance himself from such an intense and therefore traumatizing experience, she can promote an impoverished psychological organization in the child; the psychological organization of a person who might later be unable to be empathic, to experiment human experiences, in essence, unable to be fully human.
>
> (p. 302)

If emotion regulation is adequate, the child is able to *mentalize* (Fonagy & Luyten, 2014), which means that he is able to emotionally self-regulate and regulate himself through others by finding a balance in the use of cortical and subcortical areas.

Implicit Memory Circuits

Dopamine is an important neurotransmitter for development and is associated with positive reinforcement and rewards. In relation to attachment behaviors, it is intimately linked to the role of oxytocin and motivates the mutual search in the baby–caregiver dyad, as well as reproduction in adults (Panksepp & Biven, 2012). It causes a sense of satisfaction when something is achieved. The most important brain area associated with this neurotransmitter is the corpus striatum.

This region is closely related to cortical areas and is largely responsible for procedural learning (see Chapter 5). Every time an action, sensation, or emotion is stored as positive, there is an increase in dopamine; this information is stored in the corpus striatum (see Figure 3.4). It is also connected to the amygdala and hippocampus, and plays an integrative role in motivation (Damasio, 2003; Koziol & Budding, 2010).

Learned information is stored in the cortex with a positive or negative emotional valence. If a similar situation occurs again, we will have a similar sensation, emotion, or thought, without it taking place in a conscious manner (Ginot, 2015). This could explain why many impulsive actions that cannot be avoided take place, despite the knowledge that later on they will cause discomfort and/or

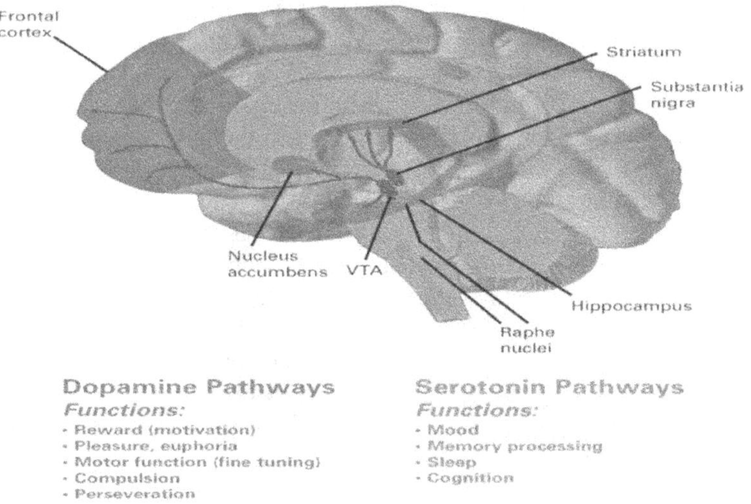

Figure 3.4 Dopamine is the neurotransmitter of reward. It is associated with gratification and motivation. If at any point something had a positive emotional effect, there will be a peak in the production of dopamine. In the future, one can try to find this same sensation with behaviors that are considered pathological.

pain. It is very likely that dopamine will greatly influence impulsivity, which is very important in psychopathology.

When Liam first came in to his appointment, he made a very good impression on me on a personal level – we had a very pleasant conversation, he had a good sense of humor – but it was hard to know exactly what his reason was for coming to therapy. In the third session, he told me he had a gaming problem. He was a pathological gambler.

Working on this topic (which was the one that truly brought him to consultation), he explained that he felt an overwhelming desire to hit the slot machines. This only happened on weekends, when he had more time off; during the week, when he was busy working all day, he felt no desire to gamble. When the weekend was over and he realized how much money he had lost (sometimes, he would win but, obviously, this was rare), he felt deep remorse and swore over and over that he would not do it again, only to repeat it the following weekend.

Koziol and Budding (2010) maintain that dopamine circuits are also involved in interpersonal relationships, as they are connected to the orbitofrontal cortex. Thus, people with secure attachment who have experienced personal relationships in childhood as positive will tend to create healthy bonds with others, and the sensation of seeking healthy relationships with friends or partners will be strengthened.

This does not mean that the brain acts rigidly in terms of what it has learned in childhood. Procedural learning is very useful for acting repetitively and spending as little energy as possible, but the neocortex, through awareness, allows flexibility in behaviors and emotions that are often spontaneous and/or repetitive. Most of the time, it will be easy to change them, but they will be more difficult to change or remove based on their anxiolytic effect.

Individuals who have not been able to learn to regulate themselves in childhood (see Chapter 5) do not have the ability to integrate new learning and are doomed to repeat emotions and/or behaviors even if these are harmful. The reward circuit may explain why many of the pathological behaviors learned in childhood and adolescence are so difficult to change or eliminate later on in life. This would explain, for example, the difficulty in treating addictions or eating disorders.

Elijah is a 31-year-old patient who comes to consultation because he is overweight. He wants to eat less, but at lunchtime or dinnertime he eats a lot. A little while later he feels hungry and has to eat again.

T: Have you ever felt a sensation of emptiness?

C: Yes. Ever since I can remember. I've always had the feeling there was something missing inside.

T: And how did you calm this down when you were little?

C: I ate. I remember being with my grandmother, having fun and, yes, always eating. She was the typical person who was always cooking and giving you food. I was happy with her.

T: Have you ever thought that maybe you are using food as a means to be happy and not feel the anxiety?

C: I've never seen it that way.

Many of the disorders that we are going to see in our practice are related to things that happened in childhood; the mechanisms that were used to reduce discomfort then will continue to be used no matter how long it has been.

Conclusions

Children are born with several innate biological systems. In this chapter, we have talked about attachment and defense, both of which are vital for the survival of the baby. The mother figure is crucial during the first 2 years of life to regulate and care for the child, both physically and emotionally. If the mother is unable to self-regulate, she will be unable to regulate her child.

In many cases where the mother is not present physically or emotionally, the child will be forced to regulate himself through something that can replace that absence (other people, material things, tasks, etc.). If these absences are excessive, or if the mother is a source of threat or discomfort for the child, all brain circuits responsible for fear and anxiety will be activated. In order to deal with the discomfort, the child dissociates psychically and somatically, with traumatic consequences. The mother is necessary for calming the child, but if she does not do this, or if dysregulation increases, damage might be pathological and permanent.

As a result, the child grows with an insecure attachment and is unable to self-regulate and regulate himself with others. This can lead to anxiety disorders, social phobias, panic attacks, or personality disorders.

The importance of attachment relationships with caregivers is, literally, vital to the child's physical and emotional survival. If these do not exist or when they are defective, the damage could be permanent and irreparable. In some cases, there may be substitute figures that allow for the child's resilience and, subsequently, an acquired secure attachment may emerge.

References

Aguado, L. (2010). *Emoción, afecto y motivación*. Alianza editorial.

Botella, L. (2005). Neurobiología de la autorregulación afectiva, patrones de apego y compatibilidad en la relación terapeuta-paciente. *Revista de psicoterapia*, *XVI*(61), 77–103.

Bowlby, J. (1985). *Attachment and loss: Volume II. Separation*. Basic Books.

Crittenden, P. (2005). Attachment theory, psychopathology, and psychotherapy: The dynamic-maturational approach. Teoria dell'attaccamento, psicopatologia e psicoterapia: L'approccio dinamico maturativo. *Psicoterapia, 30*, 171–182.

Coan, J. (2008). Toward a neuroscience of attachment. In J. Cassidy & P. Shaver (Eds.), *Handbook of attachment. Theory, research and clinical applications* (pp. 249–261). Guilford press.

Cozolino, L. (2016). Why therapy works: Using our minds to change our brains. W. W. Norton & Company.

Crittenden, P. (2015). *Raising parents: Attachment, representation, and treatment*. Routledge.

Damasio, A. R. (2003). *Looking for Spinoza: Joy, sorrow, and the feeling brain*. Harcourt.

Eco, U. (2013). *The search for the perfect language*. Fontana Press.

Fonagy, P., & Luyten, P. (2014). Mentalising in attachment context. In P. Holmes & S. Farnfield (Eds.), *The routledge handbbok of attachment*. Routledge.

Ginot, E. (2015). *The neuropsychology of the unconscious*. Norton.

Hill, D. (2015). *Affect regulation theory. A clinical model*. Norton.

Hilburn-Cobb, C. (2004). Adolescent psychopathology in terms of multiple behavioral systems: The role of attachment and controlling strategies and frankly disorganized behavior. In L. Atkinson & S. Goldberg (Eds.), *Attachment issues in psychopathology and intervention* (pp. 95–137). Routledge.

Koziol, L., & Budding, D. (2010). *Subcortical structures and cognition. Implications for neuroppsychological assesment*. Springer.

Marrone, M. (2009). *La teoría del apego. Un enfoque actual*. Psimática.

Montgomery, A. (2013). *Neurobiology essentials for clinicians*. Norton.

Nijenhuis, E. (2000). Somatoform dissociation: Major symptoms of dissociative disorders. *Journal of Trauma & Dissociation, 1*(4), 33–66.

Panksepp, J., & Biven, L. (2012). The archaeology of mind: Neuroevolutionary origins of human emotions. W. W. Norton & Company.

Porges, S. (2009). Reciprocal influences between body and brain in the perception and expression of affect: A polyvagal perspective. In D. Fosha, D. J. Siegel, & M. F. Solomon (Eds.), The healing power of emotion (pp. 27–55). W. W. Norton & Company.

Scaer, R. (2014). *The body bears the burden: Trauma, dissociation, and disease*. Routledge.

Schore, A. (1994). *Affect regulation and the repair of the self*. Norton.

Schore, A. (2001). The effects of a secure attachment relationship on roght brain development, affect regulation & infant mental health. *Infant Mental Health Journal, 22*, 7–66.

Schore, A. (2010). Relational trauma and the developing right brain. In T. Baradon (Ed.), *The neurobiology of broken attachment bonds. Psychoanalytic, attachment and neuropschological contributions to parent-infan psychotherapy*. Routledge.

Trevarthen, C. (2009). The functions of emotion in infancy: The regulation and communication or rythm, sympathy, and meaning in human development. In D. Fosha, D. J. Siegel, & M. F. Solomon (Eds.), *The healing power of emotions* (pp. 55–86). Norton.

Tronick, E. (2007). *The neurobehavioral and social-emotional development of infants and children*. Norton.

Van der Hart, O., Nijenhuis, E. R. S., & Steele, K. (2006). *The haunted self: Structural dissociation and the treatment of chronic traumatization*. Norton & Company.

Vargas, A., & Chaskel, M. D. (2007). Neurobiología del apego. *Avances en psiquiatría Biológica*, *8*, 44–56.

4 Attachment as a Means of Emotion Regulation

What is Attachment?

A few years ago, I heard about attachment for the first time. I was impressed with how it allowed me to understand the behaviors and emotions of human beings beyond childhood, even in adult life. For me it was a revelation, something that united and gave sense to a big part of my knowledge regarding psychology and biology. As I studied and explored the subject, I was increasingly surprised by the importance of childhood bonds in the biological organization of the brain and the way in which it explained many of the disorders that patients present in consultation.

I firmly believe that, in the future, the two fields where most psychological research will be carried out are 1) attachment and 2) the neurobiology of the brain, especially the way in which it is modeled to adapt to the circumstances of the environment. While there is no doubt that genetics play a fundamental role in mental development, we know from epigenetic studies that genes can also be influenced by environmental conditions. For example, the genetic predisposition to produce higher amounts of cortisol or serotonin is strongly influenced by how the mother felt during pregnancy and during the first months of the baby's life (Yehuda, 2016).

The relationships we establish with our attachment figures help us understand how we see the world, how we experience conflict, and how we relate to others. Bowlby (1977) defines attachment behavior as: "any form of behavior that results in a person attaining or retaining the proximity to some other differentiated and preferred individual, who is usually conceived as stronger and/or wiser" (p. 292). Yet, attachment is more than physical closeness; it also includes the need for an emotional connection, from which the child gains the necessary security to explore his environment.

In Figure 4.1, we see a mother with her child in her arms. The relationship between mother and child is perceived as one of affection and harmony; the two mutually regulate each other in a healthy way.

The internal working models created during childhood and stored in our implicit memory determine how we see the world and how we expect it to behave towards us. They contain the expectations we have about ourselves,

DOI: 10.4324/9781003646341-5

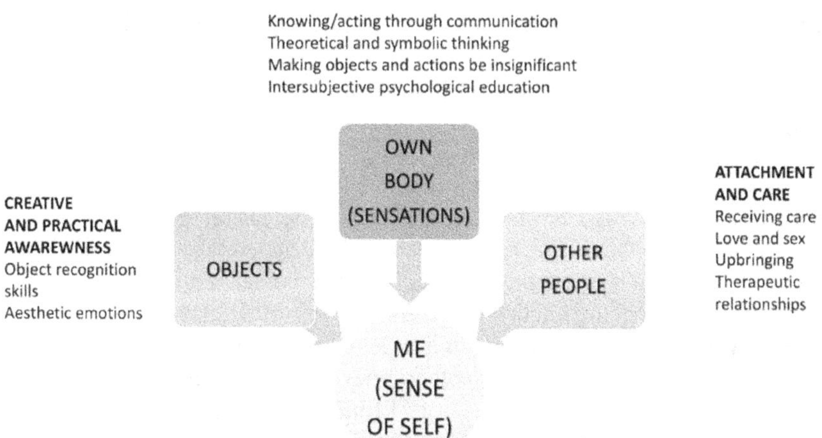

Figure 4.1 The relationships of the individual are marked by attachment relationships with other people, external objects, and with our own feelings. In order to achieve healthy emotion regulation, a correct balance between these three factors should take place.

about significant people, and our relationships with them. These models, learned in childhood, will be vital in adulthood, because they determine how we relate to others.

Children who had attachment figures that were available and attentive to their needs will create a representation of themselves as worthy people. Those who had inconsistent or abusive attachment figures will develop a defective or invalid sense of self (Cassidy, 2000).

If we close our eyes and spend a few seconds remembering the people closest to us in our childhood, we will experience different sensations: love, fear, disgust, admiration, and so on. Those people with whom we felt safe gave us a sense of calm that helped us feel accepted and important. On the other hand, those who generate unpleasant sensations when we remember them are those that made us feel alert. As we saw in the previous chapter, fear and alertness are incompatible with healthy mental development.

From the moment of birth, the baby maintains contact and relates to internal (sensations) and external factors, such as caregivers and physical objects. As we can observe in Figure 4.1, all these aspects are interrelated and mutually influence one another to construct a sense of self.

In order to study the child's relationship with his or her caregivers, Ainsworth, heavily influenced by Bowlby, conducted a series of experiments to evaluate how children behaved when a situation of fear was induced. As a result, they could study the reaction of children and their relationship with their parents.

This experiment consists of two parts. During the first part, the mother and the child (about 18 months of age) were visited at home, and the way in which they related to each other was observed. The second part was done in the laboratory, inducing stressful situations in the child and observing how he reacted towards his mother. Both were in a room; the child played with toys while the mother watched. After a few minutes, a stranger entered and spent a few minutes with them. Then, the mother left the room. Soon, the mother would return and the stranger would leave. A few minutes later, the mother would leave again and leave the child alone for another couple of minutes (Hill, 2015).

Following the results, they established three styles of attachment depending on the child's relationship to the mother. They showed that maternal sensitivity determines the quality of attachment at 12 months. Inconsistent mothers have anxious children, rejecting mothers have avoidant children, and sensitive mothers have secure children. Subsequently, they saw that some children did not enter any of the previous classifications and created yet another additional category: *disorganized attachment.*

In later investigations, they concluded that the children's attachment almost always coincided with that of the parents. In 70% of the cases, the same

Table 4.1 This table shows the strategies associated with different attachment styles in both children and caregivers. Extracted from Holmes (2001).

Attachment Style	*Parent's Strategy*	*Child's Developmental Strategy*
Secure attachment (TYPE B)	Long-term, capable, and willing to invest a lot of effort in the responsibility of looking after the child.	Maximizes long-term learning. Maintains the investment of the "healthy" parent.
Avoidant attachment (TYPE A)	Short term, not willing to invest in the child. Indifference or rejection towards the child.	Maximizes short-term survival. Avoids the non-protective parent or caregiver.
Insecure attachment (ambivalent) (TYPE C)	Short term, unable to invest energy in the child. Makes efforts to be a good parent but with inadequate resources. Inconsistent, worried, but does not reject the child.	Maximizes short-term maturation. Maintains role reversal. Parentification occurs.
Disorganized attachment (TYPE D)	None or very little investment in the child. The attachment figure is also a source of abuse or fear.	Spends a lot of energy on defense, cannot mature. Lack of coherence in everyday actions, with partners, etc.

attachment style occurs regarding both parents, and in the remaining 30%, there may be different attachment styles with the father or mother, grandparents, siblings, or other relatives (Feeney et al., 1996). The classification according to the attachment style is shown in Table 4.1:

The four phases of the child's development in relation to attachment to the caregivers are (Bowlby, 1983):

1. *Pre-attachment phase* (first 2 months): Behaviors activated in the baby regardless of the attachment figure. They are indiscriminate and innate, that is to say, instinctive, and occur in the presence of any human figure (e.g., looking at a person, stop crying in the presence of an adult, smiling).
2. *Attachment formation phase* (2–6 months): The baby can recognize the mother from other unknown individuals. The previous behaviors focus more exclusively on the mother. If the mother is not able to emotionally regulate the child, the circuits of attachment and fear will be activated simultaneously, with disastrous effects for the child's emotional development.
3. *Attachment phase* (from 6 months to 3 years): At this stage, the attachment relationship with the mother and the main caregivers is consolidated. The hippocampus develops and starts to regulate the activation of the amygdala. Three other behavioral systems are fully developed, which will be imperative for the rest of the person's life:
    a. *Defensive system*: reactions of fear or caution against unknown people or situations. The child uses caregivers as a secure basis and safe haven, and can begin to assess the source and intensity of the threats.
    b. *Affiliative system*: This is the consolidation of affection with the figures that will become attachment figures. If these do not meet the child's needs or are a source of threat (i.e., they activate the fear system), the child will not be able to develop systems of emotion regulation.
    c. *Exploratory system*: This allows the child to gradually develop independence. It is closely related to the fear system, since exploration and play are impossible when fear is activated. If the attachment figure is anxious and/or overprotective, the child will not be allowed to develop his autonomy, which will lead to a lack of resources and self-esteem in adulthood. Barg (2010) states, "Under normal conditions, as exploratory/approaching behaviors occur, the child will be able to build his or her secure basis and safe haven. The place where to leave from safely and where to return to without fear."
4. *Formation of a mutual relation phase* (from 3 years onwards): With the appearance of language, the child learns to internalize social behaviors and begins to have impulse control. Self-regulation is consolidated in relation to others.

These four phases are important for the occurrence of two aspects which are fundamental to the healthy development of the child's mind: affiliation/attachment and exploration. These two systems allow the child to feel loved and safe to play and explore. If there is fear, exploration is impossible, and the proximity of the caregivers will be sought. If they are also the source of the threat, the child will find himself in a paradoxical situation of simultaneously seeking closeness and withdrawing. In severe cases, it will lead to collapse and dissociation, as we saw in the previous chapter.

If the caregiver is anxious, the child will perceive that exploration can be dangerous and will inhibit play behavior and autonomy. When he reaches puberty, he will neither have the resources to be a secure person nor relate to others properly. If the caregiver is cold and the child does not feel loved and validated, he may experience problems with self-esteem and self-confidence. Figure 4.2 shows how the attachment style varies according to the level of alertness of the child in relation to the caregivers, that is, to his perceived safety.

Bowlby (1983) suggested that there are three circumstances that determine the relationship between attachment and the subsequent emergence of disorders in adulthood:

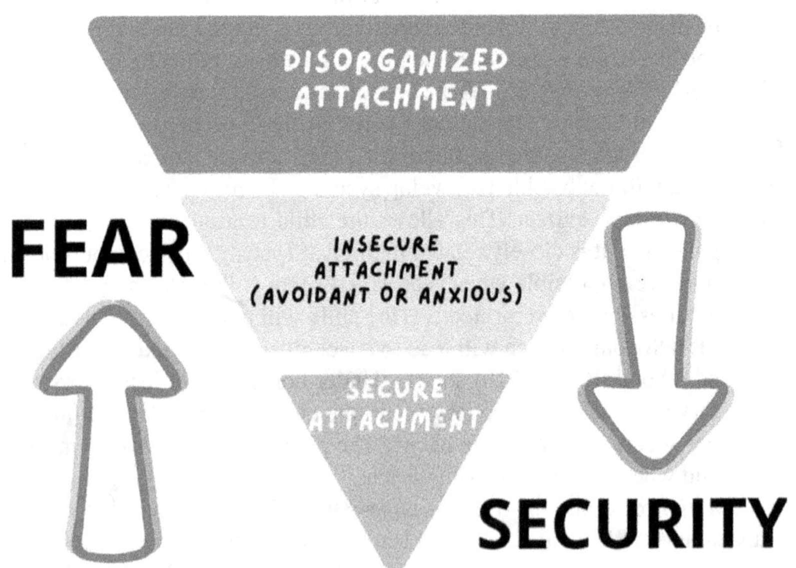

Figure 4.2 The sense of security and the absence of fear allow the child to have secure attachment. The less safety there is and the greater the fear or alert, the more pathological the attachment relationships with the caregivers will be.

- When one parent (or both) dies and the child perceives no control over events, he develops a sense of hopelessness and helplessness about any subsequent traumatic event;
- When the child is unable to develop (after many attempts) a secure attachment relationship with the parents, he will develop a sense of being defective. When events of loss or rejection occur later on in life, the person will perceive that he is defective;
- When the parents give the child the message that he is incompetent or does not deserve to be loved, he will assess himself as a person who does not deserve love and, therefore, that no one can love.

Marisa came to consultation suffering from strong anxiety and a generalized fear of almost everything. Taking on any task or doing something out of the ordinary could turn into a torment of fear and anxiety. When asked about her relationship with her mother, she gave me an example that was quite significant.

"My father worked nights and my mother was extremely fearful. So in the summer, when my father went to work at 8 p.m., my mother would lower all the blinds and tell us that it was nighttime and that we had to go to sleep. She would go to bed and cover herself all the way up to her head for fear of being alone. It was easier in winter, but in summer, when it was still daylight, I listened to the girls play in the street and I felt terrible that I could not have a mother like the others."

Antonio was a patient in his 40s. He made an impression because of his good manners; they were excessive, I could almost say cloying. Everything was correct, and he seemed to be constantly holding back. His issues were that he felt lonely and did not understand why he could not have a relationship like other men his age. He had never had a girlfriend, he had not even flirted. His relationship with women was limited to prostitutes.

It was very difficult to get him to give details about his childhood. His mother was a widow; his father died when he was very young. The mother raised him all by herself, with no relatives to help her. He did not remember having any friends in childhood or having suffered any major trauma.

When questioned about how his relationship with his mother was, he replied that she was a very religious person (he remembered praying the Rosary together every night) and very strict regarding food, order, and cleanliness. When I asked him if he could remember any display of affection from his mother, he was not able to give me a single example.

These two cases show us two pathological forms of interpersonal relationships with caregivers. In the first case, the mother's fear prevented the patient from feeling like a normal child who could do the same things her friends did. In the second case, Antonio's life was an emotional desert in which there was not a single sign of affection; the only important thing was how to face others. Both cases are equally traumatic: one because of overprotection and the other because of lack of affection.

Children with an avoidant attachment sacrifice closeness to avoid rejection or aggression; the child learns that he has to fend for himself and cannot trust others. On the other hand, those who tend towards anxious or ambivalent attachment cling to the caregiver, even in the absence of danger, due to hyperactivation of attachment behavior. They learn that it is dangerous to be alone without a protector nearby. In disorganized attachment, there is an approaching-distancing of the attachment figures that causes the impossibility of creating a secure basis (Holmes, 2001).

Balbi (2008) defends two different models within the anxious attachment:

- *Hyperprotective* style: Parents are permanently frightened and afraid that something may happen to the child. They are usually phobic parents or parents with personality disorders. Their explanations about having to overprotect the child include such reasoning as: "the world is a very dangerous place," "if something bad happens to you, I would die," "I really like being with you and I do not want to be alone." Instead of direct coercion, there is

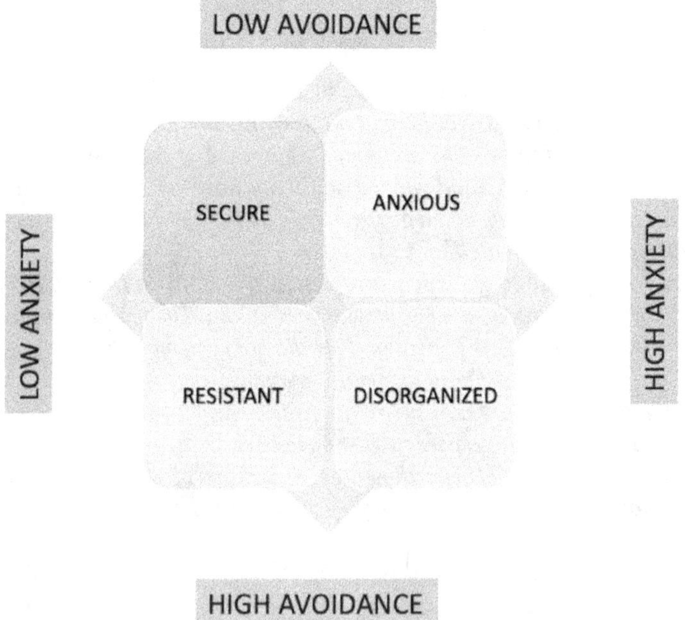

Figure 4.3 The type of relationship established with caregivers will determine the attachment style of the child. The two main factors are the degree of family avoidance (lack of affection) and the degree of anxiety (alertness or fear).

emotional blackmail that makes the child unable to become independent of the parents and perceive coercion as a token of affection from the parents.

- *Coercive or threatening* style: They maintain closeness through threats, letting the child know that if he walks away something bad may happen to the parent. There is an inverted attachment relationship (parentification), in which the child has the obligation to care for the parent.

In both cases, the child will feel that he has to be close to the parents in order to feel good. In turn, he will be chained by the fear of moving away from them and, therefore, will not be able to develop the exploratory behaviors necessary for proper emotional development.

Patricia Crittenden, a doctoral student of Mary Ainsworth, created a more complex model that she called the Dynamic-Maturational Model (DMM), based on her teacher's model. (This model varies from the original proposal.

According to Crittenden (2015), there is a direct relationship between the attachment strategies acquired in childhood and the selection of partners in adolescence and adulthood. The two vital goals of the human species are, firstly, surviving childhood and, secondly, being able to reproduce. The child will live with one attachment style or another depending on two criteria:

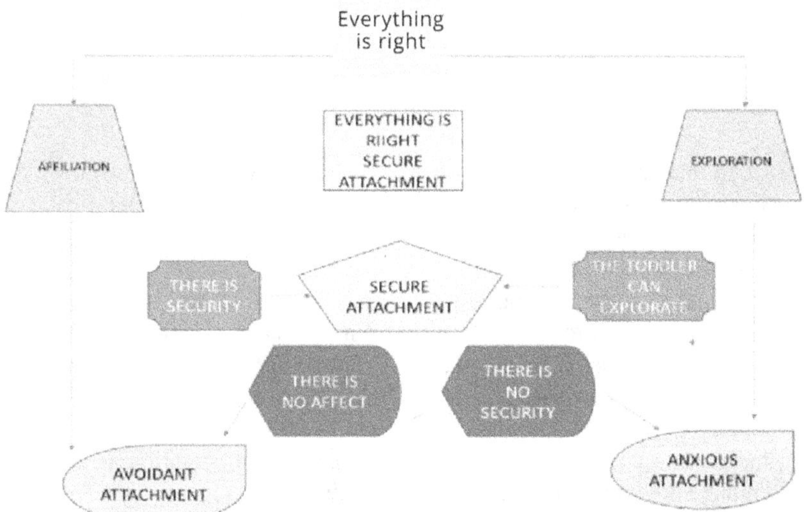

Figure 4.4 This figure details how secure attachment allows the child to emotionally regulate himself in contact with the caregivers and feel there is affection. Avoidant attachment involves a lack of affection, and anxious attachment does not allow the child to regulate himself because the parents themselves do not know how to do it.

- *Source of information*: cognitive versus affective (rational or emotional). This is related to *when* one can expect something good (a kiss) or something dangerous (anger and criticism). It is supposed to be related to the cortical areas;
- *Degree of integration of information*: integrated versus non-integrated. This is related to the subcortical areas and refers to the relationship between good and bad, that is, between comfort and discomfort.

Rose comes to a session after having called three times with doubts about the effectiveness of therapy. She has visited many psychologists and none have been able to help her. She is sick of therapy and makes it clear from the start that I am her last hope.

"What brings you to therapy? How can I help you?"

- *"I have a lot of anxiety. I can't sleep. I think my boyfriend's going to leave me because every time we're together we argue, and when I'm not with him, I call him asking for forgiveness. I very much regret the things I say to him when I'm upset, it's just that when I'm with him, he gets on my nerves."*
- *"Who do you live with now?"*
- *"My mother. She's very nervous and I believe that what happens to me is largely her fault. She's always scared: because I'm going to lose my job, because I should be careful in the streets, because she doesn't like my boyfriend. She's always been like this. I remember when I was 12 or 13 and my friends went out together on Saturdays, and she wouldn't let me go because she told me it was dangerous."*

The following circumstances may occur:

1. Cognition and affection develop in an integrated way. This is what we call *secure attachment* (type B). These individuals use both the subcortical areas related to emotions and the cortical ones related to control and cognition in a balanced way.
1 They adapt to the circumstances and are flexible in their responses. They can both be close to and walk away from their caregivers in a healthy way. When faced with stressful situations in adulthood, they are able to come up with balanced responses that involve the rational and emotional areas of the brain.
2 Individuals with an *avoidant pattern* (type A) use cognition as a way of coping with uncertainty and lack of affection. The use of cortical areas predominates. Children with this regulatory strategy organize their behavior cognitively, based on the predictable responses of their parents. They inhibit the manifestation of negative affect by doing what they believe their parents expect from them, trying not to be a nuisance or a burden (which is how they

feel). In adulthood, they will want to have everything under control, and anxiety will appear when those control strategies fail or are overwhelmed.

3 *Ambivalent* or *anxious* individuals (type C) give predominance to emotion, to subcortical areas. Cognition is scarcely used, and they do not plan as a way to regulate themselves against the uncertainty of not knowing whether to expect something good or bad. They use exaggerated affection to relate to caregivers. They learn to alternate emotions of anger and submission.
4 The individual gives priority to emotions because it is very difficult to predict what will happen. This strategy is based on seeking constant emotional and physical contact. He cannot be away from his caregivers and always feels fear and anxiety. When he becomes an adult, he will perceive that he is unable to have any control. He will feel constant anxiety and will not know how to create strategies to be able to regulate himself and diminish it. They may be adults who either do not trust the intentions of others or are extremely trusting: there is no middle ground.
5 The child with *disorganized attachment* may not prioritize any brain area because the people who should protect him are the source of the threat. They will exhibit extreme behaviors, from total absence of emotions to excessive emotional liability. They will be bullies or bullied. In adulthood, they will be problematic people with situations of risk in academic, work, and family aspects. In women, a tendency to suffer borderline personality disorder may develop and, in males, antisocial behavior.

Annette is a very skinny 26-year-old woman with bags under her eyes; she looks disheveled and gives the impression of great suffering. She works odd jobs and cannot pay for therapy, but an aunt of hers ("the mother I never had") makes her come and pays for her treatment.

"What is the happiest moment of your life?"

"The happiest moment? I don't remember much about my childhood. But I do remember that it made me very sad when I left the hospital after an angina operation I had when I was 8. The 15 days I spent there were maybe the happiest of my life."

"A stay in the hospital and at that age is something very traumatic."

"You wouldn't understand, Manuel. There, I had children to play with, the nurses took care of me. My parents came to see me every day and they never fought when they were there. They even gave me a stuffed animal one day. I still have it. The bad part was leaving the hospital. I went home and saw that everything was still the same. My parents' fights, the drugs, beating me over anything ..."

Crittenden redefined Bowlby's concept of the internal working model and called it *dispositional representations*. They are the representations that the child creates between the context and the caregivers, along with the expectation of the response he will obtain as a result of his actions. These representations change with age as threats change and new resources appear (Crittenden, 2015). According to this author, early experiences will make the child seek strategies of regulation during childhood to interact with caregivers. These will be used in adolescence when choosing a partner and will strengthen in adulthood.

The model presents different strategies that will change or strengthen during the different phases of childhood, adolescence, and maturity. Crittenden (2012) classifies each attachment style into different subtypes:

In a circular diagram, it would be represented as follows:

The diagram shows the different attachment styles and the fact that, as the threat increases and/or the available resources decrease, different attachment subtypes with different personality traits may occur. The process is dynamic throughout life: some subtypes of attachment will appear in childhood, others in adolescence, and others in adulthood. These subtypes can vary over time because of a relationship with a friend or partner, or a therapeutic relationship that allows the person not to feel threatened and/or helps to enhance the existing resources. This will enable the individual to modify his or her attachment style to what is known as *acquired secure attachment* (Feeney & Noller, 1996).

Conclusions

All mammals are born with basic emotional circuits. One of the most important ones is related to the attachment relationship with the mother during the first year of life and with other caregivers later on in life. The child will try to restore the bond if it is broken because of neglect or aggression and, if unable to do so, will create strategies for self-regulation. If this happens frequently and in a traumatic way, it will cause permanent changes in the child's emotional development later on.

A child with stable parents will develop a secure attachment; a child with cold or unloving parents will have an avoidant attachment. Furthermore, if the parents are anxious or unpredictable, the attachment will be anxious. When caregivers are never available or are the source of the threat, a disorganized attachment may be developed.

Some authors (Crittenden, 2002, 2015) have established different attachment subtypes based on previous classifications founded on two factors: the predictability of parental behaviors and their affective capacity. Children will act and regulate themselves differently depending on how their parents do it (in addition to the genetic traits that determine character). The strategies to manage uncertainty or lack of affection will sow the seeds of the personality that will grow during adulthood.

From a very early age, children will have to adapt their behavior to that of their caregivers and create strategies to reduce uncertainty based on parental actions or omissions. In adolescence, the threats and the available resources

Table 4.2 Crittenden (2015) believes that the three main attachment styles can be further divided into sub-styles that more accurately define regulatory mechanisms in terms of resources and threats. She does not believe in the disorganized model and replaces it with the a/c type.

Style	*Name*	*Description of the Children*
A1-2	Socially Facile – Inhibited	They idealize attachment figures by not integrating their negative qualities (A1) or denigrating the self (A2).
A3	Compulsively Caregiving	They protect themselves by protecting their attachment figures. During their childhood, they will try to cheer up (using positive affection) those attachment figures they perceive as sad or depressed.
A4	Compulsively Compliant	They try to protect themselves by doing everything they think their parents want them to do, especially when they are threatening or angry. Oftentimes they think they will only be loved if they excel at something.
A5	Compulsively Promiscuous	As children, they have learned not to trust others and they relate superficially, without affection. Adults in this model tend to maintain superficial relationships of both affection and sexuality. This strategy appears in adolescence when intimate relationships can be perceived from the point of view of betrayal.
A6	Compulsively Self-Reliant	They protect themselves by trusting no one but themselves. This protects them from others at the cost of paying the price of solitude. They avoid intimacy in adulthood.
A7	Delusional Idealization	They have suffered a lot of abuse in their childhood and protect themselves by imagining that the figures who have mistreated them will protect them. This pattern only occurs in adulthood.
A8	Externally Assembled Self	Due to abuse during their childhood, in adulthood they protect themselves by doing what they believe others want.
B1-5	Secure and Balanced	Integration of temporary and affective predictions. They have a wide range of adaptive behaviors. In adulthood, they transmit safety to their partners and their offspring.
C 1-2	Threatening Disarming	This group divides, exaggerates, and alternates a display of negative feelings to attract attention and manipulate others.
C3-4	Aggressive/Feigned Helpless	They often alternate aggressiveness with apparent helplessness, to make others obey out of fear, or help them for fear of not being able to fend for themselves.
C5-6	Punitive/Seductive	They are obsessed with revenge and/or rescue. They blame others for their problems and exaggerate their negative affection. This strategy is developed in adolescence.
C7-8	Menacing/Paranoid	This implies the will to attack anyone combined with a fear of everybody. It is either narcissism or extreme paranoia.
A/C	Psychopathy/BPD	These individuals take the more extreme patterns of A and C. They mix deception with the distortion of reality.

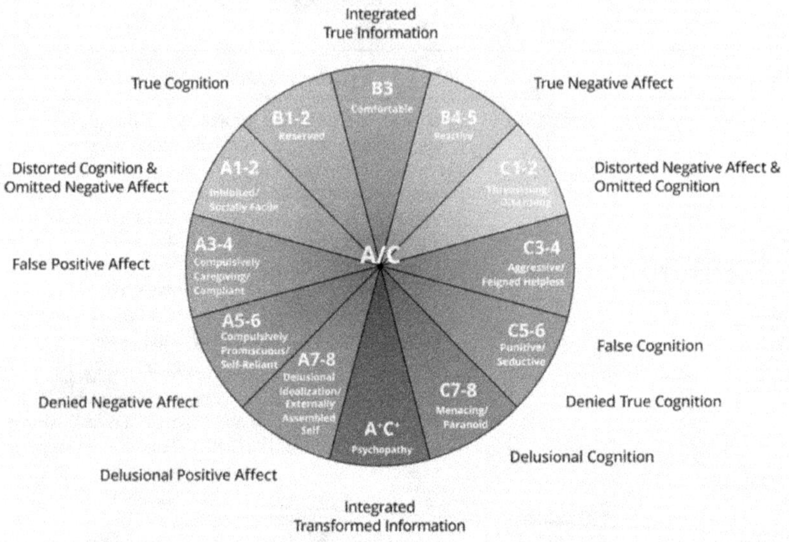

Figure 4.5 Crittenden (2002) creates a circular model in which the top part would be the secure type (B). As threats become greater, regulatory strategies change and become more pathological. Depending on whether the strategies have more to do with control (type A) or emotions (type C), the descent will go in one direction or another. In the extreme of both cases, psychopathy is reached.

change. Regulatory strategies become more complex – involving people outside the family – and sometimes pathological, such as addictions, eating disorders, or personality disorders. Regulatory mechanisms, when defective, become pathological.

References

Balbi, J. (2008). *El síndrome agarofóbico desde la perspectiva postracionalista*. CETEPO. Centro de terapia cognitiva postracionalista.

Barg, G. (2010). Bases neurobiológicas del apego. *Revisión temática. Ciencias Psicológicas*, *V*(1), 69–81.

Bowlby, J. (1977). The making and breaking of affectional bonds. *British Journal of Psychiatry*, *130*, 201–210.

Bowlby, J. (1983). *Attachment and loss: Volume III. Loss*. Basic Books.

Crittenden, P. M. (2002). Transformations in attachment relationships in adolescence. *Journal of Psychotherapy*, *12*, 33–62.

Crittenden, P. M., Dallos, R., Landini, A., & Kozlowska, K. (2012). *Attachment and family systems therapy*. Open University Press.

Crittenden, P. (2015). *Raising parents: Attachment, representation, and treatment*. Routledge.

Cassidy, J. (2000). The complexity of the caregiving system: A perspective from attachment theory. *Psychological Inquiry, 11*(2), 86–91.

Feeney, J., & Noller, P. (1996). *Adult attachment*. Sage Publications.

Hill, D. (2015). *Affect regulation theory. A clinical model*. Norton.

Holmes, J. (2001). *Attachment theory and therapy: Seeking a secure base*. Whurr Publishers.

Yehuda, R. (2016). *¿Can the effect of trauma be transmitted intergenerationally. Congress attachment and trauma. Relationships and compassion*. Rome.

5 Emotional Regulation and Mentalization

Wagner's tetralogy, *The Ring of the Nibelung*, consists of four operas. In the first one, titled "The Rhinegold," a fat and ugly Nibelung named Alberich, who lives in the depths of the earth, plunges into the Rhine to seduce the nymphs who live there. At first, they make him believe they are interested, but he soon discovers he is being mocked. When he is about to leave, flouted and angry, he notices something shining at the bottom of the river. He asks about it, and one of the nymphs tells him, "It is the gold of the Rhine, and we guard it. Whoever owns it will be the most powerful being in the universe, but only the one who renounces love can own it." She asks herself, with irony, "Who would be so foolish as to give up love?"

Alberich spitefully renounces love and steals the gold, with which he forges a ring that makes him the most powerful being in the universe. However, he who owns it pays a high price, since he will end up alone and dead one way or another. Wagner teaches us that power and love are incompatible.

In real life, children who do not feel loved and have no control over what is happening around them will look for anything that gives them the feeling of comfort they are lacking. In adolescence and adulthood, lack of affection can be replaced by material things, knowledge, power, substances, and so on, anything that will serve to fill the emptiness originated by this same lack of affection.

At birth, all children need the love and affection of their caregivers to survive. Babies attempt to regulate themselves emotionally through their relationship with them but, if this is not possible, they are forced to seek out other regulation strategies. These can involve objects, activities, or friends that contribute to the sense of calmness they have not been able to find in those who should have provided it. Naturally, there comes a time when it is therapeutic to explore activities or objects that encourage separation from the caregivers, but it becomes pathological when it has to be done desperately for the sake of emotional regulation.

The Development of Regulation Strategies

Hilburn-Cobb (2004) puts forward three proposals for developing a model that describes how children and adolescents seek regulatory strategies, both to create a secure basis that is different from their parents and to self-regulate.

DOI: 10.4324/9781003646341-6

In humans, the emotional relationship with others acts as a regulator to obtain safety. Parents who offer a safe attachment create a "safe zone" where the child can explore, knowing that the caregivers will be available if needed. Mother and child will regulate each other. The mother acts as a secure basis so that the child can self-regulate later on in stressful situations.

While the most efficient mechanism for self-regulation is establishing contact with a mother who acts as a caregiver, the child will seek out any other available self-regulating resources if there are frequent ruptures in the attachment.

Contrary to the goals of healthy attachment, a necessary element to reduce anxiety or discomfort is the acquisition of regulatory tools. These can be games, food, sports, drugs, or alcohol. All of these in excess may turn into severe pathologies. These regulatory mechanisms may or may not include other people to self-regulate in adulthood.

In early life, the perception of well-being depends on the attachment bond. Little by little, the child begins to show behaviors aimed at achieving congruence between his needs in the present moment and his caregivers' responses. If the child achieves his goal, the behavior will be reinforced and he will have a sense of control, but if there is no consistency between his behavior and the caregiver's response, a feeling of lack of control, lack of safety, and alertness will be developed (Grawe, 2006).

Based on the need to be on the alert or in control as experienced in childhood, different convictions will be established as to whether the world is a safe or a dangerous place. Childhood attachment ruptures with their caregivers will violate the rule of being in control. This is healthy if it helps the child to use techniques of exploration outside of the attachment figures and to relate to other people (other children at first, friends in adolescence, and partners in adulthood), but it will become pathological if the feeling of not being in control, and therefore of anxiety, is excessive. A certain degree of anxiety is necessary to perform tasks and do so with interest, and it will remain level as long as we feel we can perform them successfully. The initial phase of stress is identical, both in situations we control and in those in which we do not, but if the situation is beyond us, the circuit of fear that we saw in Chapter 2 will be activated.

Human beings organize themselves on the basis of the best protection strategy available to them; these can be based on age, past experience, and/or on the resources they have at any given time. This protection comes mainly from caregivers in childhood, friends in adolescence, and partners in adulthood (Crittenden et al., 2012). If the strategies were found to be defective in childhood and/or the resources are not available at present, information regarding an external or internal threatening sensation can be processed as something that overwhelms a person's capacities. The individual will act to resolve the uncertainty (and consequent discomfort) in the short term, without regard for long-term consequences. The urgency to resolve the discomfort will cause much more discomfort in the medium and long term. Grawe (2006) explains it in as follows:

> violation of the need of control are toxic for mental health. The importance of the need for control among patients with anxiety disorders is also evident because desperate efforts to regain control are often among the cardinal symptoms of the disorder and the compulsions in OCD can be regarded as dysfunctional attempts to regain control over something that has become uncontrollable, In order anxiety disorders, control in the form of avoidance plays a central role.
>
> (p. 229)

Regulatory strategies will change with age as one moves from childhood to puberty and into adulthood. As resources increase, needs change. In every stage of life, different mechanisms will be sought to reduce anxiety and allow for a new balance.

In puberty, with increasing sex hormones and the resulting anatomical changes, psychological needs also change. A transition takes place towards the search for like-minded people and possible partners. Although at this very important stage of development, social needs predominate and substances, activities, or partners are also used as regulatory mechanisms, caregivers are still necessary for healthy regulation. Friendship relationships are symmetrical: each seeks to be cared for by the other. However, they do not see themselves as caregivers.

> *Peter, 19 years old, comes to therapy accompanied by his parents, because he is very depressed over a break-up. His parents fear he will hurt himself or his ex-girlfriend, because he already had trouble managing his anger and aggressiveness in the past. When I look deeper into his emotional biography, I discover that when he was 15, his mother was busy caring for his younger brother who had a disease that required many hospitalizations. Apart from that, his father was always travelling because he was a salesman.*
>
> *How did this 19-year-old young man learn to survive? How did he overcome the loneliness he felt? Pedro's answers to these questions were the following: "I really liked football and I joined a group of hooligans from the local team. I felt I was part of something important. I did a lot of things that weren't good, like fighting and destroying, but I felt accompanied. Nobody judged me, and I knew that if I needed them, they'd always be there for me."*

After adolescence and with the onset of adulthood, priorities begin to change again: moving away from caregivers, taking on more work and family responsibilities, finding partners to form strong bonds with, and creating a new family. Adults either learn to regulate themselves with a partner or on their own, or they continue to use external regulatory mechanisms to reduce discomfort and anxiety. In a mature adult relationship, each person will be attached, but will also be an attachment figure for their partner (Crittenden, 2002).

From Regulation Strategies to Pathology

The strategies used as a way to control or regulate the internal sensations associated with discomfort or anxiety – which were useful at some time during childhood or adolescence – are behaviors that initially produced an anxiolytic or reassuring effect and served to manage what was deemed uncontrollable. The reason for the perseverance of these strategies is that they have been stored as effective in the unconscious mind, since they were reassuring at the time. Each time the amygdala is activated and anxiety is felt, it generates an urgency to behave in a similar way. Although the individual is aware that the behaviors are pathological, he cannot avoid them and feels drawn to them. Anxiety and discomfort encourage these behaviors that alleviate the symptoms and cause more anxiety in the medium term, eventually becoming an added pathology. That is, what was first used as an attempt to solve the problem will become another problem to solve.

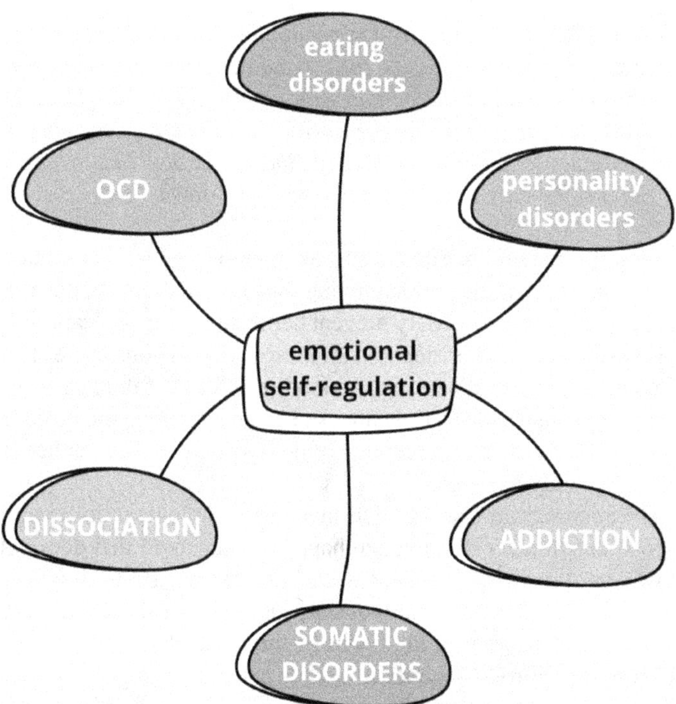

Figure 5.1 Pathologies seen in consultation begin, in most cases, as regulation mechanisms that are used to increase a sense of control, but end up becoming a bigger problem than the one they tried to solve.

All our patients use strategies to attempt to bear the discomfort. Although at first some of them may have been successful, at present, by force of repetition, they have become an additional disorder.

> *Mary is a 24-year-old patient who comes to therapy complaining about deep anxiety that has sometimes led to panic attacks. She has dealt with them by taking some anxiolytics, given to her by her mother, who takes them regularly. She has lived with her mother ever since she can remember. Her father abandoned them for another woman when she was three, and she has never heard from him again. She describes her mother as anxious and more as a friend than a mother.*
>
> *She was a good, studious child, but she met new classmates in high school and started studying less and hanging around bad company, with whom she frequently smoked pot and drank. Her mother never scolded her; she even found some drugs in her room and said nothing. This memory causes a lot of discomfort for her because it makes her think that her mother does not really care enough about her.*
>
> *She cannot currently work or lead a normal life because of her anxiety, which makes her feel very scared of relating to others. She spends nearly all her time smoking drugs using the little money her mother gives her. Her goal in therapy is to be a normal person with a normal life, but she is incapable of doing so out of fear of facing the world; she does not see herself fit as long as she continues to suffer from anxiety. She would also like to stop smoking weed, but it is the only thing that helps her calm down.*

In the case of this patient, marijuana acts as an emotional regulator (anxiolytic), but it has become part of the problem rather than the solution. On the other hand, the lack of self-esteem and anxiety prevent her from facing her fears and living a normal life, which makes her step into an inescapable vicious cycle. These feelings of impotence, unworthiness, and lack of hope for the future cause more and more fear, which makes the anxiety attacks become stronger and more frequent, leading to panic attacks. The perception of not having control over her emotions and her life gradually increases.

It is very important to bear in mind that all psychological disorders have an organic component, since nothing can happen in our mind that does not occur, in some way or other, in our brain as well (Purves et al., 1996). It is essential to clarify that, although the main cause of some psychological disorders is organic, in most cases said disorder is the result of the mechanisms that were used to obtain a sense of control. Epigenetics studies teach us that genes are expressed in terms of both the genetic conditions for which they are programmed and the environmental circumstances (Yehuda, 2016). In certain environmental conditions, regulatory mechanisms can activate the genetic expression of proteins that cause certain disorders. In other conditions, it is likely that this disorder would not have occurred. The debate on the influence of genetics and the environment on the origin of diseases still has no clear answer.

The mechanisms of regulation, as we will see throughout the chapter, are varied and change depending on the childhood attachment style. Although the list of pathologies that may be suffered as a result of these emotional regulation attempts to alleviate the discomfort is long, we can highlight eating disorders (bulimia, anorexia, or obesity), personality disorders (BPD, OCD), addictions (emotional dependency, alcoholism, gambling) and, as in the case of Pedro, belonging to violent groups or sects. The attachment style with which the individual has learned to self-regulate in relation to his caregivers during childhood will determine many of the strategies he will use later on in adolescence and adulthood (Crittenden, 2002).

One of the paradoxes of human psychology is that completely different initial situations can generate identical pathologies. The regulation mechanisms in all attachment styles are similar, even in secure attachment, where they are adaptive. Whether childhood has been marked by a lack of affection or protection (avoidant attachment), by overprotection that prevents exploration (anxious attachment), or by numerous traumatic situations (disorganized attachment), the outcomes can be surprisingly similar.

Adults with secure attachment (whether original or acquired) are not aware of needing external elements to regulate themselves. However, those with insecure attachments feel that any negative contingency could destabilize them, and they seek external elements in order to obtain that security which they are unable to find within themselves. This is what is commonly known as "controlling personalities" (who often have an avoidant attachment style) or "people who are always on the alert or anxious" (who usually have an anxious attachment style.)

Individuals with secure attachment (Type B) have learned to alternate between the need to be with their caregivers and the ability to explore or play fearlessly. In adolescence, they tend to be trusting, because they have never needed to be on the defensive. If they are able to maintain the tendency towards a secure attachment, they will be able to regulate themselves and do it with others in an appropriate way, without looking for external elements to compensate for the deficits. They learn from their mistakes and are able to recognize them in order to improve.

Individuals with insecure avoidant attachment (Type A) are predictable because they have learned to behave as expected. In their experience, appearance is paramount, while at the same time their true emotions must be concealed, even to themselves. They seek to self-regulate either via activities that require a lot of physical or mental effort (e.g., studying or practicing intense sports like running marathons) or with substances that prevent them from feeling anxiety (e.g., drugs). They tend to have everything under control and, in many cases, the resulting exhaustion leads them to lose control of everything and they end up suffering from depressions and/or panic attacks (Nardone, 2004).

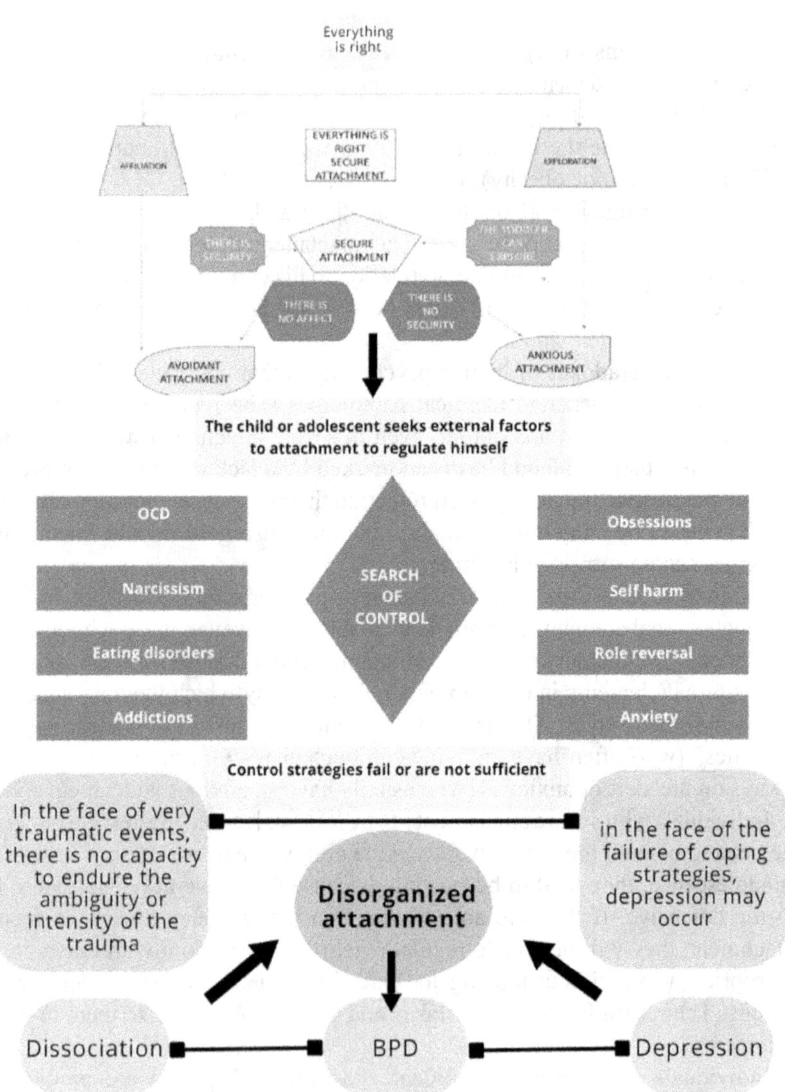

Figure 5.2 Regulatory mechanisms can be pathological if the attachment relationship with caregivers fails. If these mechanisms are not sufficient, this can result in depression, traumatic dissociation, or serious personality disorders.

Individuals with anxious insecure attachment (Type C) omit the cognitive aspect in their relationship with others, because the behavior of the parents, although affectionate, was unpredictable. These people do not try to control because they have never felt they had any control whatsoever. The negative feelings of discomfort are exaggerated and alternate with periods of calm. Their goal is to maintain constant emotional contact with someone. Their emotion regulation is a continuous search for closeness and they would do anything to achieve it, from entering violent groups, to using sex as a way to get affection, or taking drugs so as not to feel excluded from social relations.

Individuals with a disorganized attachment style have the experience that the same people who should have taken care of them were also a source of threat. Regulatory patterns can be pathological, such as self-harm, drug abuse, or extremely conflictive intimate relationships. External regulatory mechanisms are not sufficient and lead to even greater dysregulation, creating a vicious cycle of unpredictable consequences.

The main objective of these strategies, as previously explained, is to avoid the anxiety produced by the feeling of lack of control. To recover a certain balance, the individual can resort to directly avoiding the aversive stimuli, which is the most common and basic strategy, and one we share with all animals. The drawback is that, as patients avoid something that is scary (speaking in public, getting out of the house, or thinking of something painful), the amygdala reinforces the assessment that such behavior is dangerous, leading to greater avoidance.

The most basic strategy consists of avoiding something that is physically scary for us. It can be a place, a person, or a task. But there are also more complex avoidances, such as not feeling unpleasant sensations, avoiding parts of our personality that we do not like, or thinking that we are guilty or defective.

Some of these strategies may be:

Rumination/rituals: In situations of anxiety, individuals can perform certain reassuring rituals and generate superstitions about them, such as the idea that in doing so it will prevent something bad from happening. Thus, anxiety regarding situations that cause discomfort will make the person feel obliged to repeat the ritual, eventually resulting in a pathology. Obsessive thoughts can occur alone or can be accompanied by compulsive behaviors that try to alleviate them, turning into obsessive-compulsive disorders.

Addictions: Avoidance through substances, gambling, shopping, or compulsive sex all have in common that they help avoid internal discomfort; they do not allow that which harms us to become conscious. Except in very extreme cases, they do not usually appear until adolescence, along with the appearance of sex hormones and the consequent maturation. In all cases, they allow the person to avoid connecting with the degraded and/or empty internal world.

Eating disorders: Food intake and restriction act as regulators of anxiety and discomfort and help to avoid contact with emotions. The use of this regulatory strategy generates disorders such as anorexia (food restriction), binge eating (overeating), and bulimia (overeating and then vomiting).

Dissociation: A biological strategy used for avoiding psychological pain that is too excessive for the resources that are available to the individual. To dissociate means to avoid the intensity of the experience. Dissociative strategies may start either in childhood, in threatening situations that go beyond the child's resources, or in adulthood if there is a trigger that serves as a reminder of previous trauma or of some situation that poses a very serious threat and overwhelms the capacities of the individual.

Other strategies to reduce anxiety and increase a feeling of being in control can be carried out through personality patterns that help manage uncertainty in relation to others. These begin in childhood and are consolidated in adolescence and adulthood.

Care-giving personality: When children learn that their needs are not important, it will make them feel guilty and defective. They will adapt their behavior to what they believe others are expecting. One way of doing this is through parentification, or caring for parents or siblings. This strategy will usually generate an angry part that cannot be expressed for fear of provoking rejection, so it will eventually dissociate. These individuals are always aware of the needs of others, putting them before their own, and this could lead to severe anxiety or personality disorders.

Perfectionist personality: Similar to the previous one, this is a strategy that finds its origin in childhood. It consists of the magical thinking that "as long as I am perfect, I get good grades, I do everything well, etc., things will work out; my parents will love me and everything will be fine." The child tries hard to be perfect, but when nothing changes he will keep trying. This pathological search for perfection will become a personality trait with the added paradox that, since these individuals are never satisfied, they must increase their perfectionism. On the other hand, many patients with a perfectionist pattern tend to procrastinate for fear of not doing things well, which brings up much anxiety because they feel useless and a failure. This is a trait that can be part of various personality disorders.

Narcissistic personality: The child will develop a very high opinion of himself as well as an exaggerated form of self-esteem, either because he discovers that he cannot expect anything external to satisfy his needs for affection and feels that only he alone can take care of himself, or because he has been overprotected and exalted in excess, which makes him feel that others should take care of him and therefore his priorities must always be above those of others (Millon, 2011). This can lead to a narcissistic personality disorder.

Indolent personality: The person avoids any type of activity that may involve the risk of failure and blames others for everything that does not work without making any effort to change it. While it may be a natural stage during adolescence, it becomes pathological if it continues into adulthood.

Dissociation

Given its special relevance, a specific section is dedicated to dissociation, one of the most important emotion regulation mechanisms of the human psyche. As we have seen in Chapter 2, we are born with seven basic biological systems: rage, play, fear, seeking, lust, care, and panic (Panksepp & Biven, 2012). From the moment of birth, the child will do what is necessary to affectively bond with his mother and, later, with other caregivers (Schore, 2001). In a natural way, the child will develop systems focused on attachment and systems focused on exploration. Both are basic to a child's normal emotional and maturational development.

If the parents do not care for the child (by not attending to him or assaulting him), or if they overprotect him (by not allowing him to explore or play, and/or instilling in him a fear of everything), the child will have a normal development of his biological systems thwarted.

If something dangerous or annoying occurs, the child will turn to his caregivers to help him regulate himself and return to a state of well-being. But what if the very people who have to take care of him are the ones that hurt him? Or if he feels that there is no one available to help him regulate himself when things are not going well? In this case, two incompatible systems are activated: the system of attachment to the parents and the system of defense towards those same people who should protect him. These ruptures in the emotional connection provoke separation anxiety, fear, and rage. Most of the time, this involves a healthy maturational process that allows the child to learn to self-regulate in stressful situations. However, in more pathological cases, it will cause problems in his ability to regulate the relationship with himself as well as with others.

When there is serious abuse – be it physical, emotional, and/or sexual – the child's brain will try to create control or regulation strategies to survive the threat. If fear exceeds the child's capacity for defense, there will be physical immobilization, an emotional stupor, an activation of the dorsovagal nerve that, as we saw in Chapter 2, is known as traumatic dissociation (Hill, 2015). If the threat comes from the caregivers, the child will experience an irresolvable paradox: on the one hand, he will tend to seek their protection and, at the same time, he will feel the need to move away from them. The brain will create neural networks (engrams) focused on attachment to their parents and, at the same time, it will create networks that will maintain a level of alertness towards the attachment figures, in case there is another threatening rupture in attachment. These divided senses of self and its associated patterns are what we call "dissociated parts of the personality" (Boon et al., 2014).

According to Van der Hart (2006):

> *TSDP thus postulates that in trauma the patient's personality ... is unduly but not completely divided among two or more such dissociative subsystems or parts. These dissociative parts are dysfunctionally stable (rigid) in their functions and actions, and too closed to each other, resulting in adaptive compromise. One prototypical personality subsystem is metaphorically called the Emotional Part of the Personality As EP, the patient is fixated in sensorimotor and highly emotionally charged reenactments of traumatic experiences.*
> (p. 69)

Dissociation acts as an avoidance mechanism of that which exceeds our coping skills and which is impossible to handle at the time; it might have serious and traumatic consequences that may forever harm the individual.

Threats can be varied, such as an accident, an illness of the individual or his caregivers, or the death of a close relative. The parents' way of regulating themselves and regulating the child will be fundamental for the brain to work on the resolution of discomfort and uncertainty. The child must maintain the affective bond with his caregivers at all costs, which is why failures in the dyadic regulation will be internalized in his mind as faults of his own (Fosha, 2000). It is as if the mind of the child had to decide between "my parents are not perfect" and "I'm not worthy" and, at all times (until adolescence), the child's mind will assume the second option (Knipe, 2014). It is preferable to feel that "I am not worthy" than to lose the emotional and physical bonds with the caregivers. The biological reasons for this are obvious: physical contact with caregivers is a matter of life and death in all mammals. However, humans need proper emotional relationships as well. In children, the feeling that parents are faulty prevents them from being able to restore or solve what does not work, that is, it annuls any possibility for control and, therefore, the restoration of the attachment bond.

The child will continue to play, go to school, and so on (ANP), but there will be parts of his mind that will make him afraid of suffering the traumatic situation (EPs) again and he will do everything necessary so as not to feel that fear. The conflict between approaching and distancing from caregivers that cannot be solved by the child promotes a structural dissociation between parts fixed in attachment actions and in defensive actions that are in conflict with each other.

Busch et al. (2012) comment that:

> *Trauma victims defend themselves against the full implications of their traumatic experiences and the often unbearable feelings of pain, humiliation, rage, and helplessness that accompany them via various unconscious defensive maneuvers, often including the experience of dissociative states, in*

which patients feel disconnected from others, reality, or their own emotional states. Dissociative states can alternate with intense affects, including anxiety, triggered by reminders of the horror experienced. This pattern includes the reemergence of painful aspects of the trauma (intrusive memories, intense emotions, and flashbacks) and attempts to defend against the reemergence of the memory or its reminders through avoidance and dissociation (the avoidance of certain people or activities felt to be associated with the trauma and pervasive numbing).

(p. 142)

Hill (2015) argues that there are two very important moments in the development of emotion regulation throughout life. The first one includes the first 4 years of life, when the child is completely dependent upon his caregivers, and the second begins with the appearance of language, with what is known as mentalization (Fonagy & Luyten, 2014). Mentalization consists of the child's ability

Figure 5.3 There are conscious parts that are focused on the task of everyday life (living) and other unconscious ones that are related to the defense and the avoidance of the memory or re-experimentation of the trauma (surviving.)

to self-regulate and relate to others, and even to be able to regulate them through their actions.

Mentalization and, therefore, the ability to regulate oneself and know how to set boundaries with others will depend on past learnings. In other words, our ability to face new situations in the present and in the future will depend on what we have experienced in the past. This will be recorded in our neural networks as learning encoded in different types of memory.

Types of Memory

According to Hebbs' law, the more often two neurons are fired together, the more likely they will be to reconnect in the future. This means that the more we repeat something, the more likely it will be that, in the future, it will occur automatically without any intention (Siegel, 2002). It is a clear process of energy economy, which allows our brain to save resources that can be used more efficiently.

Our brain will keep memories of our actions, feelings, and emotions. Some memories are conscious and we can access them voluntarily, and others are unconscious and we cannot remember them at will. A memory will arise when a stimulus evokes the sensations, images, and emotions linked to it.

Following the DMM model we saw in Chapter 3 (Crittenden, 2002), there are seven types of dispositional representations that manage the intra- and interpersonal expectations of individuals:

Preconscious or implicit memory: Non-verbal, non-symbolic, and unconscious. It consists of emotional responses, behaviors, and skills (Wallin, 2007). It cannot be remembered at will, although it can arise if something recalls the emotional stimulus that generated it. Every day during therapy consultations, my patients remember things they had forgotten, related to the discomfort that makes them seek help.

There are, in turn, three types:

Procedural: This is related to procedures, to knowing how to do something. It is, therefore, the type of learning and memory about how the things we usually do are done, without thinking about how we do them. Its expression is, to a large extent, automatic and difficult to verbalize.

Somatic: The body stores memories of emotional events (Van der Kolk, 2014; Damasio, 2003) in order to use the sensation associated with that memory as an alarm signal; a shortcut for not having to consciously check if something is harmless or dangerous. For example, feeling a pain in my belly when I feel ashamed.

Perceptive: It refers to us remembering something due to an emotional activator that reminds us of the original situation. It can be an image, a smell, and/or a memory that emerges during the therapeutic work.

Conscious, verbal, and explicit memory: Commonly known as memory, this refers to the *"knowing."* It is related to what we can remember at will, which is stored as images or language, and can be expressed with words. These are the memories that the patient will be able to explain to us in therapy when we ask him to narrate his personal history or talk about some specific event. As we saw in Chapter 2, the hippocampus encodes the information for storage in the cortical areas and converts it into accessible memory with no extreme emotions associated to it. It is divided into several subtypes:

Somatic body language: being able to verbalize the sensation that we feel in our body. It is the personal and interpretative explanation of what is felt in the body (e.g., "my arm hurts" or "I am excited.");

Semantic memory: related to conceptual knowledge that has no relation to concrete personal experiences (e.g., European capitals or multiplication tables). It is also used to make the world more predictable (e.g., "if I am good, they will love me.");

Episodic: memory related to autobiographical events, places, associated emotions, and other contextual knowledge that can be evoked voluntarily (e.g., remembering a school trip during adolescence).

Dispositional representations or working memory: These are conscious, verbal, and integrative. They integrate preconscious and conscious memory. They are related to the planning of future activities and the achievement of goals. They help understand written texts or remember things from the past at will so as to be able to plan the best course of action for the future. It is the kind of memory accessed in therapy when a trauma is remembered and a new meaning is given to something that was stored in an emotional and traumatic way.

Reflective integration contrasts and compares all representations or memories to decide which one best fits the current situation. If there is conflict between some representations, reflective integration cannot be achieved.

Unconscious representations operate half a second faster than conscious ones (Cozolino, 2016). However effective that makes them, it may lead to errors. Children are born only with the capacity to perform unconscious learning and will create more complex representations as they grow up, until they reach explicit memory in childhood (around 4 years of age) and can integrate information more appropriately as their brain areas develop. An adult has seven different types of memories and a child only three; therefore, every time the adult interacts with a baby, the baby will have to transform the information in order to adapt it to his cognitive and emotional capacities (Crittenden, 2002).

Reflective integration is only achieved in childhood when brain development allows for cognitive maturity. In adolescents and adults, it takes place when there is a balance between explicit and implicit memory. If the emotional

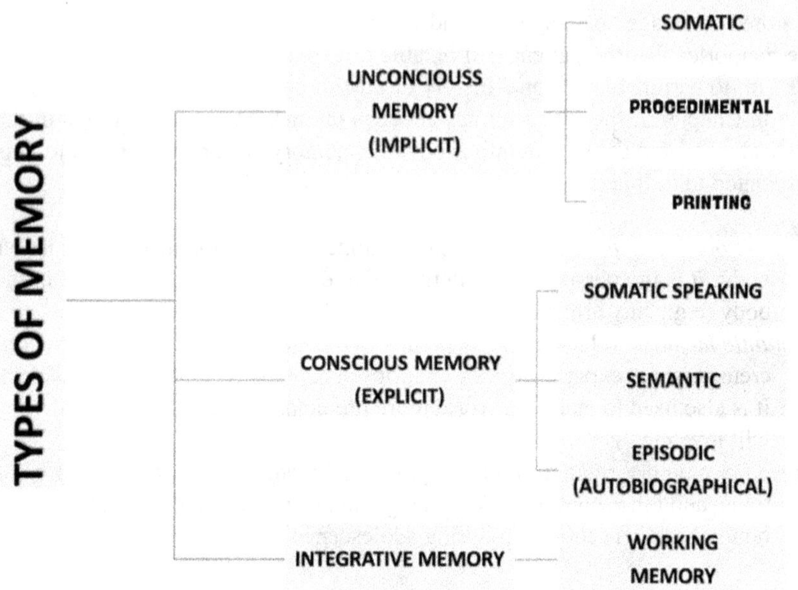

Figure 5.4 There are different types of memory, depending on the type of storage. Unconscious memory is one to which we do not have voluntary access; conscious memory is memory we can evoke at will; and integrative memory is the result of the joint work of both.

situation goes beyond the capacities for information processing and reflection, an adequate working memory cannot be produced. In order to balance the different types of memory, emotion regulation with the appropriate caregivers must have existed in childhood. If there are no adults who are able to regulate the child, he will not learn to self-regulate or effectively use the working memory.

Implicit memory models regulate everyday preconscious behavior throughout a person's life; for example, we do not have to think about how we walk or that we have to put our clothes on in the morning. We act automatically and, if the expected effect does not occur, we will turn to our working memory to consciously act in a different, more sophisticated way that brings about a new learning.

But what happens when the situation has a high emotional charge? Then we will not be able to process what is happening with our awareness, thus activating recollections of the implicit memory associated with fear, defenselessness, and/or aggression. We will not be able to act using our working memory since we will be hijacked by our emotions, which will prevent us from evaluating the pros and cons of the different possibilities for action.

Implicit memory also includes models or personality schemes of adulthood that we learned in childhood so as to know how to behave. In our intimate adult relationships, we tend to reproduce the internal models we learned in childhood, since they were coded as implicit memory.

While we unconsciously store fears and pleasures, we also remember the regulatory mechanisms we used in the past to achieve homeostasis. By repeating them, they will become automatic and involuntary, and, in many cases, even something we could do against our will. If something was useful or beneficial in the past, it is stored in our implicit memory (probably linked to an increase in dopamine levels) and, with a similar stimulus, we will repeat it, although it may be currently inconvenient or pathological. Let us look at a practical example of a patient:

> *Eva is a 25-year-old woman who comes to therapy because of morbid obesity. Although she has tried many diets, she cannot lose weight, because she is unable to stop binge eating. When asked about her childhood, she reports being raised by her grandmother, because her parents worked long hours. Her grandmother was always cooking and heavily insisted that she eat. She still remembers with pleasure when she used to finish her meal and her grandmother, very happy, asked her if she wanted more. When asked if she thinks that she may be using food as a way to avoid her anxiety – given that her happiest moments where with her grandmother and she constantly insisted that she ate – the patient says she had never seen it that way before, but that she cannot help eating every time she feels nervous.*

In Eva's case, food acts as a mood stabilizer, since she learned at a young age that eating satisfied her grandmother and she felt better in doing so. Her unconscious mind has associated food with satisfaction, pleasure, and tranquility, so every time something affects her, she eats compulsively, beyond the limits of satiety.

Individuals with a secure attachment have all three memory systems well integrated and, therefore, act in a coherent way depending on the circumstances. On the contrary, people with insecure attachments cannot easily do this and spend a lot of energy reviewing processes, fearing not doing what is most appropriate, or simply being scared of what might happen if they act in a certain way (Crittenden, 2002).

In the initial intake, patients report narratives collected from their episodic memory: they talk about memories, experiences, beliefs, and so on. As therapists, we must find the underlying unconscious mechanisms that belong to implicit memory. In my experience, the vast majority of problems that patients bring to session are generated by automatic processes that they cannot modify on their own. As I like to explain, it is a struggle between their conscious and their unconscious.

For different reasons, we have all had to repress, disassociate, or simply forget past events, which, due to the biology of our brain, influence our responses towards different, current stimuli. Integrating these implicit memories into the narrative of our life, once they become conscious, allows us to use them or reject them at will. To achieve this, we must help patients know their own history and integrate explicit and implicit memories into what some authors call *mentalization* Siegel (2002) writes:

> While these implicit mental models exist in all of us, we can begin to free ourselves from the powerful and insidious ways they create our here-and-now perceptions and beliefs. Seeing deeply and clearly into the inner world ... promotes the integration of memory. When memory is integrated, these separate implicit puzzle pieces of the past are linked together into the more complex – and flexible and adaptive – form of explicit memory.
>
> (p. 197)

Mentalization

As a father of two daughters, I cannot help but think quite often what my daughters' image of me will be like in the future, if they have felt cared for and loved, and at the same time, if they have been well educated. The relationship with my daughters goes beyond the intellectual and connects directly with my personal self. No doubt I have influenced a lot regarding who my daughters are today and who they will be, but it is no less true that they have also shaped much of who I am.

The therapeutic process is based on two major aspects: one is the attachment relationship (therapeutic alliance) that is established between the patient and the therapist; the other is the ability of both patient and therapist to mentalize in order to achieve a mental and physical balance that will make the patient healthy. Mentalization is the reflexive function that allows us to observe our mental states (desires, goals, values, and/or attitudes) and those of others (Fonagy & Luyten, 2014). When born, a baby is completely dependent upon his caregivers, who will be the mirror in which he will look at himself to subsequently see himself. The image he sees reflected in his caregivers will be what he internalizes as his true self.

If the parents are able to mentalize, that is, to regulate themselves emotionally and to do so with others, the child will have a secure base from which to explore the world and a safe haven to return to when there is uncertainty. As we have seen throughout the chapter, if this does not happen, the child will have to look for different regulatory strategies in order to feel that he has the ability to control the environment (Hart, 2011). Mentalization takes place in parent–child relationships, at school, in friendships, or in intimate relationships.

Joseph is a 34-year-old high school teacher who comes to therapy because of a depression that leaves him exhausted and without energy. He has always been an athletic person and this asthenia bothers him. His partner lives with him, and one can tell from the start that there is much complicity between them. I ask her to wait in the waiting room and am left alone with him. When I ask him about his past, the first thing he says is that we psychologists love to talk about childhood and that his was a disaster with an alcoholic father and a mother exhausted because of her fibromyalgia.

T: How is your relationship with your partner?
C: It's the best thing that's ever happened to me; ever since we met and fell in love we have mutually supported each other. We both have complicated families, and can't rely on them. When I am by her side, I feel completely safe. We have our differences, but I know we'll overcome them, somehow.
T: We psychologists like to say that you feel seen by her, that she can see inside of you.
C: That is exactly it.

Within the different parts of our personality, Lorenzini and Fonagy (2013) initially described a reflective self or internal observer of mental life. Without this observer, we are not able to differentiate subjective experiences from objective realities. When there is a flood of emotions that prevent us from reasoning or thinking clearly, the differences between feelings and facts cannot be assessed (Allen, 2013). Attachment and mentalization are two concepts that go hand in hand, since parents who are able to regulate themselves emotionally also help their children to do so. The more secure the attachment has been, the greater the capacity for mentalization in children, both in childhood and throughout their lives.

The capacity for mentalization in adolescence and adulthood is based on the affect regulation systems we had in childhood. Underlying the disorders, what we work on in this book are experiences and learning that have had a very strong emotional charge since the early years of life; they have caused both a need for constant alertness and, consequently, for regulatory strategies to maintain emotional stability. In many cases these strategies become the pathology.

As we can see in the following figure, parents relate differently to their children depending on their own attachment type. Parents, serving as a mirror in which the child reflects himself, generate different psychological variables in the child depending on how he sees himself reflected in his parents' minds.

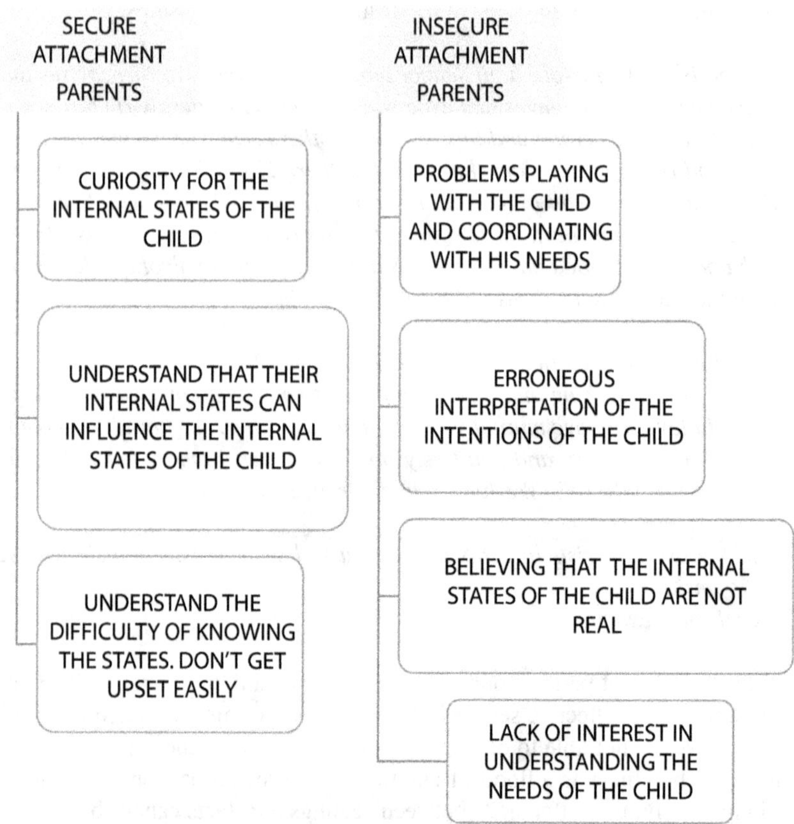

Figure 5.5 Differences of parents in relation to their offspring, depending on their attachment style (secure or insecure).

There are four variables that are essential when describing the mentalization processes (Fonagy & Luyten, 2014):

Automatic vs. voluntary: In the first part of this chapter, we have seen how human beings create regulatory strategies to withstand uncertainty when faced with alarming situations. These can be adaptive, or become rigid and pathological. In these cases, they become automatic patterns. Individuals with a high mentalization capacity can increase their repertoire of behaviors and emotions to act flexibly and voluntarily regarding different circumstances.

Internally vs. externally focused: Individuals with a high capacity for mentalization can recognize both their own internal emotional states and those of others. They are capable of not being overpowered by negative internal states and not being constantly suspicious or fearful of the reactions of others.

Self-oriented vs. oriented towards others: People who felt guilt and shame in childhood find that their relationships with others can be very painful and, thus, create strategies to protect themselves from the discomfort. The most common strategy is to take care of others (caregiver) or only take care of oneself (narcissistic). We will see this in much more detail in the following chapter. For example, people sense that they do not deserve to be loved for who they are and need to do things for others to be accepted or, on the contrary, expect nothing from anyone and consider that everyone should take care of them (narcissistic).

Cognitive vs. affective: Parents, depending on their own mentalization, will influence their children. As we saw in the last chapter, depending on their learning, parents will tend to give more importance to either cognitive or affective values. Being able to vary from a more rational to a more emotional approach and vice versa, depending on the circumstances, is important to achieve emotion regulation, both internally as well as in relation to others.

As we will see in more detail in the second part of this book, our goal in therapy will be to help patients learn to "mentalize" – to teach them to do what they could not learn in the early years of life. As transitional attachment figures, therapists must give them the space and confidence to get to know themselves, helping them to understand their problems and giving them the tools to achieve this. With mentalization, we transform the patterns that have become rigid and pathological and make them adaptive and flexible. Mentalization is flexibility, contrary to rigid and automatic control strategies.

To remember something is to create a new memory, and the presence of a therapist that generates trust in the patient can help reprogram the emotional value of what happened. Facts cannot be changed, but their emotional value can. This allows the response patterns in the present to be relaxed in situations that recall past events.

Much of what happened in the early years of life remains in our implicit (unconscious) memory in a procedural and egosyntonic way. As we will see in detail, the clients' immersions in the sensations of the past in the presence of the therapist allow them to relive what happened, integrating it in explicit memory. To be able to mentalize, we must work with both implicit and explicit memories; by integrating them, we can use working memory. Only human beings have the capacity to mentalize.

Once patients feel safe with us, as therapists and as people, their behavior patterns will become more flexible, and they will be able to access their memories without fear, in an integrated way (cognitive and emotionally); there will be no need to continue to repress or dissociate from them. This will allow them to use more sophisticated resources to solve present situations. Paradoxically, we give patients back a sense of control over things they once felt were uncontrollable now no longer need to be controlled.

Conclusions

In the first years of life, the child explores the world using his caregivers as a secure basis. If these are not available in an appropriate way, the child will look for different elements that will serve as a secure basis and safe haven to self-regulate.

If the child sees his parents as unpredictable and/or uncaring, he will create control strategies to regulate himself trying to avoid uncertainty and discomfort. There are many types of regulatory strategies, among which we find avoidance, perfectionism, substance abuse, and eating disorders. Some may appear in childhood, although they usually appear during adolescence or even in adulthood, in light of a traumatic event that can overpower existing control strategies. Often, the mechanisms for emotion regulation, used as instruments to deal with uncertainty or discomfort, become another problem.

There are different types of memory where learning is stored, which can give rise to behavioral and emotional patterns that remain rigid by being strongly consolidated in implicit or emotional memory. With the help of the therapist, mentalization allows patients to get to know these unconscious patterns, and thus they can begin to change them for others that are more adaptive. Knowing yourself and reprogramming emotional experiences will allow you to manage them and assess which is the most appropriate response.

Mentalization helps to know why these memories were generated. Furthermore, it also allows them to be modified, to increase flexibility of coping responses, and to relocate the secure basis within the patient. This helps him self-regulate and respond voluntarily and not automatically to events that cause fear or anxiety. Mentalizing is to help integrate experiences in narrative memory and recognize implicit memories, helping patients to self-regulate and regulate themselves in harmony with others.

References

Allen, J. (2013). *Mentalizing in the development and treatment of attachment trauma*. Karnac.

Boon, S., Steele, K., & Van der Hart, O. (2014). *Living with traumatic dissociation: Skills training for patients and therapists*. Routledge.

Busch, F., Milrod, B. D., Singer, M., & Aronson, A. (2012). *Trauma focused psychodynamic psychotherapy: A step-by-step treatment manual*. Routledge.

Cozolino, L. (2016). *Why therapy works. Using our minds to change our brains*. Norton.

Crittenden, P. M. (2002). Transformations in attachment relationships in adolescence. *Journal of Psychotherapy*, *12*, 33–62.

Crittenden, P. M., Dallos, R., Landini, A., & Kozlowska, K. (2012). *Attachment and family systems therapy*. Open University Press.

Damasio, A. R. (2003). *Looking for Spinoza: Joy, sorrow, and the feeling brain*. Harcourt.

Fonagy, P., & Luyten, P. (2014). Mentalising in attachment context. In P. Holmes & S. Farnfield (Eds.), *The routledge handbbok of attachment*. Routledge.

Fosha, D. (2000). *The transforming power of affect. A model of accelerated change*. Basic Books.

Grawe, K. (2006). *Neuropsychotherapy: How the neurosciences inform effective psychotherapy*. Psychology Press.

Hart, S. (2011). *The impact of attachment*. Norton.

Hill, D. (2015). *Affect regulation theory. A clinical model*. Norton.

Hilburn-Cobb, C. (2004). Adolescent psychopathology in terms of multiple behavioral systems: The role of attachment and controlling strategies and frankly disorganized behavior. In L. Atkinson & S. Goldberg (Eds.), *Attachment issues in psychopathology and intervention* (pp. 95–137). Routledge.

Knipe, J. (2014). *EMDR toolbox: Theory and treatment of complex PTSD and dissociation*. Springer.

Lorenzini, N., & Fonagy, P. (2013). Attachment and personality disorders: A Short Review. *FOCUS: The Journal of Lifelong Learning in Psychiatry*, *11*(2), 155–166.

Millon, T. (2011). *Personality disorders in modern life*. Wiley.

Nardone, G. (2004). *No hay noche que no vea el día. La terapia breve para los ataques de pánico*. Herder.

Panksepp, J., & Biven, L. (2012). *The archeology of mind. Neuroevolutionary origins of humans emotions*. Norton.

Purves, D., Augustine, G. J., Fitzpatrick, D., Lawrence, C. K., Lamantia, A.-S., & McNamara (Editor), S.Mark Williams, J. O. (1996). *Neuroscience* (2nd ed.). Sinauer Associates.

Schore, A. (2001). The effects of a secure attachment relationship on roght brain development, affect regulation & infant mental health. *Infant Mental Health Journal*, *22*, 7–66.

Siegel, D. J. (2002). *The developing mind: How relationships and the brain interact to shape who we are*. Guilford Press.

Van der Hart, O., Nijenhuis, E. R. S., & Steele, K. (2006). *The haunted self: Structural dissociation and the treatment of chronic traumatization*. Norton & Company.

Van der Kolk, B. (2014). *The body keeps the score: Brain, mind, and body in the healing of trauma*. Penguin Group.

Wallin, D. J. (2007). *Attachment in psychotherapy*. Guilford Press.

Yehuda, R. (2016). *¿Can the effect of trauma be transmitted intergenerationally. Congress attachment and trauma. Relationships and compassion.*

6 The PARCUVE Model

When Bowlby began to develop his theories of attachment in children in relation to their caregivers, he was influenced by ethology studies that pointed to the importance of the caregiver in the behavior of their offspring. Experiments like those of Harlow – who investigated the behavior of monkeys when they were raised without their mothers – or Lorenz's studies on imprinting heavily influenced Bowlby. He began to wonder if human beings perhaps shared much of their psychology with other animals, since much of their physiology is already shared (Karen, 1998). This may have been why I fell in love with the theory of attachment at first glance: how gracefully it blended the psychology and biology of the nervous system.

Unlike reptiles, the relationship of mammalian and bird offspring with their caregivers is vital during the first stages of life. It is a matter of life and death. This relationship will not only involve care and nourishment, but also certain learning that will be necessary in later stages, such as reproduction. It has been observed that primates raised with no maternal contact subsequently have many problems regarding their ability to bond with their progeny and give them the necessary care (Hart, 2011).

What could happen to a pup of any mammal or to a human baby if there is no caregiver available? Under natural conditions, the offspring would be condemned to certain death. There are multiple studies showing that physical contact and the care of the mother helps the development of a healthy brain.

In Chapter 3, we studied the brain circuit related to parental care and the separation/panic that becomes activated in babies when this care is not available (Panksepp, 2004, 2009). When this happens, the baby searches for the company of other creatures who will help provide a sense of security. If this is not possible, there is an activation of the fight/flight mode. And if the threat is excessive, the parasympathetic system becomes active, which could lead to dissociation.

This circuit is phylogenetically constructed over a more primitive one, the fear and pain circuit, which is shared with all other vertebrates. The terminology may lead to confusion, but these two cerebral circuits imply different anatomical and physiological areas (Panksepp, 2004, 2009; Panksepp & Biven, 2012). The separation/panic circuit is related to a lack of opiates in the brain. While benzodiazepines are effective in deactivating fear, they are not as good at calming

DOI: 10.4324/9781003646341-7

down panic. With opiates, the contrary happens: they do not decrease fear, but are quite effective in reducing separation anxiety.

Panic is what a baby feels when it perceives the caregiver as inaccessible, whereas fear is the emotion when faced with a concrete or imaginary stimulus that may imply danger. That is to say, one can feel fear and not feel separation/panic, but the opposite cannot happen. It is also known that the cerebral circuits for fear and anxiety are intimately related to pain and anger – so much so that it is believed they are mutually activated and inhibited (Panksepp & Biven, 2012; Hart, 2011). Therefore, every time there is a rupture in the attachment relationship, the fear, pain, and anger circuits will activate simultaneously.

As we can see in Figure 6.1, emotions are interrelated. The activation of the separation/panic circuit leads to the emergence of fear and subsequent anxiety, simultaneously provoking anger in a cascade of biological and unconscious events, independently from the will of the person.

In Chapter 2, we explored the detailed functioning of the separation/panic circuit. In this chapter, I will develop the effects of its activation on the different emotions in human psychology, such as fear and anxiety, anger, guilt, and shame.

Fear

Fear is a basic emotion in all living beings, crucial for survival, which is activated when the brain perceives a situation that may potentially endanger physical integrity. In humans, the absence (physical or emotional) of attachment figures causes a feeling of fear because of the lack of protection it entails. Panksepp and Biven (2012) quotes:

> We found indicators for a clear association between separation anxiety and future problems of anxiety and panic attacks. These results support a conceptualization of the psychopathology of the development of anxiety disorders … Children who suffer from separation anxiety disorder may lack, from a young age, skills to help them tolerate anxiety and strong emotions, which will be very important for a healthy development.
>
> (p. 342)

We have all felt fear at some point. Now, what determines if the situation is traumatic or not is the subjective assessment of risk (i.e., the feeling of control). In childhood, we lack a sense of control, which will be acquired in relationships with adults. However, if the necessary care is not provided by the caregivers, either due to neglect or abuse, alert mechanisms that simultaneously activate fear and anger circuits are switched on. The brain keeps memories of these attachment ruptures as dangerous and painful events. These traumatic memories

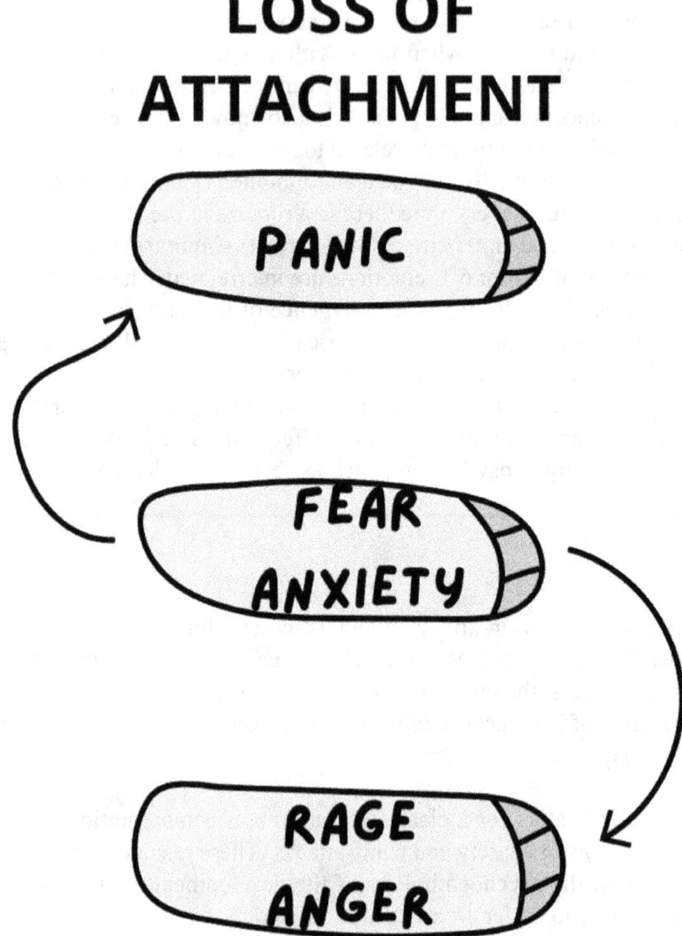

Figure 6.1 We can see how different emotions which imply different cerebral circuits create cascading processes that affect the brain and, subsequently, emotions and behaviors.

are dissociated and stored in what is called the unconscious or implicit memory (Ginot, 2015).

The child becomes a prisoner of an affective Stockholm syndrome. Since children neither have the emotional nor cognitive resources to mentalize what happened, they are incapable of structuring their maps of cognitive and affective experiences and meanings. In an attempt to find balance, they modify behaviors

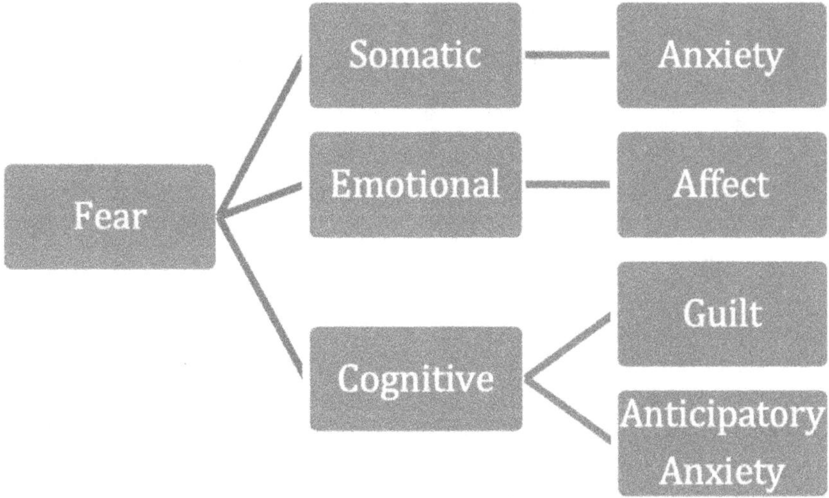

Figure 6.2 Fear generates changes in implicit memory in order to avoid repeating a situation or to be prepared if it happens again. These changes will come about on a somatic, emotional, and cognitive level.

and emotions, trying to avoid feeling the fear again. In order to do this, they must change the way they relate to their caregivers (changes in the type of attachment) and, if the fear has been extremely intense, there is a resulting traumatic dissociation at brain and body level.

Fear is an unpleasant and painful experience, and its mission is to protect the physical and mental integrity of the individual. These experiences lead to changes on three levels (see Figure 6.2):

- *Somatic level*: In a situation of fear, the body changes its physiology in order to face danger. This includes muscular tension, tachycardia, hypertension, and so on (Sapolsky, 2004). Moreover, it stores a somatic memory of what happened in order to be more alert in future (Damasio, 2003). In extreme cases, somatic dissociation occurs (Nijenhuis, 2000). Either way, the individual feels circumstantial anxiety if the situation were to reoccur, or recurrent anxiety if the fear becomes permanent.
- *Emotional level*: The activation of alert circuits affects emotions, producing changes in intensity and how they are handled.
- *Cognitive level*: With every experience, there is learning; the stronger the intensity of the stimulus, the deeper it will be recorded in implicit memory. Human beings are the only animals capable of remembering the past at will

and predicting what will happen in the future. When we do this in a negative way, it can take two different forms:

- *Anticipatory anxiety*: This occurs when our mind goes to the future, trying to plan possible warning situations that have not yet occurred and may never happen.
- *Guilt*: This happens when the mind revises, reviews, or cannot stop remembering something that happened in the past. Its function is to learn from something painful so as not to repeat errors that have already been committed.

The only way to deal with threats in the early years of life is through bonding with attachment figures. If they are unable to provide security, they become the source of fear. The brain and body store the memory of the pain associated with the experience, and this learning is recorded in the unconscious mind. Throughout the years, more resources will be developed to address risks and threats, but these will also be different. As we saw in the previous chapter, regulatory mechanisms to tolerate pain and anxiety are going to be modified and, if they are useful at some point, they will be utilized more often (Crittenden, 2015).

Lucas is 37 years old and seeks hypnosis due to his difficulties when speaking in public. His job demands that he explains some aspects related to job performance to his co-workers, and this makes him feel very uneasy. The situation has worsened over the last months, since he feels that talking and being observed is becoming increasingly scarier. He will be presenting in front of a lot of people in an upcoming convention, and he is considering quitting his job as a way to avoid this continuous suffering.

T: Lucas, we're going to work with regression, searching for situations from the past that may be related to what you're experiencing right now. Can you remember a moment or situation from your childhood where you felt similar sensations to the ones you have now?

C: I recall a Christmas play at school. We had to perform a live Nativity scene and I had a small role in which I explained the arrival of the Three Wise Men. My mom and I had rehearsed it at home many times, because I was afraid I wouldn't do it right. When I saw myself in front of all the parents at school, I went blank, I couldn't speak. I remember my mother reciting the text back to me from below the stage, but I saw her and felt such shame that I found it even harder to remember a single word. I'm telling you this and my throat's hurting a lot.

At that point, Lucas started crying like a child.

The type of attachment generated in childhood will be crucial to determine the strategies to be used throughout life to face challenges. As can be seen in Figure 6.3, fear is primarily responsible for the type of attachment in childhood and adulthood; it will be determined by the predominant self-regulation strategy. No strategy is better than others; they are just different. Coping strategies vary from person to person depending on the ability to mentalize as well as on the predominant type of attachment in childhood:

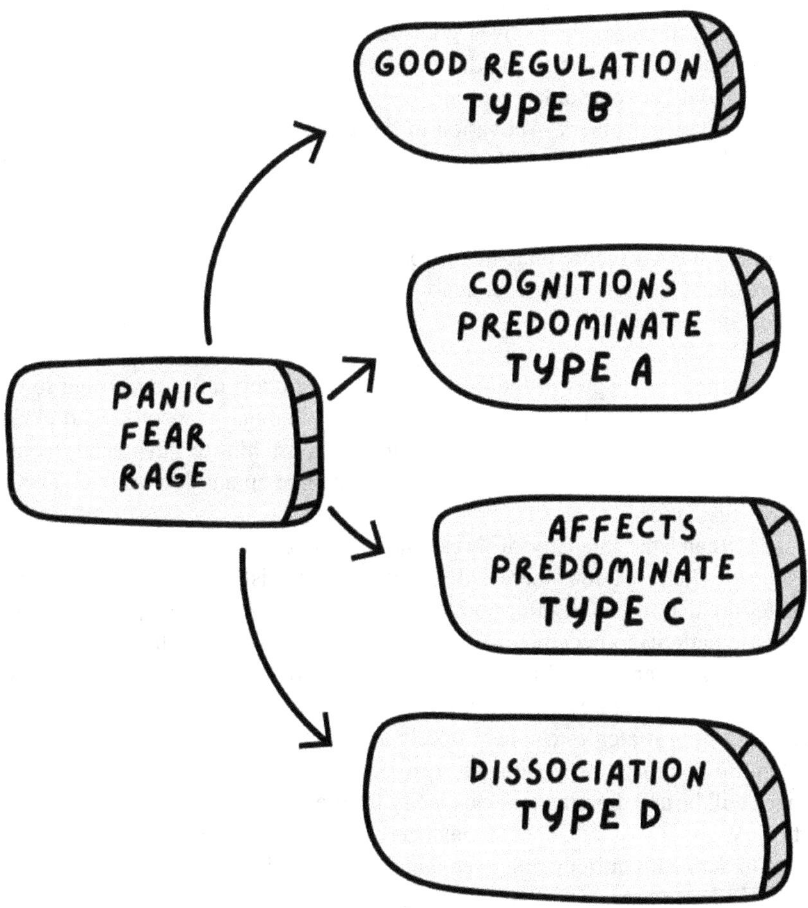

Figure 6.3 Fear in childhood in relation to the parents evokes a different type of regulation in the child depending on the personal characteristics of both the child and the caregivers. This will result in different types of attachment that will condition the way to cope with stress in adulthood.

- Cortical areas are predominant (Type A). These individuals experience anxiety when they cannot control their environment or their sensations, so there is greater activity of the parasympathetic branch of the ANS. They tend to avoid emotional closeness with other people and barely feel emotions nor their body.
- Subcortical areas are predominant (Type C): These individuals try to regulate themselves by seeking emotional connections with other people and feel discomfort when that connection occurs. They constantly feel emotions and are motivated by their feelings. There is a greater activity of the sympathetic branch of the ANS.
- No particular area predominates (Type D): These individuals try to simultaneously regulate themselves with the two previously mentioned aspects. They alternate proximity and distance, without relieving the discomfort. Fear and anxiety are constantly present. These individuals are unable to mentalize themselves nor others. Activation of the sympathetic branch may occur and then the system collapses due to the activation of the dorsovagal branch of the parasympathetic.
- Optimal regulation between cognition and affection (Type B): These individuals have a secure attachment (original or acquired). They are reflexive, flexible in responses, and act adaptively. There is a balance between activation and relaxation.

As explained in Chapter 4, the internal working models differ according to the figure with which we relate. When the individual counts on people who evoke safety and comfort, this healthy learning will allow him to have safety/confidence when facing challenges and threats; it will be an antidote to fear. This is called "resilience."

The greater the intensity of threats in childhood and the less availability of resources, the more fear there will be of making mistakes and, therefore, the greater the distortions of information (e.g., not assessing danger), which causes response patterns to become ever more rigid and instinctive. The probability of giving a wrong answer will increase. This can also lead to overidentification of danger, which generates alarm when facing harmless stimuli. Neither the danger nor the coping strategies can be properly assessed.

On the contrary, the greater the resilience, the less the fear of facing challenges will be and the greater the capacity for mentalization and emotional regulation. Without fear or anger, a balanced person has many more resources in order to deal with difficult and even dangerous situations.

Anger

Heinicke and Westhemer (1966) conducted a 2-week study of ten children aged 13–32 months who either lived permanently in boarding schools or attended a daycare center on a daily basis. When the behavior of the children was compared, it was found that those who remained separated from their parents were four times more aggressive than the children who lived with their families. In the study, the children received dolls to play with, and the aggression was always directed towards the dolls that represented the role of the parents.

We know through Bowlby (1977) that children who are separated from their parents experience anger, mostly towards them, and that many times this hostility is the expression of a reproach for not being there when they were needed.

> Whenever loss is permanent, as it is after a bereavement, anger and aggressive behavior are necessarily without function. The *reason* that *they occur so often* nonetheless, even after a death, is that during the early phases of grieving a bereaved person usually *does* not believe that the *loss can really be permanent*; he therefore *continues to act* as though it were still possible not only to find and recover the lost person but to reproach him for his actions. For the lost person is not infrequently held to be at least in part responsible for what has happened.
>
> (p. 271)

As we saw earlier, anger does not just show with something as serious as the death of a parent; it can also occur in cases of ruptures in the attachment relationship between the child and the caregivers.

Fear and anger are two emotions that feed each other, modulating conjointly. The anger response (or its synonyms: rage, frustration, or impotence) can be expressed at will from the time the person is approximately 2 years old. It is at this stage that the expression of frustration begins to be valued as either something that is tolerated or that should be inhibited, depending on the caregiver's response. Bowlby (1977) argues that anger is a normal reaction to restore the attachment bond. If there is no affective repair, one moves from a rage of "hope" to a rage of "despair."

Some authors (Hart, 2011; Schore, 2001) argue that there are two types of anger: aggressive or calm. The former is modulated by hyperactivation of the amygdala and activation of the sympathetic nervous system; it is expressed as marked aggressiveness (screams or fights). It is more normal in individuals with Type C attachment patterns. In extreme cases, it would be considered an antisocial personality.

Calm rage is modulated by the hypothalamus and the parasympathetic branch of the nervous system. It is associated with bradycardia and low anxiety, and is shown in a controlled and cold manner. It is often related to somatic disorders such as irritable bowel or gastritis. It is common in personalities with a Type A attachment pattern (Mikulincer, 1998).

There are many reasons for a child to learn to hide his discomfort:

- The parents have definitively disappeared, either due to death or abandonment. The child cannot express frustration because the parents are not available;
- The child feels that their caregivers are weak or sick, and therefore he should take care of them and not burden them with his problems. In this case, role reversal (parentification) will take place, in which parents are likely to burden their children with their illnesses, concerns, and so on; the child will feel obliged not to be another burden;
- The parents are very aggressive, either through physical violence or by imposing excessive discipline that prevents the child from expressing his needs for fear of retaliation.

Luis works in the food industry, the typical family business where everyone helps to "get the job done" when there is too much work. His childhood, he says, was not very happy. His father worked all day and his mother, as a housewife, did what she could to raise four children with the little money they had.

Luis complains of severe hypochondria that prevents him from concentrating at work and at home. He spends his time visiting doctors and searching the Internet for potential illnesses based on his symptoms, although his doctors have not yet found any organic disease and have recommended that he see a psychologist. He is obsessed with everyone who feels well: he wants his children to study and give them the education he didn't have; he wants his wife to work no more than is needed, so as not to aggravate her joint pain; he wants the psychologist to finish the session a little early so he can rest ...

My experience with this type of people whom I call "compulsive caregivers" is that they hide a lot of anger inside; anger as a mixture of rage and impotence that they are afraid to let go as they could lose control. So, I always ask the same question: "Have you ever been afraid of losing control and hurting the people you love? Or of losing control and hurting yourself?" When a patient starts to get emotional and cries, it means we have touched upon something important and sensitive.

C: I feel very embarrassed talking about this, I feel like shit, but sometimes I'm afraid of picking up a knife and hurting my family, or drowning them, or driving off a cliff. But I swear I could never hurt them. I'm going crazy and I feel terrible just thinking about things like that. There is no hope for me, right?

T: This is difficult to explain, Luis, and we will work on it throughout the therapy. There is something inside of you that is very angry because you always take care of others but never of yourself. It's as if a part of you wants to get away from the people you love so you can take care of yourself, something that, by the way, you don't know how to do.

This inability to express one's own needs creates a feeling of deep discomfort and inadequacy (guilt), as well as a sense of not deserving attention or care (shame). On the other hand, people who use anger as a way of getting themselves noticed accomplish two evil effects. The first is not to be treated normally and the second is to be in a permanent state of anxiety and discomfort, which also causes feelings of guilt and shame.

Individuals with secure attachment in childhood (Type B) are able to restrain their anger adaptively, that is, they can mentalize in different circumstances (Mikulincer, 1998):

- Taking time to assess the most suitable response in any given situation;
- Avoiding anger so as not to suffer ruminating thoughts;
- Avoiding emotions that can be harmful for the person himself or for others.

Individuals with avoidant attachment (Type A), as we have seen, mask anger as a way of avoiding conflict, maybe showing false emotions (e.g., smiling when angry) or passive-aggressive behaviors.

Anxious individuals (Type C) will show anger and annoyance all too often without being able to assess the suitability of when or how to do it. Individuals with disorganized attachment (Type D), due to the dissociative states, will have responses of both excessive rage to any stimulus that disturbs them as well as pathological indifference where defensive behavior is necessary.

In a gradient of lesser to greater inhibition, at one end, anger would be totally hidden, never manifesting itself externally (individuals themselves may not even feel it) and directed towards the self in the form of self-criticism. At the other extreme, anger is always outwardly focused and can lead to antisocial behaviors (see Figure 6.4).

People suffering from panic attacks and social phobia have trouble expressing their needs. They feel angry, but dare not show it for fear of being rejected. This pent-up anger ends up becoming toxic; it will prevent relaxation and cause a permanent state of alert. Anxiety often generates avoidance of objects or situations that are considered dangerous when in fact they are innocuous (superstitious behaviors).

From the very beginning, anger (also referred to as impotence or frustration) becomes a somatic feeling of discomfort (anxiety) that, every time it is felt, is coded as "shame." Once language begins (3–4 years) – and, therefore, the capacity for reflection on the internal state (mentalization) – thoughts may arise in order to reason how to avoid it. This constant revision is what leads to ruminating thoughts in adolescence and adulthood (Ginot, 2015). The process of assessing (with a negative bias) what happened in a cognitive way is what we know as *guilt* (see Figure 6.5).

Emotions that are common to all mammals are called primary emotions. Human beings, in addition, feel other more complex emotions called secondary

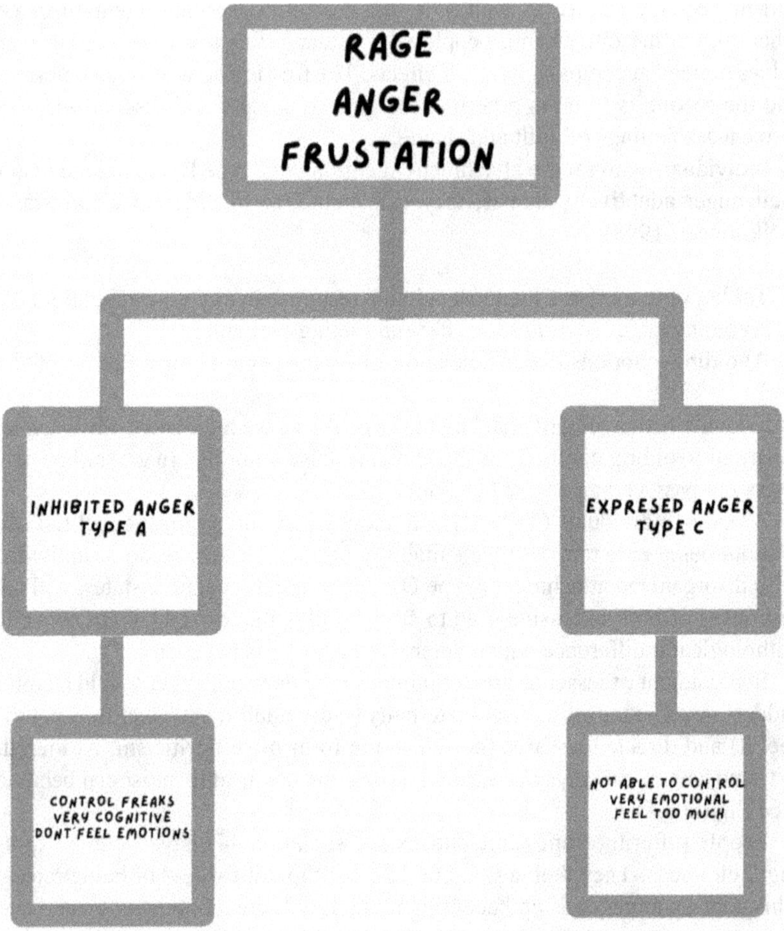

RAGE
ANGER
FRUSTATION

INHIBITED ANGER
TYPE A

EXPRESED ANGER
TYPE C

CONTROL FREAKS
VERY COGNITIVE
DONT FEEL EMOTIONS

NOT ABLE TO CONTROL
VERY EMOTIONAL
FEEL TOO MUCH

Figure 6.4 There are two different ways to deal with anger: inhibiting anger and expressing anger. The first is conditioned by an activation of the sympathetic branch of the ANS, while the second is regulated by the parasympathetic branch.

emotions, which are of a social origin (Aguado, 2010) and can be a major source of discomfort. The most important emotions are guilt and shame. These emotions are learned in childhood depending on the family context and on how the parents dealt with emotions. As discussed in Chapter 3, there is a relationship between the behaviors and emotions of children and their caregivers: they sustain each other.

Figure 6.5 This figure illustrates the PARCUVE model. Rupture in the attachment relationships (real or imaginary) generates fear and anger. If this cannot be adequately managed, feelings of guilt and shame are developed, which can become pathological when recurrent.

Most of the time, when there is emotional disconnection, a correction immediately follows and a healthy balance emerges. This helps the child tolerate certain levels of discomfort and frustration (Schore, 2001). In cases where there is poor mentalization, there is a tendency to rigidly repeat roles. In general, this becomes a vicious cycle in which caregivers and children dysregulate each other. In all cases, guilt and shame become alarm signals to help anticipate the actions of caregivers and thus be able to modify the behavior to avoid future suffering (classical learning). Figure 6.6 illustrates how the emotional styles of parents and children influence each other.

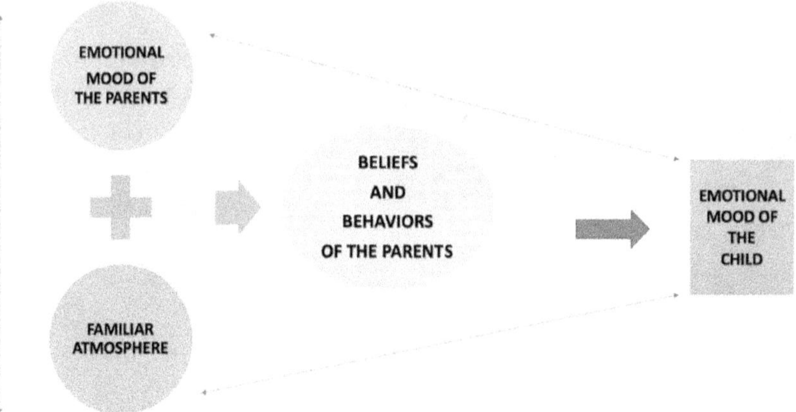

Figure 6.6 Guilt and shame are generated in a family context, which is composed of a system of emotional and behavioral relationships among people who mutually influence each other. If the relationship is healthy a virtuous circle of well-being will be created, but if the individuals connect in a pathological manner, the vicious circle will lead to pathology.

If these toxic sensations and emotions are felt often, they become innate and spontaneous, and are incorporated in the implicit procedural memory, thus becoming a part of an individual's personality. There are longitudinal studies showing that measurements of guilt and shame at 4 years of age are the same as those at 12 years of age and those in adulthood (Tangney & Dearing, 2002).

Shame

We find the first written documented case of shame in the Bible, specifically, in Genesis, when Adam and Eve, after biting the apple of the tree of knowledge, are punished to earn their hard-earned bread and feel shame when seeing their naked bodies. Being aware of their shortcomings, they must leave the paradise of the unconscious that they shared with the rest of the animals and become fully human, aware of their own being in front of others.

Shame and guilt are secondary or self-assessment emotions, universal in humans. Shame fulfills a social function: it regulates our behavior when facing our peers and inhibits negative emotions and behaviors. The causes of shame differ according to personal, religious, and cultural variables.

Shame is experienced in the first years of life in relation to the caregivers; a result of an activation of the parasympathetic nervous system, it serves to inhibit a behavior that is viewed as wrong (Schore, 1994; Nathanson, 1992). By scolding their children, most often in a controlled way, parents create a sense of shame and discomfort in order to educate them and avoid dangerous or inappropriate behavior. These memories of inhibition and fault, if recurrent, are stored long-term in the form of somatic memory.

In secure attachment (Type B), these momentary ruptures of the attachment bond are healthy and allow for learning and for the autonomy of children, who will gradually learn to regulate themselves in social contexts in the absence of their caregivers.

In avoidant attachment (Type A), the child accommodates his behavior to what he believes his parents expect of him. His behavior is based on the inhibition of his desires. By prioritizing the cortical parts, he is able to avoid feelings of discomfort. Sometimes this results in somatic illness, anxiety, or compulsive behavior such as addictions or anorexia in adulthood, because of the inability to face certain sensations from which it was necessary to dissociate.

Individuals with anxious attachment (Type C), as we have seen, have a dominance of the subcortical areas, which leads them to feel too much. They base their behavior on their sensations and are permanently activated. They tend to suffer from panic disorders, obesity or bulimia, generalized anxiety, or depression.

The sense of pathological shame is always related to the belief of "I am unworthy," that is to say, "I am defective." This distorted perception of reality is compensated by actions that help reduce discomfort. I want to highlight the gradient of two common personality types to reduce the feeling of discomfort:

Caregiver

The caregiver belongs to Type A. Since the child has learned that he is not worthy, generally because his needs have not been attended to, he can try too hard to be worthy; that is to say, he can care for and worry about others as a way of being accepted. "Since no one will love you for who you are, they may love you for what you do."

These behaviors tend to be highly boosted by caregivers (teachers, parents, siblings, etc.) as they are usually very good children who are not at all conflictive. The problem is that the more they strive to please others, the more difficult it is for them to see and feel their needs, which they are unable to express.

Rage and discomfort during childhood (and later during adolescence and adulthood) are fully dissociated, avoiding conflict at all costs for fear of being rejected. They are often afraid of real or imaginary affective separation.

In this type of people, shame always manifests itself in the form of apologies, unrequested care, and so on. They often present somatizations and anxiety, and seek a doctor or psychologist to help them attenuate them, without being aware that it is their constant behavior and submission that causes their discomfort.

The main characteristics of people with a caregiving pattern of behavior are:

- Excessive worry over others' well-being, ignoring their own well-being; they often fall into anxious behavior;
- Negligence in self-care;
- Constant feelings of shame and guilt. They never consider themselves good enough or having done all they should have done for others;
- They avoid conflict at all costs, making very important compromises to avoid problems;
- They observe others so that they can evaluate how they should feel; they are the typical patients who, when they enter the therapy office, are more concerned with how the therapist is doing than with how they are.

Lola is a 28-year-old only child living with her mother, who was widowed when she was young. I point out to her that the peculiar thing is the way she expresses herself regarding this: it is not that she lost her father, it is that her mother was widowed.

Her request is that I help her explain to her mother that she wants to leave home and live alone. Every time she tries to explain to her that she wants to be independent, her mother recriminates and blackmails her so she does not leave, saying things like, "Where are you going to be better off than here?" "What am I going to do alone without you?" and the well-known "Is this how you pay me back for everything I have done for you?"

Role reversal, negligent parental care, and real or emotional abandonment lead the child to constantly invest a lot of energy in sustaining the bond of attachment. This develops the physiological, behavioral, and emotional characteristics that make the child feel anxiety when facing any stimulus that is perceived as a threat, mainly in relation to emotional connection with others. From the time they were children, they have learned to analyze how others feel, spending lots of energy on strategies so that there are no conflicts. They live worrying about others, which makes them both afraid to explore the world and unable to feel calm around others for fear of being rejected.

Narcissist

Similar to the previous case, these children learn that no one will attend to their needs. However, by giving predominance to the more cortical areas, they assess the world in a cold and non-emotional way. It is as if they think, "Since nobody is going to take care of me, only I can take care of myself." These individuals do not feel shame in adolescence and adulthood because they were unable to tolerate it when they were young (Solomon et al., 2001).

As with the compulsive caregiver personality, there is a lot of anger. But unlike the previous case, it will be shown externally, trying to make everyone do what they want. Anxiety does not exist because they do not waste a second observing it, but when it appears, it becomes intolerable. These patients are very reluctant to go to therapy and when they do it is because the discomfort is intolerable or because a family member has forced them to do so.

They can often mistreat family and friends in an attempt to achieve their goals, regardless of the consequences (tendency towards psychopathy). They will do anything to avoid feeling the sensation of not being worthy.

Tom has worked as a doctor in the public administration his entire life and is about to retire. He comes to therapy because he has very strong chest pains which his colleagues discard as being organic. He is very angry with them because he considers that they do not take his discomfort seriously; he is also very upset with the Andalusian health care system because he believes that he has worked hard and that they are not rewarding him for it by giving him a pension he considers he deserves. He is also upset with his wife and daughter because they do not give him the care he needs and they complain that he protests too much. He is angry with the politicians because they do not help solve the country's problems and he doesn't speak to almost anyone in his family because of a problem concerning his father's inheritance.

T: Are you sure you're right about everything? But, haven't you considered the possibility that maybe what you're feeling is anxiety because you're constantly tense?
C: That's why I'm here, because everyone insists that I have to see a psychologist, but I see no point in this.
As a psychologist, I start feeling he is getting angry at me, too.

The main features of people with a narcissistic personality are:

- They do not empathize. Apparently, they need no-one;
- They pretend to have no fear of rejection;
- They show pathological self-care that does not take into account other people's needs;
- They have sensations of guilt and shame, but they are hidden deep down. They are never satisfied and demand more and more from others;
- Apparently, they are not afraid of conflict, but they are good at assessing whether the other person might be a rival and act submissively. They tend to relate to caregiving people who tend to all their needs.

Figure 6.7 shows how different personality traits can help tolerate and avoid the feeling of unworthiness in relation to oneself and others. This is another example of how, in psychology, we may arrive at opposite situations based on the same symptom.

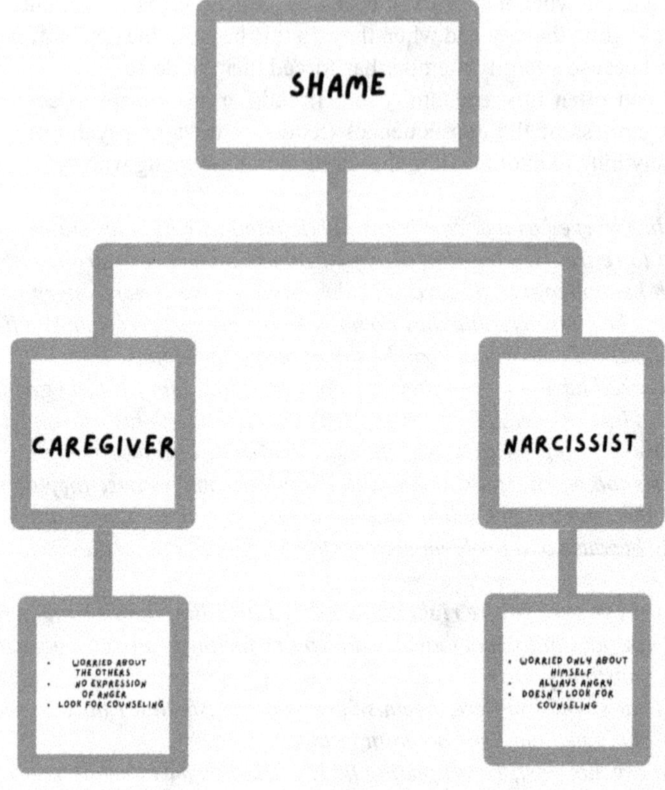

Figure 6.7 When shame (feeling of unworthiness) becomes a disturbing sensation, children develop different personality patterns in order to tolerate it. On the one hand, they may avoid conflict at all costs and, on the other, they may be completely indifferent towards how others feel.

Ideally, a person would find a balance between both extremes, what we call a "selfish" person: an individual who is able to take care of himself and who, at the same time, takes into account the needs of others.

Guilt

Guilt is closely related to shame. But while the latter requires the eyes of another person (as adults, it means imagining how others see us), feeling guilt does not require the judgment of other people, since it is a reflexive process related to language, to the way in which we speak to ourselves. There are studies indicating that with guilt, only the right hemisphere is activated, while when there is shame, there is an activation of the corpus callosum (the organ that connects the two hemispheres), which would indicate a relationship between the emotional and the verbal (Solomon, 2001).

While shame is an inhibitory emotion, guilt is an emotion that seeks out reparation of the damage that may have been caused. There are mainly two types of guilt:

- *Empathic guilt*: This becomes activated when we feel that we have hurt others and has a positive effect since it helps to restore and maintain social relationships;
- *Pathological guilt*: This becomes activated by an event, in relation to a thought, emotion, or behavior. It originates in childhood as a defense mechanism and encourages constant submission and/or obedience in order to avoid the aggressiveness of the caregivers. Over time, it can result in ruminations and may cause great suffering.

Chronologically, the origin of guilt is posterior to shame. These emotions also fulfill a socializing function. In the event of frequent and/or threatening ruptures of attachment, the feelings of shame and fear will cause great discomfort, so children will review their behavior in an attempt to avoid them next time. If this process is repeated too often, it will remain encoded in implicit memory as constant thoughts of guilt and self-condemnation (Ginot, 2015).

In order to alleviate feelings of guilt and regain a sense of control, the child uses strategies that allow for the recovery of the bond with the caregivers, but, unlike shame – in which strategies are somatic – with guilt these will be cognitive. As we saw in Chapter 4, the attachment bond in childhood must be maintained above anything else to avoid triggering the separation/panic circuit. Thus, whenever there are situations of discomfort in relation to the caregivers, they will generate associated thoughts of guilt and lack of worth. At puberty, this guilt can be targeted towards oneself or towards others, that is, to hold others accountable for one's own failures. In a dimensional continuum and depending on the circumstances, we find two opposite strategies:

Perfectionist

Being a perfectionist is quite positive; if I were not one, you would not be reading this book now. However, as Nietzsche said, "Everything that is absolute in human beings belongs to the realm of psychopathology." Individuals with an ailing perfectionism try to do everything perfectly in childhood as a way to please parents, teachers, and so on. The underlying thought is, "If I am perfect, they will be proud of me and there will be no more problems, and they will finally love me." The main features are:

- They completely neglect their needs in order to fulfill those of the caregiver (parents, siblings, teachers);
- They tend to be caregivers, with a tendency towards parentification;
- They are very responsible. Behaviors are greatly reinforced by others in childhood and adolescence; no one worries about what they really need;
- They have low self-esteem, a pathological fear of failure, and, therefore, fear of rejection;
- They have a tendency towards procrastination. They do not do their homework for fear of not doing it perfectly;
- They need to have everything under control. They feel anxiety if they lose that control because of the infantile sensation of needing to control their impulses and needs to please adults.

Louise is in her first year of law school. She comes to therapy because she has serious trouble concentrating. When she studies, she is unable to sit for more than a minute in front of her notes or pay attention in class.

When I start talking to her, I realize she spends her days procrastinating; she is incapable of doing anything, because it is useless if it is not perfect. And, of course, perfection is a mirror: if you look in it, you will see yourself deformed.

T: Tell me Louise, when you start studying, how do you do it? Do you use university manuals, your own notes, or those of your classmates?

C: I'm really obsessed with getting good grades because my parents are making a great effort to pay for my studies. So, when I get home, the first thing I do is sit down to study and recopy my notes. But, of course, I realize I haven't made my bed, haven't swept my room, or that I'm missing something to make my meal. I do these tasks, so I can focus completely on my studies, but by then many hours have gone by and I'm exhausted, so I decide to rest a bit.

T: I get the impression that you have very good intentions to study, but there is always something more important that demands your attention.

C: Yes, I'm just scared of not having everything organized and perfect and being able to concentrate on what's important, which are my studies.

Indolent

The etymology of the word says it all: those who do not feel pain, remorse, or guilt. They decide to sabotage the caregivers' efforts by sabotaging themselves. In some cases, this personality trait may appear in adolescents who really tried as children, but when these strategies fail, they shift to the other extreme. Their motto is, "If I do nothing, I cannot go wrong nor fail."

It is as if they thought, "I have failed because you did not give me what I deserved and, therefore, I will sabotage you in your efforts to help me." Normally they have narcissistic and ego-syntonic tendencies, and have no interest in changing this.

They have the following characteristics:

- They are extremely dependent upon others, using them to satisfy their needs (they surround themselves, if they can, with caregiving people);
- They mask their anxiety behind drugs or other types of addictions;
- They blame their parents, families, or society for their failures;
- They don't try any solutions for fear of failure. They lack self-esteem;
- They know they are rejected, but that feeds their indolence under a mask of indifference.

Paul is a 21-year-old man who spends his days smoking weed and playing on his PlayStation. His mother brings him to therapy because she wants me to motivate her son – who she loves and spoils – to study or work.

T: Hi Paul, tell me, how can I help you?
C: Well, I have no idea, I don't know what the hell I'm doing here. I don't have a problem, and besides, I don't believe in psychologists.
T: Why did you come, then?
C: Because my mother made me. Because she insists, I have to study or work, and I don't do that shit. I am an anarchist; I don't believe in society or in any of the shit they try to sell us.
T: But you'll have to do something in order to eat, live ... ?
C: I could care less about all that shit, I'm a free spirit. I like rap and sometimes I compose songs. I'm going to have a YouTube channel and post them on there. I can make a lot of money without having to deal with a boss and all that crap.

Types of Attributions

Abramson et al. (1978) created a model of three types of causal attributions:

- Internal or external attributions;
- General or particular attributions;
- Stable or variable attributions.

This model helps us know how a person understands the world. For example, if something works out for a depressive person, he will tend to attribute his success to something external ("I had nothing to do with it"); particular ("this

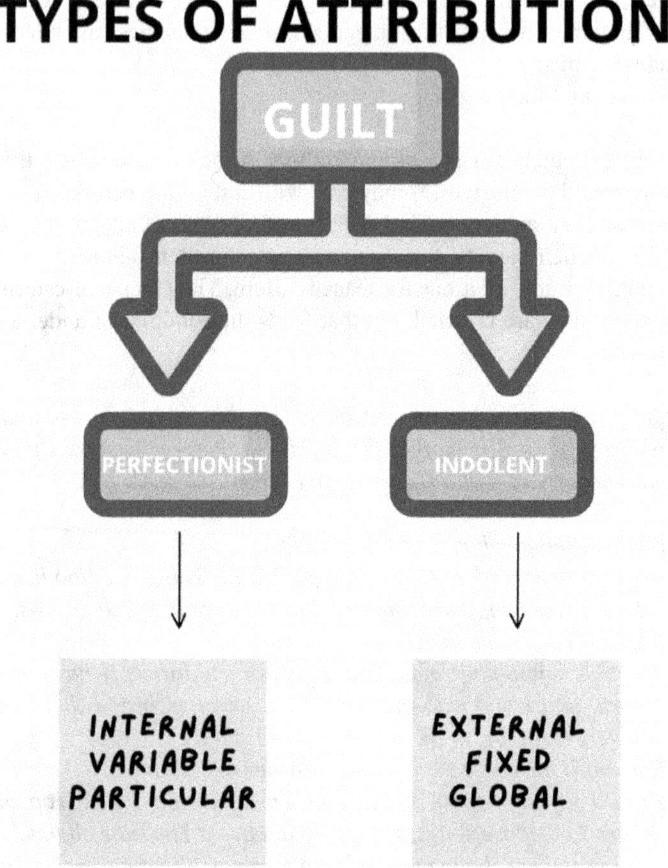

Figure 6.8 People who feel a lot of guilt during their childhood may take on different types of personalities in order to feel a sense of control. On one end, we would find those who are perfectionists and, on the other, those who are indolent.

time I have been lucky"); and variable ("it has happened, but surely it will not happen again"). When he fails, he will attribute it to something internal ("I am a disaster"); general ("nothing works out for me"); and stable ("it will always happen like this").

The way in which each of us experiences guilt and shame will depend mostly on the type of attributions that are made. According to Tangney and Dearing (2002), shame is based on internal, general, and stable attributions. Guilt is based on internal, particular, and variable attributions.

We will find the following variables regarding guilt:

- Individuals who become perfectionists in order to redeem guilt have an unconscious "if I am perfect, they will love me and accept me" thought. They use internal ("I have to do better"), particular ("there are times when I get things right"), and variable ("when I do it well everything will be different") attributions.
- Individuals who become indolent to make up for their guilt use a "I'd better do nothing so I cannot go wrong" type of thought. Attributions are external ("no-one is going to help me" or "others are to blame for my failures"), stable ("nothing will change no matter what I do"), and general ("no exceptions").

Regarding the sensation of shame (remember that it is somatic), we may find two opposite extremes:

- Individuals who become caregivers in order to bury shame make internal ("I am defective"), variable ("if I try hard I'll be accepted"), and particular ("I must care for others more than for myself") attributions;
- Individuals who become narcissistic so as not to feel shame make external ("people are wrong and only I am right"), stable ("things can't be any different"), and general ("everyone is wrong") attributions.

Beliefs about oneself and the ability to be congruent also affect behaviors. People who feel flexible are able to cope with their failures, while those who feel rigid feel a lot of negative affect when facing problems; they consider themselves incapable of modifying their behaviors.

Tangney and Dearing (2002) have also found that congruence greatly affects guilt and shame. On one end, there are the extremely congruent people ("you are what you do") and, on the other, the incongruent people ("I make promises I can't keep"). Alternatively, flexibility is related to the possibility of changing coping strategies depending on the circumstances. The greater the threat, the more need for control there will be and, consequently, the more rigidity in behavior, thoughts, and emotions.

Fear, anger, guilt, and shame are the basic negative emotions that we will find in patients who come to our offices. Failure in regulating these emotions causes psychological pathologies. As we will see in the following chapters, both therapist and patient will have to walk the path traveled by the patient together in order to help him face his fears, learn to handle anger in an adaptive way, and live with a sense of inner peace that leaves no room for guilt or shame.

Conclusions

In order for the person who has placed their trust in us to heal, he will need the therapist to become the attachment figure he did not have when it was needed. In some cases, the encounter will be brief and will require few sessions, but

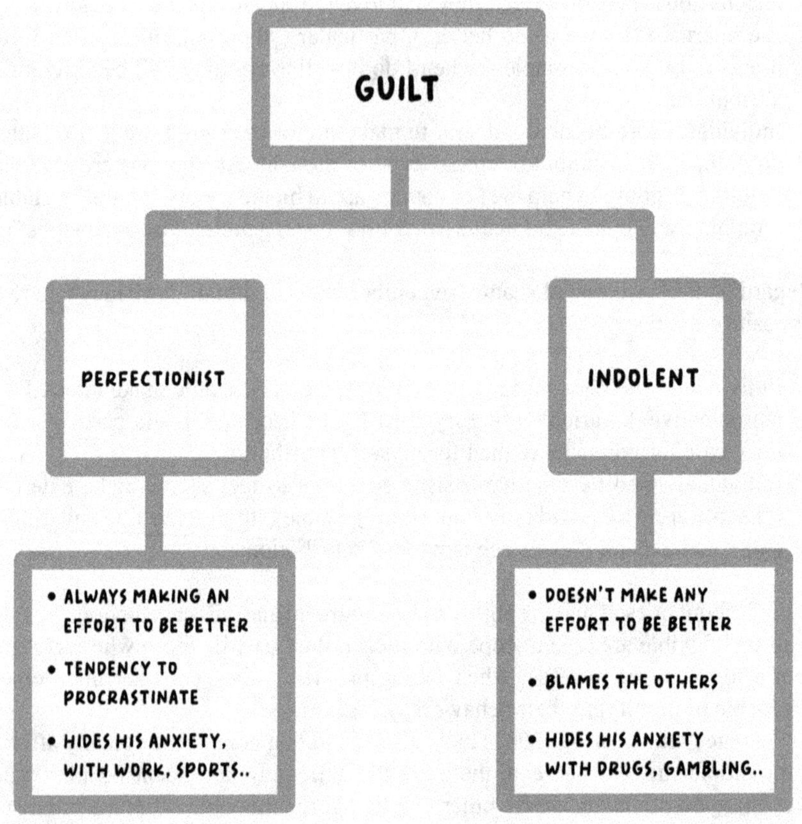

Figure 6.9 Attributions govern the way in which individuals see the world. The more rigid the need for control and defense, the higher the degree of pathology.

sometimes it will take a long time to heal emotional wounds. In all cases, if the person does not feel safe, there will be no therapy.

We cannot forget that what caused the trauma – the emotional wound that the mind could not heal on its own – was the lack of safety, and what eventually caused the pathology were the regulation mechanisms that developed to achieve a sense of control. It is the therapist who, with his physical and emotional presence, will create the safe environment in which anger, guilt, and shame can be treated without fear, yet with safety. As my grandmother use to tell me in my childhood: "Alone you can't but with friends you can."

The PARCUVE model explains how attachment influences anxiety and panic disorders throughout a person's life. It explains how the rupture in attachment

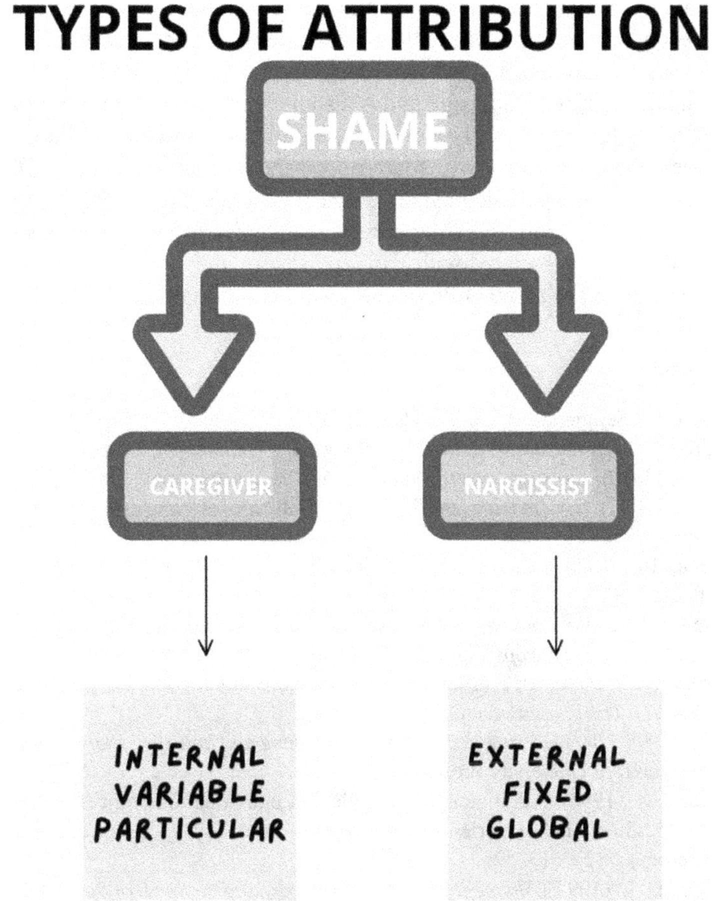

Figure 6.10 Feelings of shame are disturbing and the child will try to avoid them, rehearsing behaviors that will allow him to feel a sense of control and repair the attachment bond. Depending on the way of understanding the world, a different personality type will be adopted.

bonds with the caregivers activates the panic circuit. In humans, this can be activated either by a real (e.g., death, hospitalization) or imaginary (e.g., the mother's depression) loss.

This panic circuit is built on the fear and pain circuit, which is phylogenetically more primitive and causes feelings of anxiety and discomfort in the body. Similar to this, the anger circuit is activated, which in humans can take the form of a feeling of frustration or impotence.

All of the above is common to all mammals, but in humans there are also two emotions that have a social origin and are not shared with any other species. These secondary emotions are guilt and shame. Guilt appears with language at 4–5 years of age; its function is to encourage reflection and rectifying mistakes. Shame is prior to language and is a somatic emotion. According to many authors, it has the function of curbing exploration and teaching children to set boundaries. Both emotions, which are necessary for human beings to develop socially, can become pathological and as such generate much suffering.

Starting in childhood, individuals create strategies to avoid feelings of discomfort which are associated with guilt and shame; they either become perfectionists or indolent to avoid guilt, or caregivers or narcissists to avoid shame.

References

Abramson, L., Seligman, M., & Teasdale, J. (1978). Learned helplessness in humans: Critique and reformulation. *Journal of Abnormal Psychology*, *87*, 49–74.

Aguado, L. (2010). *Emoción, afecto y motivación*. Alianza editorial.

Bowlby, J. (1977). The making and breaking of affectional bonds. *British Journal of Psychiatry*, *130*, 201–210.

Crittenden, P. (2015). *Raising parents: Attachment, representation, and treatment*. Routledge.

Damasio, A. R. (2003). *Looking for Spinoza: Joy, sorrow, and the feeling brain*. Harcourt.

Ginot, E. (2015). *The neuropsychology of the unconscious*. Norton.

Heinicke, C., & Westhemer, J. (1966). *Brief separations*. International Universities Press.

Hart, S. (2011). *The impact of attachment*. Norton.

Karen, R. (1998). *Become attached. First relationships and how they shape our capacity for love*. Oxford University Press.

Mikulincer, M. (1998). Adult attachment style and individual differences in functional versus dysfunctional experiences of anger. *Journal of Personality and Social Psychology*, *74*(2), 513–524.

Nathanson, D. L. (1992). *Shame and pride. Affect, sex, and the birth of the self*. Norton.

Nijenhuis, E. (2000). Somatoform dissociation: Major symptoms of dissociative disorders. *Journal of Trauma & Dissociation*, *1*(4), 33–66.

Panksepp, J. (2004). *Affective neuroscience. The foundations of human and animal emotions*. Oxford University Press.

Panksepp, J. (2009). Brain emotional systems and qualities of mental life: from animals models of affect implications for psychoterapeutics. In D. Fosha, D. J. Siegel, & M. F. Solomon (Eds.), *The healing power of emotion* (pp. 1–26). Norton.

Panksepp, J., & Biven, L. (2012). *The archeology of mind. Neuroevolutionary origins of humans emotions*. Norton.

Sapolsky, R. M. (2004). *Why zebras don't get ulcers: The acclaimed guide to stress, stress-related diseases, and coping*. Holt Paperback.

Schore, A. (1994). *Affect regulation and the repair of the self*. Norton.

Schore, A. (2001). The effects of a secure attachment relationship on roght brain development, affect regulation & infant mental health. *Infant Mental Health Journal*, *22*, 7–66.

Solomon, M., Neborsky, R., Mccullough, L., Alpert, M., Shapiro, F., & Malan, D. (2001). *Short term therapy for long term change*. Norton.

Tangney, J. P., & Dearing, R. (2002). *Shame and guilt*. Guilford Press.

Part 2

Treatment

7 Transversal Elements of Therapy

"Reason cannot defeat emotion, an emotion can only be displaced or overcome by a stronger emotion." *Spinoza*

Psychology is the realm of subjectivity; no two people are the same. Everyone has their own experiences, longings, fears, and frustrations. Getting to know a person's individuality demands a personal approach in therapy which will multiply the possibilities of help. However, there are several transversal elements throughout therapy, which will have to be taken into account from the first to the last session. These factors are independent of the type of therapeutic model applied and are universal for all patients.

This does not imply they will be stable or rigid. Instead, they will change throughout the sessions. We should always take them into account during treatment and be very flexible in order to modify the course of our work when changes are detected. They can and should change throughout treatment, and we will need both the therapist and the patient to be aware of this.

There are three transversal elements I consider fundamental throughout the entire treatment:

1. The first element is the problem presented, the reason why the patient has come to therapy. Problems can vary from insomnia to marital problems, from social phobia to panic attacks to obsessions, and so on.
2. As we have seen in previous chapters, there are four basic emotions at the root of most disorders. We should keep these in mind at all times: fear, guilt, shame, and anger. These emotions have overwhelmed the alert system in the patient's brain and will generate symptoms of anxiety apart from activating the emotional regulation and control mechanisms to deal with this anxiety.
3. The third element is the therapeutic alliance, that is, the relationship established between patient and therapist. As we have seen, a crucial aspect of the origins of pathology is the patient's attachment relationship with his caregivers during childhood. As therapists, we should teach them to bond in a different, healthier way, developing a corrective bond that can create a secure basis, so they can use it as an example in their daily life.

DOI: 10.4324/9781003646341-9

The Therapeutic Goal

The therapeutic goal is that which the patient asks to work on in therapy. It is crucial to agree on a clear goal, because if we do not know where we are going, we can end up in the middle of nowhere. Patients will often come in with a clear request, such as getting rid of their anxiety, quitting certain habits, or not being so self-conscious. In other cases, they will simply come in searching for help, and the therapist will have to guide them to decide their therapeutic goal.

When the therapeutic goal is not clear enough, it is necessary to dedicate some time to redefine it and make sure it is operational for both the therapist and the patient. Our clients will often not know how to explain their problem and sometimes will have goals that are unrealizable either because they are unrealistic or impossible.

Sometimes a symptom-based goal can be negotiated with the patient, such as reducing anxiety or resolving insomnia or eliminating pain. The therapist must be clear at all times that it is important to work on the cause that led to the symptom and not only on the symptom itself; if the root of a problem is not solved, the problem will reoccur in one way or another creating new symptoms. This is very common in addictions; for instance, when a person stops smoking or drinking and tries to calm anxiety by eating sweets; or when a person with panic attacks falls into a deep depression as soon as the panic attacks diminish.

Michael is a 30-year-old patient who comes to therapy because of social phobia and insomnia, which worsened recently because he was relocated to a different city and had to leave Malaga, where his partner and family live.

He feels anxious in situations where he considers being observed or judged. For example, when he attends a workshop and is afraid of being asked questions, or when he is with his in-laws and feels afraid of expressing his opinion and making a fool of himself. Sometimes, he is also afraid of transpiring or blushing in public. On one occasion, he suffered a severe anxiety attack that could be diagnosed as a panic attack.

In the fourth session, being asked about situations in which there could have been physical or emotional separation from his mother (with whom he has an anxious, dismissing-needy relationship), he reported being hospitalized in the ICU for 15 days due to an acute intestinal infection when he was 3 years old. He did not remember anything, with the exception of an image of a machine, nor did he feel anything.

In the following session, he told me that he had talked to his grandmother. She believed this event could have affected him because he was placed in a plastic bubble (to avoid infections) and had to use a respirator. The doctors forbade his mother from coming to see her son because, whenever she did, the boy would strip off all his devices and start kicking and punching the plastic. After 10 days, the doctor asked her to come in, to avoid causing the child a psychological illness.

While disclosing this, he began to feel anxiety in his chest, but no image or memory came to him. I asked him to close his eyes and tapped on his knees. At that moment, he began to cry and memories of the fear and loneliness he once experienced came to mind. I asked him to imagine himself as an adult, walking in with his mother to visit the child. He saw the child hugging the mother rather angrily and gradually, after several sets of tapping, the child started to calm down and finally hugged him and merged with him (integration of parts).

Later, an image came up of going back home and not seeing his brother. He had always had a very bad relationship with his older brother, who acted as if he were his father, setting rules and scolding him. He spontaneously told me he now understood his brother had been frightened during his hospitalization, as a result of which, according to his mother, his school performance had greatly decreased. His older brother was afraid that something might happen to him and, in order to avoid this, he started overprotecting him unconsciously. Once the negative bodily sensation stopped and the session came to an end, he told me that he felt a strangely peaceful calmness he had not felt in a long time.

I do not know if this particular situation – the feeling of abandonment in the hospital and the fear and anger associated with not being allowed to be with his mother in a situation that is very hostile for a child – was the cause of his symptoms of shame and anxiety in adulthood, but I do believe it was an important pillar of the pathology. As a result of this session, the anxiety decreased noticeably.

The main goals for treatment that clients usually present are the following:

1. Therapeutic goals related to fear of being exposed to others:
    a. Fear and/or shame in situations in which the person has to relate to other people (e.g., fear of public speaking, playing an instrument in front of an audience, going on stage, or expressing opinions to someone who is admired or who can refute them).
    b. An irrational fear of being observed or judged because of uncontrollable physiological reactions. In my practice, I have had patients who were scared of sweating, of blushing, of their stomach rumbling, of losing control of their bowel movements, and so on. These fears, which the patient recognizes as irrational and uncontrollable, may not be related to any particular event. Nevertheless, they can lead to avoidance behaviors that prevent the person from leading a normal life.

   c. Fear of showing themselves intimately because they think they either have sexual problems (e.g., impotence, premature ejaculation, anorgasmia) or a body part that makes them feel self-conscious, which they believe could be a reason for ridicule once intimate.
2. Therapeutic goals related to fear of losing control: Once again, in most cases, there is no specific situation directly related to the fear that would suggest a phobia. Fear is irrational and excessive, and the patient fears feeling overwhelmed by excessive anxiety. The most common cases are patients who are afraid of planes but have never experienced in-flight problems, or people who are afraid of driving on highways or riding an elevator. Patients show their surprise and anger (towards themselves) because they were able to do this activity and, now, just thinking about it makes them tremendously anxious. The first attack is usually related to something traumatic that was happening in their life at that time, but patients are usually not able to make this connection without the help of a therapist.
3. Therapeutic goals related to some organic function: They are usually related to sex, food, or sleep.
   a. Insomnia: Hidden behind insomnia there is usually a need for alertness. It is important to inquire if the patient feels anxiety or not. If the answer is affirmative, we should first work on the anxiety and later on the insomnia. If there is no clear cause (e.g., a couple crisis, problems at work, etc.), we may suspect that this and the consequent insomnia are symptoms of unresolved conflicts in the patient's psyche.
   b. Food problems: Food is often used as an emotional regulator. There may be binge eating disorders, anorexia, or bulimia, which are all regulatory mechanisms to try to control anxiety.
4. Therapeutic goals related to a disorder (anxiety, OCD, insomnia, addictions, and phobias) that can be explained by a specific traumatic event (e.g., post-traumatic stress disorder).
5. Therapeutic goals related to anxiety for no apparent reason. They can have a specific reason or a disturbance of unknown origin, and the person cannot think of an event that could have caused it. In these cases, we will have to find personality traits that may be causing this discomfort.
6. Therapeutic goals related to psychosomatic disorders. These are often organic disorders for which no organic cause is found. The goal is usually to experience improvement or remission of a conversion disorder, abdominal pains, and so on.
7. Therapeutic goals related to harmful habits or addictions, including everything from being dependent on people to pathological activities or substances. In these cases, high motivation on the part of the patient is essential or the therapy is unlikely to be successful (Rollnick, 1995).

We should be extremely cautious in handling the therapeutic goal because most of the time patients have not established a connection between their anxiety and their attachment relationship in childhood. It becomes essential to create a strong therapeutic alliance from the initial interview onward in order to gradually address elements from the past that the patient does not connect with current fears.

T. *You have already told me how the panic attacks began, when it first happened, and the anxiety they generate in you. What do you think is the origin of these attacks (or of that irrational fear)?*

P. *I honestly don't know. I get them all of a sudden: I start sweating, I can't breathe. I start to notice that I'm going to have one, and I get very nervous.*

T. *Yes, I understand perfectly that they are very unpleasant but that's not what I'm asking. We will discuss all of that in detail later on. What I would like is for you to tell me where you think the origin lies, if there has been any moment in your past when you experienced a specific situation that could explain these symptoms.*

P. *Not really. I've led a pretty normal life with a very happy childhood.*

T. *OK, so they seem to come out of the blue, right? But anxiety is an alarm in your brain. What I mean is that maybe your mind is on the alert because of things you don't even suspect. Could that be possible?*

P. *Well, now that you mention it, I have always been a very shy person, I admit that I've always worried about what others thought, but it has never been very serious nor do I think it has anything to do with this.*

T. *Of course. But perhaps there are things that happened in your past that you felt then were not so important and now they're taking their toll. Don't you think we could explore things from your past that may be influencing what is happening to you now? Because, if we only treat the anxiety, we will be focusing on the symptom and we will not have discovered the cause, with the subsequent risk of relapse. Just like when I have a fever and I take an aspirin. If I have the flu, I'll feel better and, in a few days, I'll feel like new; but if it's an infection, aspirin will do nothing.*

P. *That actually makes a lot of sense, and I'd like to get rid of this forever.*

T. *OK then, shall we agree to work on the origins of the problem? Why don't you tell me a little bit about your childhood? Who was the most important person for you when you were little? Who did you feel most at ease with?*

The therapeutic goal will almost never be related to shame or guilt, but to symptoms of discomfort. Therapists should first accept these goals by agreeing with clients to find the reason for their anxiety. By eliminating the factor that causes fear, most of the symptoms will disappear on their own.

The dreaded symptoms and situations may be much worse than those described. Every therapist will occasionally be unable to assign a diagnosis that fully fits. For the therapist, the most important thing is to pay attention to case conceptualization, in order to properly differentiate whether the origin lies in a specific event that can explain the symptoms – which would make us consider phobia or post-traumatic stress disorder – or in a more diffuse and unclear issue. When we encounter the latter, we should think in terms of a hyperactivated alarm system that might result in a search for external situations or factors which could – albeit in a superstitious way – explain the origin of anxiety. It may also lead to the development of pathological regulatory mechanisms. In any case, hyperalertness is derived from major suffering.

Having a sense of not being in control, considering oneself unable to handle problems, and feeling guilt or shame will cause the patient to enter into a vicious cycle of discomfort, of fear towards their feelings, and of ruminating thoughts of guilt and fear that perpetuate the disorder.

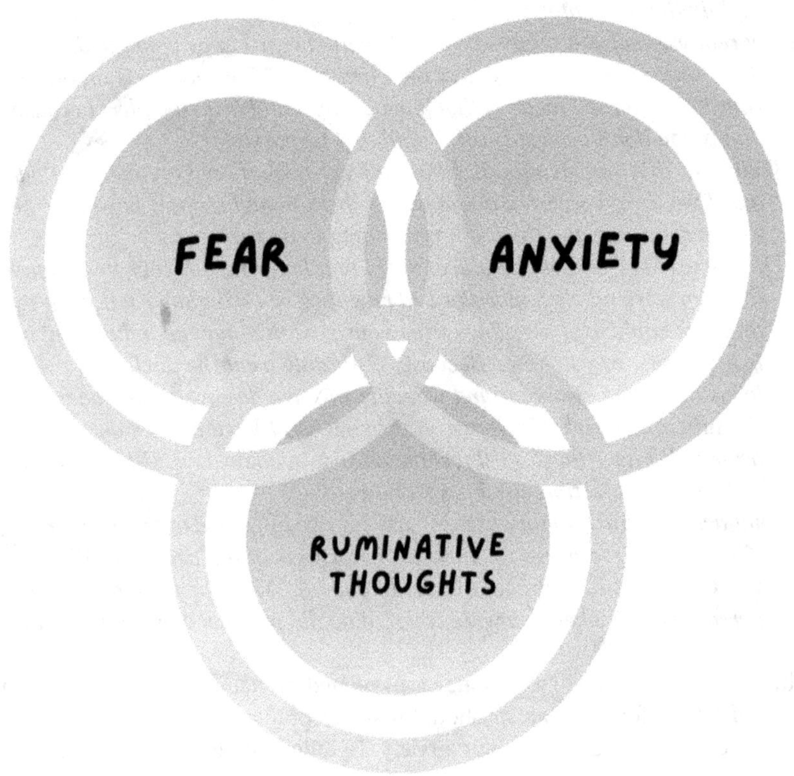

Figure 7.1 Anxiety, fear, and obsessions can become a vicious cycle in which they mutually affect each other, causing more and more suffering.

We should look beyond the clients' goals (e.g., fear of flying, blushing in public), exercise caution, and move at a pace that the patient can tolerate, properly explaining (see Chapter 11 on psychoeducation) what we believe may be the source of the problem. If we delve into their attachment relationships too fast, they may not feel heard and consequently quit therapy. One must be extremely respectful of the client's goal, create a strong therapeutic alliance, and gradually help them see that what lies behind the disorder is often shame, which was probably acquired at a very young age in relation to an attachment figure (Wallin, 2007).

Distrust and fear of being rejected or not being understood are common among patients. They will often offer us the information very slowly or in a fragmented way. Therefore, it is vital to create a relationship of mutual trust that allows us to develop a secure basis from which to begin the therapeutic work that goes beyond the symptom. This alliance between the therapist and the patient will make it possible to correct many of the situations experienced in childhood in relation to the caregivers, allowing for new, more useful, and healthy learning to take place.

Underlying Emotions in Therapy

Throughout the sessions, we attempt to change different factors such as maladaptive beliefs, thoughts, or coping strategies that the patient has developed in daily life. Most of the time these factors are related to aspects that were useful in the past, but which the patient no longer knows how to modify due to their repetitive nature. During treatment, we generate corrective experiences for our clients that will first help them to realize the ineffectiveness of their solutions, which were learned in childhood, so they can be changed later on. Treatment consists in reliving those experiences from an adult perspective of the patient with the support of the therapist.

Many emotions underlie the pathology and will be present throughout the entire therapeutic process. In this book, we will highlight:

A) *Fear*: For our patients, this is the most commonly experienced and recognized emotion. Deleting the anxiety caused by fear is the ultimate goal of therapy. The full extinction of the sensation of anxiety is an indicator that the problem has been solved.

The sense of being on the alert may have many reasons (e.g., external factors, concerns about the future), but may also have its origin in the patient's inner struggle, feelings of loneliness or remorse, and misunderstandings. That is to say, fear will be caused by anything real or imagined that generates a sense of alertness in the patient's mind, inducing a feeling of anxiety in the body (see Chapter 2).

B) *Anger*: This term has multiple synonyms, such as rage, frustration, or helplessness. Anger is an innate emotion – crucial for survival and shared with all vertebrates – provoked by the frustration of the desire for something we want and have not been able to achieve. It is a way of expressing our disagreement with something that has happened and allows for things to be different in the future. At other times, it will arise along with fear and will cause a defensive fight reaction that will biologically trigger the activation of the cerebral anger circuit.

Bowlby (1985) refers to studies comparing children separated from their parents and a control group of children who have remained in their homes; the former appears to have a greater tendency towards aggressive responses. A frequency of four times as many hostile behaviors were recorded in their games. Eight of the children attacked a doll that had been identified as a symbol of the father or mother, while none of the children in the control group attacked the dolls.

Bowlby (1985), a pioneering author in the field of anger and attachment, argues:

> The answer proposed is that as long as the separation is temporary, which in the large majority of cases it is, it has the following two functions: first, it may assist in overcoming such obstacles as there may be to reunion; second, it may discourage the loved person from going away again … as long as the loss is permanent, the anger would not fulfill any function. The reason that they occur so often, nonetheless, even after a death, is that during the early phases of grieving a bereaved person usually does not believe that the loss can really be permanent; he therefore continues to act as though it were still possible not only to find and recover the lost person but to reproach him for his actions. The lost person is often held, at least partly, responsible for what has happened; in fact, he is believed to have deserted. The anger will be unleashed not only towards the being that has been lost but to any other who may have played some role in the cause of the loss.
>
> (p. 286)

The role of anger is to retrieve the attachment figure and avoid any further separation (physical or emotional), so its function is not to break the attachment bonds but to strengthen them. This is the child's way of saying, "Don't forget I'm here" and, above all, "Don't do it again." Anger is not only a form of reproach, but also a way to prevent the separation from happening again. However, anger may be excessive, as we often see in adult relationships, and, instead of acting as a way to strengthen affection, it causes its disappearance and even the appearance of more rejection with its resulting frustration.

The inability to express anger (e.g., repression, definitive disappearance of the attachment figure) does not allow this emotion to find a way out, and there will be no effective outcome. Anger will turn inwards, taking the form of guilt and shame, as a way of not losing the affective bonds with the attachment figures (see Chapter 6 on the PARCUVE model). Bear in mind that the child will do anything to be emotionally attached to the caregivers, and it is much better to feel "it is my fault" or "I am defective" than to break that bond (Knipe, 2014).

When children feel that their needs are not taken into account and they cannot express what they need, they may assume a submissive role – and although there may be gender differences, girls may take on a more submissive role and boys a more aggressive one – they may excel academically and socially, and/or make sure everybody is feeling well. These children are often apparently exemplary, but this situation of constant frustration will generate anxiety in later years and a feeling of discomfort attributed to something inherently defective.

There are many reasons why patients may have not been able to express their needs in childhood, but we can highlight the most common:

- Definitive disappearance either due to death or to permanent abandonment of one or both parents, or negligence due to the parents working long hours and leaving the child to be cared for by an institution or a surrogate relative such as a sister or a grandmother.
- The mother and/or the father are depressed or very busy working, caring for siblings or relatives. The child does not want to be an additional burden on their parents and believes exemplary behavior will help the parents value their efforts and feel better.
- The mother and/or the father react with indifference or dislike to anything the child says or does that they deem inappropriate. The child feels the need to be very careful not to do anything that might upset the parents. For instance, the mother of a patient could spend two days without talking to her daughter whenever she was angry with her.
- The mother and/or the father react very aggressively or violently towards anything that causes them discomfort. The child will be terrified of these violent reactions and adopt a submissive role in order to avoid conflict.
- The parents are very demanding in academic, social, or behavioral aspects, making the child feel that nothing that he does is enough. The child will abandon his needs to satisfy those of the parents and will not be able to express frustration because this would generate rejection from his parents, who will accuse him of disloyalty or ungratefulness.

Certain abnormal behaviors in one or both parents may force the child to take sides or keep a secret for fear of breaking the family unit. These behaviors may range from a divorce where the child feels compelled to choose between the father and the mother, to an infidelity that cannot be shared for fear of causing harm to the deceived party. The child will feel the need to be very careful about what to say or do and will take on responsibilities far above those for which he is prepared. In many cases, one of the parents will use the child as a confidant or supporter to take sides against the other parent. The internal struggle between the hatred they are supposed to feel (or do feel) and the love they feel is too much for the child's resources. This generates a great deal of anxiety and, in extreme cases, dissociation.

Some patients may end up feeling that anger is unacceptable or they are afraid of their own emotions associated with fear of hurting others and being rejected or abandoned (Busch, 2012). In therapy, it is always necessary to explore whether the patient is afraid of losing control and hurting others. These terrifying fantasies are related to the anger that has not been expressed and usually generate much suffering and feelings of guilt. It is common for them to feel ashamed when confessing them in therapy.

The suppressed anger or frustration will have to be extensively worked on by making the patient understand that the therapist has no interest in criticizing the parents but rather understanding how the patient felt during childhood and adolescence. At first, patients usually refuse to comment on their relationships with others for fear that the therapist may believe they are bad or ungrateful towards their family members. Little by little, through the therapist's active listening and explaining over and over again that there is nothing wrong with having an opinion on things that they currently do not like or did not like in the past, they will slowly allow themselves to express the frustration and anger they have felt throughout their lives.

Working with anger must be done very carefully. If we move too fast, patients may feel overwhelmed or think they are betraying their attachment figures. This may lead to rejecting therapy, while the patient feels that the therapist is not taking their needs into account. If we move too slowly, they may feel we do not understand them.

As therapy progresses, patients will want to let go of both their current feelings and of what happened in their past. We should gradually redirect that rage, making them understand that they should take responsibility for their behavior and for changing without waiting for others to change first.

C) *Guilt*: This is a secondary emotion that makes us feel as if we have done something wrong or did not do something we should have done. According to many authors (Schore, 2001; Siegel, 2002; Panksepp, 2004; Tronick 2007), during childhood, the child's priority is to maintain the attachment bond with the parents at all costs. As we have seen, if there is an attachment rupture, the child will show annoyance and anger as a way to restore the bond. If anger cannot be expressed or is rejected, the child will sustain the bond through complacent behaviors. A second option is to conceal the anger and internalize feelings of guilt whenever that rupture takes place in the relationship with the caretaking figures. The chosen regulation strategy, based on repetition, will be a constant in all subsequent relationships in adolescence and adulthood. For Nathanson (1992), guilt is a combination of shame and fear, such as memories of doing forbidden things or breaking the rules.

Bowlby (1983) states that children with an insecure attachment will have internal models that are inconsistent with their caregivers. The real experiences of the interaction do not match with what the parents say to the child (e.g., the parents shout at the child and immediately tell him "I love you very much"). The child will try to resolve this dissonance by seeing his parents as intrinsically good and will blame himself for the rejection he suffers. Unconsciously, the child will experience anger which will be dissociated because of not being able to express it (see Chapter 12 on dissociation).

In other words, guilt is a regulation mechanism that the child will create in order to remain emotionally attached to the parents. If the parents also compare the child with another sibling or accuse him of being bad or nervous or of upsetting the parents, the child will feel even more frustrated and will certainly internalize this feeling of rejection and guilt towards the self as a pattern of his personality.

On a neurobiological level, the right hemisphere is not yet developed at an early age, which is why it will be unable to correctly interpret what is happening on an emotional level and to differentiate between what his mother feels and what he feels. This is because the right hemisphere is especially sensitive to negative affects (Schore, 2001). Paradoxically, these elements that result from childhood, and are fundamental to the emotional connection with caregivers as well as to maintaining the attachment relationship, generate a distorted image of the self that will cause much suffering in adolescence and adulthood.

According to Miller (1990):

> Many people suffer all their lives from this oppressive feeling of guilt, the sense of not having lived up to their parents' expectations … No argument can overcome these guilty feelings, for they have their beginnings in life's earliest periods, and from that they derive their intensity and obduracy.
>
> (p. 38)

We should work intensely with this emotion during the therapeutic process, because the patient has always lived with guilt and will probably prefer to live with it rather than face the terrifying sensation of criticizing his parents or not being loved by them. This is an element that will need to be worked on once and again in therapy, allowing the patient to feel understood and accompanied by the therapist, without betraying his parents until he can objectively judge reality.

In patients with a narcissistic personality, the existing defense will be the opposite: to blame everybody else without accepting any responsibility for their problems. It is very difficult for these patients to go to therapy. We do not usually find patients that fit this profile, since they are very reluctant to accept that they may have a problem.

D) *Shame*: Guilt and shame result from the internalization of the voices and the looks from others, respectively. In both cases, a person's well-being is disrupted, and negative sensations known as anxiety are generated in the body (Fuchs, 2003).

Shame is the first emotion to appear in the child when he perceives that he is not approved of by his mother. As mentioned previously, it is preverbal and felt in the body. Some people describe this bodily sensation as a feeling of emptiness.

The healthy aspect of this emotion is that it leads to the ability to relate to society by setting limits to our needs in relationship with others. As children, our parents set limits to let us know what could be dangerous or damaging to our social relations. However, if the child is not met with repair when scared, or when he has to be vigilant of the possible attachment rupture with the parents, he will begin to internalize the feeling that he is defective. This feeling will accompany him for life, preventing him from being able to relate normally, feeling shame with just about anyone.

Schore (2001) states that the image of the angry or absent mother causes a sudden break in the activation and the appearance of a state of inhibition in the child. In nature, this hypoactivation can be very positive, for example, when there is danger. However, a constant state of hypoactivation may lead to a sense of rejection throughout life.

In extreme cases, fear of rejection results in many of the pathologies described in this book. Any continued rupture in the interpersonal relationship during infancy causes feelings of shame and unworthiness that prevent healthy and normal interpersonal relationships in adult life.

According to Nathanson (1992), when it comes to working with our client's shame, we must investigate the following elements:

- Worthiness issues: "I am weak, incompetent, stupid";
- Dependency issues: feelings of helplessness;
- Competence issues: "I am a loser";
- Personal appeal: "I have a physical defect that will cause rejection";
- Sexuality: "There is something defective in me regarding sex";
- Fear of being seen, or standing out: "I could make a fool of myself";
- Fear of intimacy: "I do not deserve to be loved and, therefore, I avoid relationships with others."

In each and every instance, patients feel the unworthiness or defectiveness acquired in infancy. Along with shame and rejection comes intense anxiety. People will do anything so as not to feel the fear of being rejected again. In order to prevent such unpleasant feelings, patients may show avoidant behaviors causing a vicious cycle of shame and a sense of rejection that, as time goes by, becomes increasingly amplified.

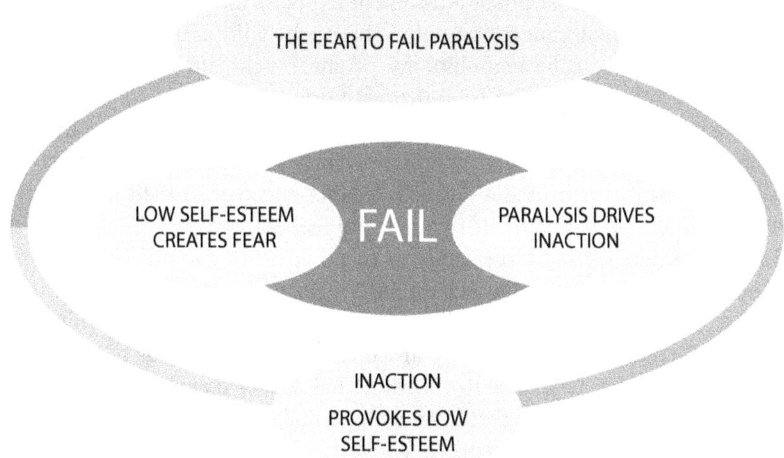

Figure 7.2 The sensation of fear of making a fool of oneself or failing causes invasive intense anxiety; this is what we know as *shame*. The person feels so frustrated that he is afraid of suffering it again and is condemned again and again to suffer the feeling of failure.

Mary is a 25-year-old patient, married, with two children. She had a traumatic childhood because of her verbally abusive father. She had an irrational fear of bumping into an old friend (she lives in a small town) with whom she had an argument. Because of this fight, she started to develop a tremendous fear of having to go to the bathroom and not finding one nearby. When I suggested the possibility of going into the restroom of any cafeteria or restaurant, she told me it could be dirty and, furthermore, someone might take notice of her urgency and she would be very ashamed.

She had stopped hanging out with friends or going anywhere slightly far away from home in case she had to go to the bathroom and did not have time to get back. What was sad was that she had never suffered diarrhea, but the fear that it could happen was all she could think about and made her avoid any kind of social activity outside her home.

I must insist that it is crucial not to get confused by the patient's therapeutic goal. We need to understand – and then inform our client – that behind many of the disorders seen in our practice, such as fear of being rejected or making a fool of oneself, profound shame is hidden that should be worked on intensely throughout therapy.

Therapeutic Alliance

What we have seen so far about attachment explains that the origin of the disorder is an emotional connection deficit between child and caregiver. As we saw in the chapter on the neurobiology of attachment, the areas of the brain that are most affected are the orbitofrontal cortex and the amygdala (Schore, 2003; Siegel, 2002). The brain maintains its plasticity throughout our life, so it also changes and develops after childhood. Through the patient–therapist relationship, the treatment provides corrective experiences that modify information processing and help patients self-regulate and feel better.

In our practice, we need to establish a relationship of complicity and trust to help our patients develop a new secure basis so as to approach life in a different way. The foundation of the entire therapy process will be the relationship established in this almost magical setting, in which two human beings try to connect emotionally in order to be able to substitute maladaptive experiences for adaptive ones. It is naïve to think that if we were to make the same mistakes that the caregivers made with our patients as children, we could make some progress and promote changes. The relationship we establish to restore the self-esteem wounds that occurred during the first years of life is as important – or even more so – than the techniques and knowledge we apply.

According to Dworkin (2005), there are several factors that determine how we relate to others and which are most important in the patient–therapist relationship:

- The *orienting response* is the attention response to any stimulus, be it positive or negative. In our practice, it is caused by first impressions in the very first meeting and, later on, when something stands out in verbal or bodily communication.
- The *assessment* is the evaluation of a new stimulus to decide if it is interesting or not and is related to the amygdala. In clinical practice, it is the patient's assessment of us, observing and assessing if we show interest or boredom, concentration or lack of focus. In consultation, it is crucial to show maximum interest because, as we have seen, this type of patient comes in with self-assessment that includes shame and the idea that no one is interested in them. Therefore, they are extremely sensitive to anything that could be interpreted as a rejection. Whenever the patient reveals anything which is considered difficult to disclose, we should offer positive reinforcement to encourage sharing anything without fear of being boring or rejected.
- *Mental models* are the schemes that are created to understand how the world functions; they are unconsciously repeated over and over. In therapy, our work will often involve changing these mental models to more adaptive ones.
- *Activation* is the reaction generated in the patient's brain after the assessment of attraction or rejection. Regarding the therapist, activation is what makes

the patient feel comfortable in the sessions, open to our suggestions, and willing to disclose intimacies and fears. In the event that we do cause a sense of rejection in our patient, we are creating blocking situations that will require intense work in order for the therapy to succeed.

- *Mental states* refer to the brain activity mode (the internal working models) that occurs at any given time. Encouraging positive mental states in the therapy (patients have negative ones in daily life) can lead to cognitive and emotional regulation, which helps patients feel much better on a day-to-day basis. In many cases, these states will be triggered by different emotional parts that take control during different times of stress.
- *Resonance* is the deepest form of emotional bonding; it occurs when we connect emotionally with the patients and they perceive that we understand their needs and concerns. It is very important to emphasize that we must not over-resonate. Patients do not want a therapist who cannot deal with their traumas or cry with them in therapy. We have to resonate with our patients, yet not let ourselves be overly affected. Too little resonance with the patient can be as negative as too much resonance.
- *Co-regulation* is the change in emotional states in both the therapist and the patient when the therapist resonates with the patient. It is also the agreement of the therapeutic goals, as well as the agreement of the price of the sessions or the clarification of misunderstandings. It is the synchronizing of objectives. In the stages of childhood, it is the vital process of attachment; the child seeks to co-regulate himself with the caregivers, and the patient will seek to co-regulate himself with the therapist.
- *Alignment* is when we change in order to approach the state of the other. Sometimes it can be done on purpose, and other times it may happen naturally. For example, with patients who feel shame, we may look down for a few seconds to make them feel more comfortable and then look at them again so they may feel they have nothing to be ashamed of.
- *Response flexibility*: Most pathologies are based on rigid behavioral, emotional, or cognitive patterns that cannot change; we should try to modify that rigidity by having the patient assess new ways of approaching the problem. In many cases, therapists may feel frustrated because our therapy is ineffective or because we are irritated by the patient; it is important that we be flexible in the way we act.

It is important to note that the patient's obligations are also part of the therapeutic relationship, such as fulfillment of payment terms, schedules, punctuality, cancelation of appointments, and so on. Fear of breaking the alliance can lead the therapist to unclearly explain all of these issues or to avoid them in case of non-compliance. This will result in frustration which will, in turn, harm the treatment. Once again, we should be empathic with the patient, but we also need to know how to set boundaries on the therapeutic relationship.

It is obvious that if what caused the origin of the disorder was the rupture of the patient's dyadic relationship with his caregivers when he was a child, in our clinical practice, we will try to foster a relationship that replaces the previous one, creating a secure basis to expand it to different situations in the patient's daily life. According to psychoanalysis, in this dyadic relationship between therapist and patient, mirror images will occur that will be a reflection of the previous experiences of both. I'd like to highlight several concepts: transference, countertransference, and vicarious trauma (Wallin, 2007).

Transference: "A term inherited from psychoanalysis, which refers to the psychic function by means of which a subject unconsciously transfers and relives, in his new bonds, his old feelings, affections, expectations, or repressed childhood desires" (Wikipedia).

If, as we have seen, the rupture of the attachment bond created the foundation for the patient's lack of confidence and its subsequent anxiety, we should create healthy bonds that replace those early experiences with ones of acceptance and self-worth. According to Wallin (2007):

> therapists must show a similar receptivity (to that of a good parent) with patients whose internal interpersonal experience is so threatening, especially because they have very little capacity for self-compassion and understanding, very little awareness of their own intents, and very little confidence that it is possible to manage their experience.
>
> (p. 120)

One of the most important elements to work on with patients will be shame, since they will feel a deep fear of rejection from the therapist, just as they used to in the past. We will have to try to gradually undermine resistance without letting the patient feel pressured or perceive that we are not interested in their problem, since these patients are extremely suspicious in their personal relationships (see Chapter 15 on defenses). Whenever there is any revelation that we feel has been important to the patient, we must reinforce it, thanking him for the effort made and the trust he has placed in us.

In my therapeutic practice, I have encountered many situations that the patient was afraid to comment on for fear of rejection: fear of murdering nephews, fear of looking at other people's genitals, sexual impotence or having had sex with a brother, having suffered sexual abuse, etc. In all cases, I react in the same way, thanking them for their trust and trying to normalize what they have told me. First, empathizing with how painful it must have been for them to live with that and explaining that they could not have avoided it since they had no tools to handle it differently.

We must be aware that patients are going to see us as saviors or magicians, or, as they express so many times, "their last hope." Nevertheless, we must be realistic and explain that we will only be companions on their journey, but that they will have to do the most important part.

To use a nautical simile, if the therapeutic alliance is the compass that will help us navigate through the therapeutic process, healthy transference will indicate the direction for us to arrive at a safe harbor.

Countertransference: If transference is what patients unconsciously place on their therapists, this term refers to what we bring into the therapeutic relationship with our patients. We all feel that there are patients who are more involved, others that make the sessions feel endless or that leave us frustrated because they neither make progress nor take into account our therapeutic guidelines.

With patients who suffer panic attacks, social phobias, or irrational fears, it is easy for the therapist to feel frustrated due to not understanding where these fears come from or because of the patients' inability to deal with them.

Something that may also happen is that the patient confesses something that is very painful to tell and the therapist is not able to remain empathic. These types of patients are experts at seeing rejection even where there is none. If they perceive in us anything similar to shame or rejection towards them, it will take an enormous effort to repair the therapeutic alliance. This does not imply that we should allow lack of respect, breaches in the agreed conditions, and so on, but we should take extra precautions to see the needs of our patients far beyond what they express.

There is a very personal matter within countertransference: the therapist's self-disclosures regarding situations in which he has felt fear or shame and how he experienced and resolved them. While these may help the patient to normalize emotions, if used in excess, the weakness of the therapist may prove harmful. This is a very personal matter, defined by the therapist's intuition and preferences. Obviously, the therapist's attachment type will be very important in the therapeutic relationship. An avoidant-style therapist will stay emotionally removed from the patient, while a more ambivalent one may be able to empathize a lot more with the emotions and shame that brings the patient to therapy, sometimes even too much.

Vicarious trauma or compassion fatigue: This is secondary traumatization suffered by those professionals who work on health issues; being in contact with people who suffer or hearing painful stories may affect the therapist because of excessive empathy, thus reducing the effectiveness or simply contaminating the private sphere.

> *One of the greatest fears of any therapist is to lose a patient due to their decision to end their life. When I started my clinical practice, I had a patient that showed up covered in blood in the hotel room where he tried to commit*

> *suicide. I am aware that a patient's suicide is something to which all therapists are exposed.*

Patients who come to our clinics do so with deep discomfort and great urgency to solve their problems, and we must be careful to not become infected with their anxiety and their urgency in solving the disorder too quickly (Leeds, 2012). As I have commented before, the health professional should be empathic, but should never allow the patient to determine the agenda of the therapy.

Patients may place high (often magical) expectations on the therapist and feel very frustrated if the therapy does not go at the pace they were expecting. They may even try to take care of their therapist and inquire about his private life.

In other cases, we will feel a lot of empathy towards patients who have suffered all kinds of abuse throughout their lives, who cannot work due to their problems, who cannot afford treatment, or who make us feel we are the only person in their life who worries about them.

Therapists with caregiving tendencies can get overinvolved in therapy, allowing phone calls at any time, accepting invitations to the patient's home, or not charging for the sessions; the result will most likely be that the therapist will become increasingly frustrated and exhausted by the lack of advancement, which will end up hurting both.

Perhaps the most advisable thing for the therapist is to check himself periodically. As soon as he feels anxiety when thinking about or being with the patient, he will have to evaluate what is happening to him and, if necessary, seek supervision in order to return to his place in therapy.

Conclusions

Regardless of the type of therapeutic orientation that we use and regardless at what moment of therapy we find ourselves, we will encounter elements that will always be present throughout treatment. Patients come to consultation with a certain amount of suffering which they want to eliminate with our help. It is important to explain from the very beginning that anxiety is a symptom of something deeper taking place in the mind, and that in order to alleviate it, we must work with those issues from the past which are affecting them in the present.

Often patients may think of psychology as a medical model in which they are passive subjects on which the doctor acts, intervening with pharmacological treatment or any other type of intervention. However, we must clearly explain that in psychology the cooperation and intervention by the patient is fundamental throughout the process. Also, there will often be short-term pain to achieve long-term improvement. The initial goal established by the patient will change as we progress in treatment, and once the intensity of symptoms has diminished and the patient's confidence has been established, we can delve deeper into the origin of the disease.

None of this can be achieved without a good therapeutic relationship, wherein the patient can fully trust the therapist and the latter is able to remain consistent and firm throughout the entire process. The patient has experienced many emotions (e.g., fear, shame, guilt, and/or anger) over a long time which will have to be sorted out and gradually worked on towards more adaptive emotions so that the patient can face his fears without so much suffering.

If the emotions that the patient brings to the session are overwhelming or are not effectively managed by the therapist, retraumatization can occur in the patient, who will once again feel that the people he trusted have failed him. Therefore, we should be empathic and professional with the patient's goals, but must not let their negative emotions rub off on us and contaminate the therapeutic work.

References

Bowlby, J. (1983). *Attachment and loss: Volume III. Loss*. Basic Books.

Bowlby, J. (1985). *Attachment and loss: Volume II. Separation*. Basic Books.

Busch, F., Milrod, B. D., Singer, M., & Aronson, A. (2012). *Trauma focused psychodynamic psychotherapy: A step-by-step treatment manual*. Routledge.

Dworkin, M. (2005). *EMDR and the relational imperative. The therapeutic relationship in EMDR treatment*. Routledge.

Fuchs, T. (2003). The phenomenology of shame, guilt and the body. Dysmorphic disorder and depression. *Journal of Phenomenological Psychology*, *33*(2), 223–243.

Knipe, J. (2014). *EMDR toolbox: Theory and treatment of complex PTSD and dissociation*. Springer.

Leeds, A. (2012). *EMDR therapy basics and beyond*. Guilford Press.

Miller, A. (1990). *The drama of the gifted child: The search for the true self.* Basic Books.

Nathanson, D. L. (1992). *Shame and pride. Affect, sex, and the birth of the self.* Norton.

Panksepp, J. (2004). *Affective neuroscience. The foundations of human and animal emotions*. Oxford University Press.

Rollnick, S., & Miller, W. R. (1995). *Motivational interviewing: Preparing people for change*. Guilford Press.

Schore, A. (2001). The effects of a secure attachment relationship on roght brain development, affect regulation & infant mental health. *Infant Mental Health Journal*, *22*, 7–66.

Schore, A. (2003). *Affect dysregulation and disorders of the self.* Norton.

Siegel, D. J. (2002). *The developing mind: How relationships and the brain interact to shape who we are*. Guilford Press.

Tronick, E. (2007). *The neurobehavioral and social-emotional development of infants and children*. Norton.

Wallin, D. J. (2007). *Attachment in psychotherapy*. Guilford Press.

8 Approaches for the Treatment of Emotional Disorders

According to a Greek legend, Procrustes was a thief who forced his victims into an iron bed. Those who did not reach the ends were stretched until it was achieved, and the ones who had body to spare, he cut it off. One of the problems of psychology is that we, the professionals, have acted towards our clients as Procrustes with his victims, forcing them to be the ones who adapt to our therapeutic approaches and not the other way around. We must have the greatest number of tools available and know how to use them properly to achieve the healing of our patients.

There are multiple models for the treatment of emotional disorders. The aim of this book is to create an integrative model that adds elements of different approaches to make treatment much more effective. Thus, we can complement the shortcomings of some approaches with the advantages of others. It is obvious that a complex problem will require complex solutions.

We will now describe some theoretical approaches of different therapeutic models and, in later chapters, how to use them in an integrated way, depending on the different needs that arise during the therapy.

Biological Models

Many researchers blame the origin of emotional disorders and anxiety on biological dysfunctions, which is obviously true. Nothing can happen in our body that does not have a biological origin. This is what we described in the first chapter as the brain, which would be the chemical part, and the mind would be the assessment and interpretation we give to reality; both influence each other.

We will always have to rule out organic disorders that can trigger the disorder but there is no doubt that behind most of these lie multiple psychological factors. As we have seen, the mind and brain interact and change each other constantly.

Theories of the main biological factors behind anxiety are:

- *Genetic studies*: These state that if it is more frequent in the same family, the origin could be genetic, but it could well be that the cause of that frequency is an environmental rather than a genetic factor. Studies have been conducted

DOI: 10.4324/9781003646341-10

on monozygotic or dizygotic twins who have been raised in different families to see if there is a greater frequency of panic attacks than in the normal population, but the results have been inconsistent (Barlow, 1988).
- *Hyperventilation hypothesis*: It has been suggested that some people hyperventilate when breathing, and that this could give them anxiety and panic attacks. This does indeed provoke alkalosis in the blood, dizziness, headaches, and derealization symptoms. People who suffer from panic attacks hyperventilate, and one of the exercises we must teach them is to better manage their breathing. But I believe that hyperventilation comes from the sensation of fear and the activation of the fear circuit that we saw in Chapter 2. Some authors (Ley, 1989) postulate that the patients first feel the asphyxia and then the panic, which does not demonstrate that the attack does not have a psychological origin.
- *Dysregulation of the noradrenergic system*: When the neurons of the *locus coeruleus* are activated (see Chapter 2), an excess of norepinephrine is produced, inducing anxiety and maybe even panic attacks. While it is necessary to dismiss it as the basis of an organic disorder, it does not justify that it can be activated by thought. It is also important to rule out hyperthyroidism, which can provoke symptoms of severe anxiety or a panic attack.

This model is very reductionist, because it states that the origin and solution of the disorder is organic; in my opinion, it is very effective for treating the symptoms, but by not resolving the cause, it can create drug dependence or frequent relapses. In many cases, in order to perform the therapeutic work with the patients, they will have to be medicated as a form of stabilization until the therapy takes effect, so it is convenient to communicate with the patient's doctor or psychiatrist so as to coordinate the use of medication with them.

Cognitive-Behavioral Treatments

Cognitive-behavioral therapies (CBTs) are the most popular and frequent in the treatment of panic attacks and anxiety (in most cases combined with pharmacological treatments).

In the words of Dattilio (2000), "CBT takes into account the roles of vulnerability predisposition (biological and psychosocial) along with other precipitating factors, both internal (bodily sensations) and external (environmental)" (p. 46).

One of the main trends in the treatment of anxiety is based on Beck's cognitive theory (Beck, 1995), according to which the emotions are not the result of the situation itself, but of how we assess it – that is, of what we think about it. Anxiety is associated with thoughts of danger or perceived threat, whether real or not. Therefore, if a person assumes, for example, that he is about to die of a heart attack, he will react by experiencing the same terror as if this were true.

The authors of this therapeutic approach argue that anxiety is the result of:

- Misinterpretation of interoceptive sensations as a sign that an impending catastrophe is about to happen (going crazy, dying or losing control);
- Exteroceptive signs that are incorrectly assessed. This catastrophic interpretation increases anxiety, which in turn increases the dreaded interoceptive sensations, since they are feelings associated with anxiety. This triggers a vicious cycle that gives rise to more anxiety;
- Irrational ideas or beliefs that distort reality in such a way that it is always lived with a constant sense of danger and alertness.

People who suffer from anxiety experience it because they have developed a stable tendency to misinterpret benign bodily sensations as indicators of an imminent mental or physical catastrophe (e.g., palpitations can be interpreted as evidence that one is having a heart attack).

Therefore, therapy consists of a series of strategies aimed at helping clients learn to correctly assess these feelings and thoughts, thus overcoming both their tendency to make catastrophic interpretations and the emotional and behavioral alterations that are derived from them.

Barlow (1988) bases his work on four fundamental aspects, which would be five if agoraphobia existed:

- *Observation and understanding of the disorder*: Cognitive restructuring through self-logging, so as to demonstrate to patients that improvement does exist. This phase is fundamental to be able to move on to the next one.
- *Physical control techniques*: Control of diaphragmatic breathing and muscle relaxation. Its function is not to reduce anxiety but to lower the level of activation.
- *Cognitive restructuring*: Changing the wrong cognitions, like the fear of going crazy or suffering a heart attack.
- *Interoceptive exposure*: This is about trying to look for sensations instead of avoiding them. At first, sensations are provoked in a controlled environment (e.g., consultation); later, patients do it by themselves and, finally, in situations that cause fear (Lacasa, 2005).
- *Exposure to dreaded situations or places*: The goal is to avoid escape behaviors. Exposure should be systematic and regular.

Whichever technique we use to help our patients, they are going to have to face the situations they fear. In my opinion, this method is too simple, carries a very high rate of relapse, and does not allow the patient to get to know the origin of his illness. This is the complaint of most patients who come to my office after having done CBT; in many cases these techniques alone have been ineffective or insufficient and they have not been able to get to know the origin of their problems, which further aggravates their sense of lack of control.

In the treatment described in this book, we will use these techniques during the final phase of treatment, when the patient is able to control his thoughts and is prepared to deal with the situations he fears.

Psychodynamic Approaches

The psychodynamic approaches, heirs of psychoanalysis, give great importance to the role of the unconscious in the appearance and maintenance of different pathologies. According to the authors of this therapeutic approach, anxiety would be due to unconscious conflicts in the patient's mind.

The authors of this psychological current argue that patients who suffer from anxiety tend to somatize their emotions and impulses, and therefore, during the course of therapy, unresolved conflicts in the patient's mind should be explored, which would not only reduce the symptoms but also help the patient to get to know themselves better and to obtain more mature personalities (Dattilio, 2000).

Busch et al. (2004) present three phases:

- The first one would be to explore the sensations and feelings associated with anxiety. Psychodynamic conflicts are based on separation and independence issues and recognition of anger and aggression towards other people or towards the patient himself. The main objective in this phase is to reduce the symptoms so as to be able to continue with the following phases.
- In the second phase, we would work towards getting to know the mental configurations of the patient in depth. The main objective is to reduce patient vulnerability by describing the interpersonal hyphens with which patients relate to others.
- In the third phase, the goal would be for patients to overcome their difficulties with separation and independence. The idea is to allow the patient to relive internal conflicts with the therapist as a way to solve them.

Some authors (Gassner, 2004; Leeds, 2012) argue that the majority of patients suffering from panic attacks or severe anxiety experienced situations of insecurity in their childhood (physical, emotional, or sexual abuse). A traumatic childhood left them with a deep sense of helplessness and deep love/hate conflicts towards their caregivers. This would produce a profound ambivalence within them regarding the closeness/separation with the attachment figures.

One of the most interesting therapies, in my opinion, that has emerged from dynamic psychology is time-limited psychotherapy (Solomon et al., 2001; McCullough 1995; Fosha, 2000), which studies patients' internal conflicts with themselves and interpersonally, so as to be able to eliminate the sensation of alertness and, therefore, the anxiety.

Psychodynamic techniques are very useful when it comes to helping the patient to get to know the origin of their problems, to know why they persist or what secondary gains they may have in suffering them. These techniques suffer from the limitation of not working with coping strategies or physical sensations; this type of therapy is fundamental for a profound approach towards the disorder, but must be complemented with other therapeutic techniques.

Strategic Therapy

Nardone (2004), the creator of this therapy, defends that in order to solve an emotional disorder it is not necessary to know its origin but to know its functioning. Therefore, it would not be necessary to know the patient's history, only to study the dynamics of his anxiety, since the patient is afraid not of what happened but of what can happen to him.

According to this author, patients provoke their anxiety themselves by triggering the fear of their own feelings and trying to control them. This leads them to losing control definitively, leading to the dreaded discomfort. In this approach, fear would be increased as a way to annul it, or behaviors or thoughts will be modeled so that, by overexposure, the fear disappears.

Therapeutic strategies are used to lead the patient, without his knowledge, to experience the overcoming of fear in a concrete way. Only when the symptoms have completely disappeared will the person be led to the full awareness of their personal resources.

Treatment is carried out in four phases (Nardone, 2004):

- Determine the specific type of pathological fear and, at the same time, introduce elements that change the patient's view on the problem;
- Suggest, direct, or prescribe actions or thoughts that induce people to perform actions of change;
- Lead the person to increase their experiences of success in managing the feelings and situations that frighten him;
- Close intervention and redefine the result.

The tasks consist mainly in making the patient see the contradictions he makes when solving the problem, and, by presenting irresolvable paradoxes, this will force him to act and think differently than he had done before treatment.

The author's statistics are his own and are not recognized by other authors, so we can doubt the success of this therapy. However, it is very helpful to be able to propose tasks that help the patient solve some of their symptoms and help him get to know the dynamics of his disorder.

Somatic Therapy

These types of therapies are based on the latest findings in neurobiology and on how the body always remembers the trauma (Damasio, 1994; Levine, 2010). As we saw in Chapter 2, our body keeps a memory of the trauma (Porges, 2011).

According to Shapiro (2010):

> There are many types of somatic therapies. Most share the idea that trauma deregulates the body, causing restrictions on emotions and movements; movements that have not been performed since the moment of trauma must be experienced, and focusing on the sensations and movements will heal trauma. (p. 308)

We can access trauma either through the memory of an image, a smell, something we have been told, or a sensation; for instance, in preverbal traumas, there can be no narrative memory. Therefore, from a bodily sensation, we can feel different sensations that will lead to trauma resolution (see Chapter 14).

Levine (2010) argues that in all animal species there is a release mechanism of the stored traumatic energy, which consists of repeated agitation until any vestige of traumatization in the body is eliminated. This mechanism does not exist in humans, which is why therapy would be focused on feeling the sensations again and performing the actions that could not be done during the traumatic event.

This therapy on its own, in my opinion, is not effective for treating anxiety, but is very useful when supplemented with other types of techniques. It is obvious that we all feel in our body (we cannot feel anywhere else), and that it is essential to explain and help our patients understand their sensations better, and how to recognize them so as to be able to control them and live without fear. It is very useful in the early stages of therapy because it helps generate an atmosphere of trust between the patient and the therapist, for example, helping them manage the symptoms in the consultation and generating a sense of control in the patient.

Family or Systemic Therapy

This proposes that the individual lives in a system with which he is constantly obliged to relate (or not to relate) (Schwartz, 1995). Family models try to understand the person's interaction with his or her family, acquaintances, or co-workers because they consider that this would be the basis of the disorder. Anxiety would be the malaise created by a poorly organized family system (Minuchin & Fishman, 1984) due to its poorly organized hierarchy; for example, when the father does not play the role that belongs to him.

This would create faulty families or social systems in which pathological relationships are formed, leading to the feeling of discomfort. In order to solve them, it is necessary to know and evaluate the relationships between the family to detect any existing anomalies in the relationships, such as failures in hierarchies, conflicts, groups within the family unit set against other groups, and overdependence or overprotection from some relatives to others.

In my opinion, it is a therapy that is completely necessary in any approach that works with emotional disorders. In fact, attachment is nothing more than the beginning of the formation of the family network, even though, as with other approaches, it is incapable of solving the emotional disturbances by itself. In fact, this approach does not address emotions as part of its therapeutic model, being based almost always on the relationships between members of the family or social system.

Acceptance and Commitment Therapy

This approach is an evolution of the cognitive therapies, for example, the use of mindfulness techniques (Didonna, 2009). Acceptance and commitment therapy (ACT) argues that anxiety is caused by a distorted assessment of reality, which leads to suffering from events that have not occurred. The discomfort can be caused by both internal (sensations) and external elements. What leads to anxiety is mainly the negative valuation of cognitions and emotions (Hayes et al., 2011). For the authors of this approach, to consider thoughts and feelings as a problem would be part of the problem.

As its own name indicates, the goal would be for the patients to learn to accept and stop fighting their thoughts, emotions, and feelings and, in doing so, the body will once again balance itself out. The main points they defend are:

- Not judging: Not making value judgements of others or themselves;
- Accepting: Trying to change things without suffering, but accepting them;
- Living in the present: Not analyzing what has already happened nor worrying about what has not yet happened;
- Not controlling: Trying to be in control and not "going with the flow" of our experiences leads to discomfort and anxiety;
- Not avoiding: Avoiding sensations, objects, or experiences is what leads to discomfort and pathology;
- Not identifying: Not becoming identified with the thoughts and beliefs. Living as if they belonged to someone else.

This technique does not work with past events, only with how the facts are interpreted in the present. In my opinion, this technique is very useful at the beginning of therapy when it is used as psychoeducation or as a form of transient emotion regulation. In some cases, when the source of anxiety is the "need for control," it will be very useful for helping to teach the patient not to always be on the alert. In cases of complex trauma, it is only effective at the end of therapy when we have worked with the situations that caused the discomfort in the past and, once resolved, it will be possible to teach the patient how to live events in a different way.

EMDR

Eye movement desensitization and reprocessing (EMDR) is a form of psychotherapy developed by Francine Shapiro that emphasizes the role of distressing memories in some mental health disorders, particularly post-traumatic stress disorder (PTSD). It is an evidence-based therapy used to help with the symptoms of PTSD. It is thought that when a traumatic or distressing experience occurs, it may overwhelm normal coping mechanisms. The memory and associated stimuli are inadequately processed and stored in an isolated memory network (Wikipedia, 2015). The model is based on Adaptive Information Processing (AIP), which consists of three principles (Manfield & Shapiro, 2004).

1. There exists an intrinsic information processing system that has evolved to allow humans to reorganize their responses to life-disrupting events, starting from an initial dysfunctional state of imbalance to reaching a state of adaptive resolution.
2. A traumatic event or persistent stress during a vital developmental phase may disrupt the adaptive processing of information. As a result of the emotional impact, the related information is stored in a "specific state" form, in the form of implicit memory.
3. There would be a process of self-healing in the brain (identical to that which can occurs with the skin or other organs) that has not been developed because of the impact of the trauma (it is as if a physical wound had become infected), but, according to Manfield and Shapiro (2004), the combination of the phases for the standard EMDR procedure with bilateral stimulation restores the balance of the adaptive information processing system (to continue with the metaphor, it is as if healing the wound).

EMDR's standard protocol is based on eight phases, rigidly sequenced and structured:

- *Case conceptualization*: Client history and treatment planning.
- *Preparation*: Stabilization and assessment of suitability for treatment.
- *Assessment*: The clinician asks for the worst image of the memory, what the patient thinks about himself (negative cognition, NC), what he would like to think (positive cognition, PC), in what part of his body he feels it, the

emotions he feels, and how intense the discomfort is as well as the rating of the positive belief.

- *Desensitization*: Bilateral eye movements, tapping, or sounds are used to activate the reprocessing of the information stored in a traumatic way.
- *Installation*: Making the patient feel the PC as completely true and uniting the PC with the feeling of well-being in the body.
- *Body scan*: Assessing if there is any unpleasant sensation in the body and if so, working with it until it disappears.
- *Closure*: Verifying that the information has been reprocessed and that there is no emotional or physical discomfort associated with the memory.
- *Reevaluation*: Working to reevaluate the process and confirm that there has not been any discomfort associated with the memory.

EMDR's basic protocol has proven to be extremely effective in treating PTSD, but in more complex traumas it becomes imperative to use complementary techniques to work with traumatic experiences (Manfield & Shapiro, 2004). We will find many traumatic situations which can be worked on with the standard protocol and others that will need more complex interventions. Some of the influencing factors are:

- The age at which the trauma first occurred; the younger the age, the more complex treatment will be.
- Which people were involved in the traumatic event; the closer they are affectively, the greater the impact.
- How long and how many times the traumatic event has occurred; obviously, the greater the intensity and/or duration, the greater the injury.
- What was the traumatic event like? Sexual abuse in which the person feels like an object is not the same as a car accident.
- What was the relationship with the attachment figures like at that time and how did they act? Were they involved? Did they protect or accuse the victim of provoking it? Did they deny the problem or act as support?

In emotional disorders, we will often encounter traumatic situations of physical, psychological, or emotional abuse, situations in which the person has been afraid of dying, has had feelings of not being in control, fear of rejection, and so on, and we may also find comorbidity with other disorders such as OCD, eating disorders, or personality disorders that will make the therapeutic work more complex.

The question that most therapists who use EMDR ask themselves is when to apply the standard protocol and when to use other complementary tools. We will develop this whole topic in detail in the next chapters. But if I had to give a simple answer, I would say that we use the standard protocol when two requirements are met:

- When the person remembers a particular event (or several events associated with it) as a before and after in his life;
- When, once the conceptualization of the case is made and the therapeutic alliance is created, the patient is able to process the trauma while being within his window of tolerance (Ogden & Minton, 2000).

We will find many situations in which, due to the type of pathology and/or the existence of dissociative disorders, it will be impossible to apply the standard protocol, and we will have to use more complex tools before we can process the traumas.

In any case, whether we use the standard protocol or a more complex therapeutic approach, the objective remains the same: to strengthen the AIP in order to restore the patient's psychological balance, and to integrate all traumatic memories into adaptive neural networks. It is necessary to emphasize that all the work with traumatic events of the past have one objective only: that the patient can live better in the present and can imagine the future with joy and well-being. We cannot change the past, but we can accept it and integrate it in our mind so we can live our present better.

Conclusions

There are as many psychological treatments focused on the treatment of PA and associated diseases as there are psychological currents. This large number of potential therapies only add more confusion for therapists and patients when choosing a treatment. In many cases, when the treatment does not improve the patient's disorder, we attribute it to their resistance or to the patient not performing the mandated tasks or not following our instructions. I prefer to think that it is we, the therapists, who have to adapt to the needs of the clients and not the other way around.

We need to create unified protocols that integrate different therapeutic models that have proven their effectiveness in the past. I take EMDR as a reference model because, in my opinion, it allows for the integration of different approaches, acting as a unifying element.

When applying treatment, it is important to differentiate what kind of trauma we are going to be working on in order to be able to know if we need to work with a standard protocol so as to desensitize isolated traumatic memories, or if we should use modified protocols to be able to work with patients who will require, because of their psychological history, a treatment more adapted to their needs.

In all cases, it is the therapist who should adapt to the patient and not the other way around, following the necessary steps according to the patient's tolerance to the treatment process and his or her degree of dissociation.

References

Barlow, D. H. (1988). *Anxiety and its disorders. The nature and treatment of anxiety and panic*. Guilford.

Beck, J. S. (1995). *Cognitive therapy: Basics and beyond.* Guilford Press.

Busch, F., & Milrod, B. (2004). Nature and treatment of panic disorder. In J. Panksepp (Ed.), *Textbook of biological psychiatry* (pp. 345–366). Wiley.

Dattilio, F., & Salas-Auvert, J. (2000). *Panic disorder Assessment and treatment trough a wide-angle lens*. Zeig Tucker Co.

Damasio, A. R. (1994). *Descartes' error: Emotion, reason, and the human brain.* G.P. Putnam's Sons.

Didonna, F. (2009). *Clinical handbook of mindfulness*. Springer.

Fosha, D. (2000). *The transforming power of affect. A model of accelerated change.* Basic Books.

Gassner, S. (2004). The role of traumatic experience in panic disorder and agarophobia. *Psychoanalitic Psychology, 21*(2), 222–243.

Hayes, S. C., Strosahl, K. D., & Wilson, K. G. (2011). *Acceptance and commitment therapy: The process and practice of mindful change*. Guilford Press.

Leeds, A. (2012). *EMDR therapy basics and beyond.* Guilford Press.

Levine, P. A. (2010). *In an unspoken voice: How the body releases trauma and restores goodness*. North Atlantic Books.

Lacasa, R. (2005). *Pánico perdido. Como curar los ataques de pánico.* Editado por la autora.

Ley, R. (1989). Dyspneic-fear and catastrophic cognitions in hyperventilatory panic attacks. *Behaviour Research and Therapy, 27*, 549–554.

Manfield, P., & Shapiro, F. (2004). Application of Eye Movement Desensitization and Reprocessing (EMDR) to personality disorders. In J. Magnavita (Ed.), *Handbook of personality disorders* (pp. 304–331). Willey.

Mccullough, L. (1995). *Changing caracther*. Basic Books.

Minuchin, S., & Fishman, C. (1984). *Técnicas de terapia familiar*. Paidos.

Nardone, G. (2004). *No hay noche que no vea el día. La terapia breve para los ataques de pánico*. Herder.

Ogden, P., & Minton, K. (2000). *Trauma and the body: A sensorimotor approach to psychotherapy*. Norton & Company.

Porges, S. (2011). *The polyvagal theory.Neurophysiological foundations of emotions.* Norton.

Shapiro, R. (2010). *The trauma treatment handbook. Protocols across the spectrum.* Norton.

Schwartz, R. C. (1995). *Internal family systems therapy*. Guilford Press.

Solomon, M., Neborsky, R., Mccullough, L., Alpert, M., Shapiro, F., & Malan, D. (2001). *Short term therapy for long term change*. Norton.

9 Working with Trauma

EMDR

EMDR was initially developed as an effective treatment for post-traumatic stress disorder (PTSD). Subsequently and over the years, given its proven efficacy, it has expanded to a multitude of pathologies. Bilateral stimulation is used to desensitize disturbing thoughts and reprocess traumatic situations. The goal is to achieve their total disappearance as well as the disappearance of the dysfunctional symptomatology that accompanies them. It is a scientifically proven technique that is very effective, fast, powerful, and stable. It is currently recommended by the Clinical Practice Guidelines in countries like the United States, England, Ireland, and Israel as well as by the World Health Organization (WHO) as an essential intervention in PTSD-related treatments.

Although at first only the basic protocol was used in the treatment of the different pathologies, it started adding techniques of other therapeutic approaches. The basic protocol is extremely effective in cases of simple trauma in which the person recalls an event that, although time has passed since it occurred, continues to cause great discomfort when he remembers it. In all our patients, we will find traumas of the past that we must work on to be able to help them live totally in the present without spending energy on suffering or repressing things that happened in the past. Many times, this will be enough to help them but, in many types of complex trauma, we will need modified protocols to help the patient.

It is very important to highlight that in order to use EMDR in our practice, we must have completed at least Level I (although it is advisable to also complete Level II) offered by the EMDR Spain Association. This technique, although very effective, if not used properly, might aggravate the pathology of our patients, so we would violate the ethical code if we used it without proper training.

Situations in which we may use EMDR:

- Reprocessing of panic attacks that are remembered as especially traumatic. It is considered that mainly the first, last, or worst one should be dealt with;
- Deaths or abandonments of loved ones with which we consider there is traumatic or unresolved grief. (Do not forget that many of the attacks will be triggered by death or loss of loved ones.);
- Spontaneous or provoked abortions, which are always very traumatic for the women who suffer them;

DOI: 10.4324/9781003646341-11

- Diverse situations such as bullying in childhood or adolescence, moving to a new house or school, patient's hospitalization, and so on;
- Any situation that the patient views as a crucial moment after which he felt traumatized or, upon remembering it, he feels a strong emotional charge.

However, in many cases we will not be able to process the trauma until there is a good stabilization of the patient and a strong therapeutic alliance. So, we will have to work for a long time in Phases 1 and 2, to which we will dedicate

Table 9.1 The Eight Phases of EMDR Treatment

PHASE	*GOALS*	*TASKS*
Phase 1 Conceptualization	Establish therapeutic alliance. Gather information on previous treatments. Rule out problems for using EMDR.	Look for processing targets and goals.
Phase 2 Preparation and stabilization	Psychoeducation, stabilization, elaboration of self-reports	Explain to the patient what EMDR is. Give metaphors to explain what we will do. Check patient's self-control.
Phase 3 Evaluation	Access information relevant to emotional, cognitive, and somatic trauma.	Obtain the worst image of the memory, the current negative and positive belief, the emotion, and the physical sensation.
Phase 4 Desensitization	Reprocess the target experience to adaptive resolution.	Do bilateral stimulation sets. Go back to target when necessary. Use interweaves if necessary.
Phase 5 Installation	Total integration of positive belief in the memory network.	Do sets while the patient keeps target in mind along with the positive belief.
Phase 6 Bodyscan	Check that no discomfort exists when remembering.	Check if there is physical discomfort and reprocess if there is.
Phase 7 Closure	Check that the patient is stabilized.	Inform the patient that the brain will keep working. Ask the patient to keep in touch in case a problem occurs.
Phase 8 Re-evaluation	Check that the work is complete.	Re-check target. Work on targets that may have come up.

Note: Table adapted from Leeds (2012)

the following chapters. In many cases, the work during these phases will make the brain function naturally and, thanks to the new information acquired, the brain can reprocess in order to unblock the neural networks associated with the trauma. Other times, we will have to apply the protocol and all of its phases.

As we have seen, the basic protocol consists of eight phases:

Phase 1. Conceptualization: During this phase, information about the patient's medical and psychological history and the existence of past issues that may interfere during the processing is collected. If, for example, the patient comes asking to work on a recent car accident and informs us that his father died in an accident when he was a child, it will be very difficult for us to work without interfering with the trauma of the loss of his father. If it were to appear during the reprocessing, we may find ourselves in a very difficult situation.

Phase 2. Preparation and stabilization. We will strengthen the bond between the therapist and the patient and evaluate what resources the patient has in order to work with the traumatic memory. We can use metaphors to explain the PAI model to the patient and how it will help him overcome the traumatic memory.

We will explain the different methods of bilateral stimulation that exist, such as eye movements, knee tapping, or bilateral sounds, and let the patient choose the one that he is most comfortable with. As much as possible, we will try to use eye movements (EM) to work with the traumatic memories and the installation of resources.

It is essential to install a safe place to help the patient in case of a strong abreaction. This consists of imagining a real or imaginary place or situation in which one visualizes oneself in a calm state. The patient is asked to think about this place/situation while installing the resource with bilateral stimulation. In case of an abreaction, the patient will be reminded of this place so as to be able to calm down and return to working with the trauma.

The goals (Leeds, 2012) to be achieved in the first two phases are:

- Establishing a therapeutic alliance;
- Obtaining informed consent for treatment;
- Determining that the patient has suitability criteria;
- Formulating case conceptualization;
- Developing a treatment plan;
- Ensuring that the patient has sufficient abilities to manage anxiety, depressive and dissociative states, and maladaptative stress reduction impulses.

This phase is essential regardless of the therapeutic approach that we use during treatment, be it AP or phobias. Therefore, we will develop this phase in great detail in the next chapters so that it can be used independently from the preferred therapy.

Phase 3. Evaluation: During this phase, we will ask for different aspects of the memory and the sensations associated with it. The questions we would ask are the following:

Image: The worst part of the memory: *What image represents the worst part of the memory?* ....

....

<u>If there is no image</u>: *What do you notice when you think about that memory?*

....

....

NC - Negative Cognition: *If you think about the image, what words come to mind that express the negative belief you have about yourself <u>right now</u>?*

....

....

PC – Positive Cognition: *If you think about the image <u>right now</u>, what words would you like or would have liked to believe or think instead of those?*

....

....

VOC: *How true do these words* .... (repeat PC) *feel right now on a scale of 1 to 7, where 1 feels totally false and 7 totally true?*

Completely false -------- 1 2 3 4 5 6 7 -----------Completely true

Emotions/ Feelings: *When you think about that event and the words 'I... ... ...* (repeat NC)', *what emotions do you feel <u>right now</u>?*

SUDs: *On a scale of 0 to 10, where 0 is no disturbance or neutral, and 10 is the highest disturbance you can imagine, how much disturbance do you feel <u>right now</u>?*

no disturbance/neutral 0 1 2 3 4 5 6 7 8 9 10 highest disturbance

Location of Bodily Sensation: *Where do you feel it in the body?* ....

....

....

Phase 4. Desensitization: The first thing is to indicate to the patient that we are going to work with dual attention, that is, he will be in the traumatic memory and in our office at the same time. We ask the patient to focus on the worst image of the memory, the negative cognition, the sensation in the body, and the associated emotion, and then we begin to work with eye movements (EMs).

It is very important that the therapist not intervene at any time unless the processing gets stuck and looping occurs, in which processing cannot proceed. In that case, we will change the way of processing.

The work would be as follows:

Bring to mind the negative words (repeat the NC) *and register where in your body you are feeling it and follow my fingers, with your eyes, without moving your head.*

(Feedback after a set of bilateral stimulation of 30 seconds ≈ 24 sets).

Let it go and take a deep breath. Then I ask: *What comes to mind now?* or *What are you noticing now?*

Processing and checking for new channels: Continue processing with various sets of EM (or tapping or tones), until no new material comes up.

Ask: *When you go back to the original experience, what comes up now? Focus on that moment.*

Examine the SUD:

When you look at the experience, on a scale of 0 to 10, where 0 is no disturbance and 10 the highest disturbance you can imagine, how strongly do you feel the disturbance now?

If the SUD is 1 or more, continue processing➔ if we cannot lower SUD ➔ incomplete session/if it stalls/*If you think about the event, the memory, the experience, what comes to you now, what do you notice?* If there is more than one emotion: fear first/ if there is more than one emotion ➔ focus on one/ accelerate or slow down.

If **SUD is 0**, reinforce with one more set of 10-second bilateral stimulation ≈ 5–6 sets and **move on to Installation.**

Sometimes, if there is looping, "cognitive interweaves" may be used, which are brief comments made by the therapist related to an idea or belief that hinders processing. An example would be: "Are you telling me that a 4-year-old child could have prevented the traffic accident?" On other occasions, we can use somatic or affective bridges that take the patient to earlier moments where he felt something similar. An example of these would be: "Close your eyes and go back in time to the first time you felt something similar."

We will continue processing until the level of discomfort associated with the memory (SUD) is zero. We will check this when, after several positive or neutral responses that are related to the memory, we ask the patient about his level of discomfort, from zero to ten, until he says it is zero. In the event that the number is higher, we will continue with the desensitization until there is no discomfort associated with the target memory.

Phase 5. Installation: The goal of this phase is to expand reprocessing and ensure that the target memory has been integrated into the memory network in a non-pathological way (Leeds, 2012). In this phase, we begin by asking if the PC is still valid or if there is another more appropriate one. If the VOC is less than 7, we will process the original experience associated with the PC and we will do sets until it reaches the level of 7. If this were not the case, we would investigate if there is something that is interfering with the processing and solve it until we reach our goal.

Phase 6. Body scan: During this phase, we ask the patient to go back to the target memory and see, with his eyes closed, if there is any remaining discomfort in any part of his body. If so, we process it again until it disappears completely. We will devote a whole chapter to how to treat the body in cases of complex trauma. Due to the importance of the body in the disorders included in this book, there is an entire chapter explaining in detail how to work with the body in therapy.

Phase 7. Closure: This phase has two purposes. The first is to ensure that the patient is stabilized and we can bring the session to an end, and the second is to make sure we explain to the patient that he can have sensations, dreams, or flashbacks the following days, that these are normal, and that he should log them in a journal to inform us in future sessions. As we will see in complex trauma treatments, many of the processes cannot be completed in a single session, so we will talk about open sessions.

Phase 8. Re-evaluation: After a few days of closure we make sure, in the following session or by phone or email, that there is no discomfort when the traumatic event is remembered and that no new memories come up that cause discomfort. If so, we will choose a new memory as target, and we will initiate a new reprocessing.

Let's see an example of a standard EMDR session using the basic protocol (T = therapist and C = client). We started the work with part of phase 2, and the complete phases 3–7. This session is reproduced with the patient's authorization.

T: EMDR is something completely natural. You've come here because of a situation in your past which was traumatic for you. We're not going to do anything weird. What happens is that, during the day, we process a lot of emotional information, but if something happens that is too painful or traumatic, our brain doesn't have the capacity to process it and it gets kind of anchored, so it may happen that we can feel it as if it were actually happening all over again.

It can happen, for example, that you are walking through the place where the trauma occurred, and you feel discomfort, or there is a smell that was present at that moment and you feel like it is happening right now.

EMDR, the treatment we will be working with, seems to have the ability to stimulate the experience you underwent and it will help you not to have any emotional connection to it when you remember it again.

It is important for you to know that I won't do anything strange, that this is a totally natural process, and that you, your brain, will control the process at all times.

It will be as if we were traveling by train and you had all these different images, memories, sensations, as if you were looking through the window and you were seeing different things. Maybe at some point you feel some distress, but we will quickly go out into the light as if that train were leaving the tunnel.

There are different ways of stimulation, but with you I'd like to do EM. This means I'll move my hand and you will follow it with your eyes. Follow my hand, are you comfortable with the speed?

C: Yes, I'm comfortable.

T: Very good. You already have a safe place. Please tell me what it is.

C: The room in my house.

T: We've said that if, at any time, you feel bad, you can imagine going back to that place to calm down and feel at peace. It is very important to me that, if you ever feel overwhelmed or you feel really bad, you have a STOP signal to let me know that I need to stop. Please give me a signal so that I know I have to stop.

T: As we have established in the treatment plan, I would like you to give me a small and brief account of what we are going to work on today, which refers to a memory about ... ?

C: A sensation of feeling inferior to others and not daring to ask for anything.

T: Very good. You have a concrete memory, right? A traumatic moment that represents a before and after.

C: Yes.

T: OK, I'd like you to tell me an image that represents the worst part of that memory.

C: The worst part ...

T: An image that represents the worst part.

C: An image? Well, I was at an office and I saw this large window and a road in the background and I felt as if they were throwing me out of it.

T: The worst image would be a window with a road in the background?

C: Yes.

T: If you think about the image, what words come to mind that express the negative belief about yourself right now?

C: That I'm not worthy.

T: I'm not worthy?

C: Yes.

T: If you think about that image now, what words would you like or would have liked to believe or think instead of those?

C. That I am very much worthy.

T: How true do you feel those words are on a scale of 1 to 7? I AM WORTHY. Where 1 feels completely false and 7 completely true.

C: 2.

T: If you think about the fact and the words I AM NOT WORTHY, what emotion do you feel right now?

C: Frustration and anger.

T: On a scale from 0 to 10, where 0 is nothing or a completely neutral disturbance and 10 is the worst disturbance you can imagine, how much disturbance do you feel now?

C: 8.

T: Where do you feel it in the body?

C: In my chest.

T: Thank you. I'd like you to take the image of the window with the road in the background, and register the words I AM NOT WORTHY, where you are feeling them in your body, and to follow my hand without moving your eyes.

EM

T: Take a deep breath and tell me what comes to mind.

C: It's come to me associated with another situation in which I was also under-appreciated. They said I wasn't worth a damn, they underestimated me.

T: Go with that.

EM

T: Take a deep breath and tell me what comes up.

C: Other images have come up in which I felt they wanted to humiliate me.

T: Go with that.

EM

T: Take a deep breath ...

C. The belief that they did it because they felt inferior to me.

T. Very good. Go with that.

EM

T: What's coming up now?

C: The belief that I am worth a lot more than them and that they wanted to take revenge, I mean, that they felt inferior and that I will not allow it to happen ever again.

T: Very good. When you go back to the original experience, what comes up now? Focus on that moment.

EM

T: What comes up now?

C: That it was a necessary experience to be able to learn certain things.

EM

T: What comes up now?

C: I now feel that I have the belief that I will let go of all my chains, the chains that paralyze me, that I am going to be like a butterfly coming out. That it is no more a chrysalis.

T. Very good, go with that.

EM

T: Take a deep breath and tell me what you feel now.

C: I now feel the conviction that I am going to break the chains for good and that I will fight for whatever I feel like, and that nothing or no one will stop me.

T: Very good J. How does it feel? What comes up now?

C. It's like the situation was close by and has become distant, as if it's gone, it's far away. It's far away ... it's like it's gone away, it's like really very far away, and I feel a sensation of tranquility.

T: Very good. If you think about the event, about the original experience, 0 being completely neutral and 10 being the worst you can imagine, how much disturbance do you feel now?

C. Zero.

T. Are the words I AM WORTHY still appropriate or would you like to change them for a more appropriate statement?

C. Yes, they are correct.

T: On a scale from 1 to 7 where 1 feels completely false and 7 completely valid, how true do you feel the words I AM WORTHY to be?

C: Totally valid, a 7.

T. I'd like to ask you to close your eyes, take the memory and the words "I am worthy," keep them together and explore your body from head to toe, and if there's any tension in any part of your body, please let me know.

C. Everything'sreally well but I do notice a small sensation in my shoulders.

T: Ok, follow my hand.

EM

C: OK, close your eyes, take the memory and the words "I am worthy" and explore your body from head to toe and tell me if you notice any sensation.

EM

C. I have the belief that I am worthy and don't have any tension.

Short installation with EM

T: What do you take away from this session?

C: The belief that I am free from all the chains that bound me. The sensation that it was I who set myself limits, I'd put up the barriers.
T: It is your mind who has done the whole process.
C: And I've taken them off. It's like I've left a sort of prison.
T: As I told you, our brains process information. During the next hours, the following days, when you're asleep, when you're awake, your brain will continue to process. If any flashback or insight comes up, I'd like you to log it and you know I am at your disposition to help you with anything you need, OK?
C: Perfect.
T: Any questions?
C: No, it's all good. Thank you very much.
T: Thank you.

Table 9.2 Situations that require more precaution are in bold.

Name: Date:
For patient's history, the severity of the worst episode is indicated.
For current situation, the severity at the moment of consultation is indicated.
0: absent, 1: minimum, 2: moderate, 3: severe.

Problem	*History Includes*	*Severity*	*Current Situation*	*Severity*
Secondary Gain/Loss		0 1 2 3		0 1 2 3
Absence of confidence or truth		0 1 2 3		0 1 2 3
Extreme crisis		0 1 2 3		0 1 2 3
Economic Instability		0 1 2 3		0 1 2 3
Health risk		0 1 2 3		0 1 2 3
Mayor depression		0 1 2 3		0 1 2 3
Suicidal thoughts		0 1 2 3		0 1 2 3
Suicide attempts		0 1 2 3		0 1 2 3
Self-injuries		0 1 2 3		0 1 2 3
Injuries to others		0 1 2 3		0 1 2 3
Risky behavior		0 1 2 3		0 1 2 3
Substance abuse		0 1 2 3		0 1 2 3
Compulsive sex		0 1 2 3		0 1 2 3
Compulsive acts		0 1 2 3		0 1 2 3
Alexithymia		0 1 2 3		0 1 2 3
Patient overwhelmed by emotions		0 1 2 3		0 1 2 3
Depersonalization		0 1 2 3		0 1 2 3
Dissociative Identity Disorder		0 1 2 3		0 1 2 3

The intervention of the therapist is very scarce, and almost the whole process lies with the client, who finds an optimal resolution to solve his problem that adapts to his own needs.

In the event that there is a complex trauma such as the cases we are working on here, the basic protocol will not suffice when solving the pathology, which does not mean that we will not use it, but that we will have to first resolve the stabilization of the patient so that he can start reprocessing. Leeds (2012) also uses a table to indicate cases in which a more extensive treatment to treat trauma will be recommended.

In cases of complex trauma, we will have to use tools taken from other approaches and use modified protocols that allow us to overcome defenses, access memories often amnesic or that the patient cannot tolerate such as idealizations of parents who have been abusers, very rigid patterns learned since childhood and so on. We will have to modify the protocols to adapt them to the needs of the clients; the phases cannot be rigid, nor can we always follow a predetermined order as is done with the basic protocol.

Conclusions

EMDR has proven to be a very effective tool in treating PTSD and those disorders associated with it. Using the basic protocol created by Shapiro, we can access neural networks associated with memories that were traumatic in the past and continue to interfere in one way or another in the present in the patient's life.

However, in many cases, we will not be able to apply this protocol either because the patient cannot bear the emotional burden associated with the memory or because there are associated pathologies, such as traumatic dissociation, that prevent the processing from being effective.

In these cases, we must modify the protocol and use tools taken from other therapeutic approaches that will allow the patient to accept what happened in a gradual way, reduce the dissociation if it exists, and finally integrate those traumatic memories in a healthy way for the patient.

Reference

Leeds, A. (2012). *EMDR therapy basics and beyond.* Guilford Press.

10 Conceptualization

Beyond Diagnostics

The Initial Interview

During consultation, every new person who places his trust in me is an enigma, someone I have to get to know little by little in order to help him get what he needs. In many cases, these people are going to be able to open up and give me all the information I need from the word "go," and with others I will be the one that will have to encourage them, little by little, to let go of their defenses, to access their most intimate feelings and memories. The people who come to see me are more than a label or a diagnosis, they are human beings who need help and they are looking for the security and support they cannot find in their lives. That is why each person who places their trust in us deserves all our attention and curiosity in order to find the essence of their individuality.

> *I like to tell my patients that each of them is like a puzzle. I have the pieces in front of me and I have to put them together to discover how I can turn that initial chaos with which they come to the consultation into a beautiful portrait, a process in which we will work together to achieve it.*

This phase will be the pillar on which we will build the foundation for the rest of the therapy; it will be vital for undertaking the therapeutic work. Intuitively, it may seem obvious that the first thing we should do is gather the patient's history, but many times this will not be possible. Psychological disorders, as we saw in the first part, find their origin in emotions of anger and fear that have led to a strong sense of guilt and shame. If the patient does not feel listened to or cared for, we will repeat the feelings of not feeling accompanied that were present during childhood and we will lose a golden opportunity to create a good therapeutic alliance.

The goal of the first sessions is not only to collect the patient's history so as to plan the treatment, but also to create a strong therapeutic alliance and to achieve a reduction of symptoms in the first sessions if necessary, and thus get the patient to increase their confidence in us and be able to overcome their fears.

DOI: 10.4324/9781003646341-12

According to Dworkin (2005):

> The first encounter is crucial, the patient carries in his memory implicit and explicit traumas and their experiences of attachment, as well as a neurobiological mechanism to establish interpersonal relationships. It is a very delicate situation in which the clinician is challenged to establish a comfortable connection with an unknown person while simultaneously having to ask personal and sometimes painful questions. It is a matter of respect and dedication to the patient to spend as much time as necessary in building a good relationship during this phase.
>
> (p. 35)

In the first sessions, when the patient makes the request for what they want to solve, we must act with extreme caution, because in many cases they can come with a request for treatment that they have self-diagnosed after having looked on the internet or they can feel very embarrassed to tell us what the problem that

Figure 10.1 Dante's divine comedy perfectly reflects the journey we make through the therapeutic process. Virgil accompanies Dante, escorting him and protecting him, as his figure of attachment, through hell and purgatory, but when they reach the gates of paradise, just as the therapist and the patient say goodbye at the end of therapy, Virgil abandons him, letting him follow his path in the company of his love, Beatriz.

brings them to consultation is. If, as we have seen, the basis of these disorders is guilt and shame, it is not surprising that from the beginning these two emotions appear as obstacles in the treatment.

> *Adele is a 42-year-old woman who comes to therapy because she suffers from insomnia and anxiety, which does not allow her to lead a normal life. The therapeutic process is a bit stuck after five sessions, which is why I decide to use hypnosis techniques to work with childhood memories that may be related to her anxiety. Upon remembering events from when she was five, she starts to remember, with a lot of pain and tears (abreaction), her grandfather fondling her when he stayed over to take care of her.*

When answering my usual question in these cases (whether she consciously remembered it happening), she said no, but that she'd always had the intuition it had happened. This insight led to us being able to work on the sexual abuse, which helped us banish the anxiety and insomnia.

The stage of conceptualization is a process of getting to know the patient and will never be completely closed during the therapeutic process, either because they spontaneously give us relevant new information or because the patient does not feel ready to share it in the first sessions until the therapeutic alliance becomes stronger. Whenever this happens, we must hide our frustration because sometimes the patient may not have told this us before. We will emphasize how difficult it must have been for them to tell us and how we appreciate the trust they have placed in us.

In no case should it appear in the first sessions that we only want to collect data to diagnose or label the patient with a diagnosis; we must ensure that he perceives a sincere interest and empathy for his suffering at all times. It is during the first encounters when we are going to create the therapeutic alliance that, as we have seen, is so important during the therapeutic process. At the same time that we are empathic, we must be directive when collecting the necessary information so as to be able to make a good conceptualization of what the history of the patient's disorder has been.

Although the stage of conceptualization should numerically be the first, it will not always be possible in practice. We will have to alternate between stabilization, understanding, and the teaching of tools to reduce the discomfort between sessions before we can elaborate a good history of the disorder. This does not mean that we cannot or should not work on collecting the patient's history in the first sessions, but we must do it with great care so that he feels that we have a sincere interest in him as a person and as long as the patient is stabilized. Do not forget that much of the basis of the disorder has been the feeling of abandonment and rejection.

According to Leeds (2012):

> Patients … often have such profound terror of reconnecting with those (early) experiences that they will only be able to consciously identify them when they have achieved some mastery of their current panic symptoms and have developed greater confidence in the therapeutic alliance.
>
> (p. 444)

Depending on the disorder, there will be a varying degree of cooperation from the patient to be able to create a good history of the pathology. Conceptualization with children or adolescents will not be the same as with adults. Addictions, antisocial behaviors, or eating disorders require an extensive phase of motivation when approaching treatment (Rollnick, S., & Miller, W. R. 1995), while in issues related to anxiety, the motivation of patients will be very high and will almost always come with an urgent need to diminish the suffering associated with the disorder. What this may mean for the therapist is that in the countertransference process he may feel a lot of pressure to reduce the patient's suffering at any price, with the disadvantages this can imply for the treatment. We should never shorten the stages because of pressure on behalf of the patient because this would be a violation of the therapeutic contract. Collecting data is essential to be able to perform good therapy; it can be postponed to stabilize the patient, but should never be ignored.

We must bear in mind that the patients themselves do not know what is happening to them and that their lives are submerged in real chaos and we must put order in the morass of emotions they feel. For that, it will be essential that we ask the pertinent questions in order to allow the patient to get to know themselves and start having a feeling of control over their disorder.

In patients with avoidant traits, it is more complicated to establish a complete history because they tend to avoid any subject related to their past. On the other hand, patients of the anxious type try to talk about their symptoms and how they feel over and over again, without going into relevant details for the treatment. In all cases, the therapist must be firm in his line of work and careful at the same time, because if we fall into the traps the patients have created to survive, they will abandon the therapy because they will not consider it effective.

During data collection, we will keep in mind the emotions we saw in the PARCUVE model in Chapter 6. How were the patient's first years and their relationship with the caregivers? How does the patient deal with fear and how does he handle the feeling of helplessness and anxiety? What are the mechanisms used to self-regulate emotionally? Is there guilt or a sense of failure (= shame)? The questions are asked openly, with interest from the therapist, which allows for a solid therapeutic relationship in this first phase of therapy.

The questionnaires that I detail below are a reference script when it comes to knowing the patient. When did the problem begin and why does it persist? How does he try to solve it? What symptoms does he have? What personality traits predominate at the time of relating to others?

Data to Be Gathered during Conceptualization

The main issues that we will have to reflect in this phase are:

1. Triggers of the disorder, especially the associated anxiety;
2. List of symptoms;
3. History of the disorder and current situation;
4. Previous and current psychological and psychiatric treatments;
5. Existence of dissociative disorders;
6. Presence of unresolved grief in childhood or adulthood;
7. History of attachment relationships in the past and in the present.

We must make a detailed history and as complete an evaluation as possible. It is vital to understand the full complexity of the disorder. The questions should take into account comorbidities, avoidance behaviors, rituals, traumas, or personality disorders that may interfere with the treatment. Does the patient have significant traumas? Does he have symptoms of phobic or avoidant behaviors? Symptoms of depression? All questions that the therapist needs to better understand the client should be answered

T. Hello Buffy,you told me what brings you to therapy over the phone, but I'd like you to explain it to me in detail so I can get to know you better.

C. Yes, of course. I have a lot of anxiety and the truth is I don't sleep well. I'm taking medication but it doesn't help. I'm desperate. I've come to you because I saw your website and found it trustworthy. I thought maybe you could help me. Although I feel like a lost case.

1. Anxiety Triggers

The basis of all pathologies is fear and, associated with this, anxiety. It is going to be the most frequent symptom that we will find in the consultation. Anxiety is a sensation that alerts the brain to make the necessary changes to react and find a new balance that reduces the level of alertness. We find disease and the anxiety associated with it when this is not possible.

Anxiety crises can appear associated with multiple disorders, such as phobias, OCD, eating disorders, or PTSD. It is important to take into account situations in which anxiety usually increases. These can be of several types:

- *Unexpected*: The patient perceives the crisis as unexpected without any reason that may cause it; this is most typical in cases of panic and anxiety attacks that do not have a specific trigger. There is no reason or place that causes crises, and patients avoid all kinds of situations that relate to anxiety, including, in severe cases, leaving home.
- *Situationally determined*: Crises occur in specific situations which the patient knows about. They can be of three types:
  - Environmental: These are places or situations that the patient perceives as dangerous, such as crowded or closed places or situations that the patient perceives that he does not have control over, such as driving on the freeway, riding an elevator, or getting on an airplane, as well as phobias, like fear of dogs or heights.
  - Relational: The patient is afraid of rejection or making a fool of himself in front of others because of some characteristic that evokes shame, for example, fear of going to the beach for having to show one's legs or fear of going to a restaurant for fear of sweating.
  - Causal: There is a known reason that causes anxiety, but it cannot be avoided, for example, performing a compulsive ritual, insomnia, frustration or anger, or the need to have everything under control.

T: I'd like you to explain to me when you feel that anxiety overwhelms you. Can you give me an example?

C: I have a horrible fear of having my stomach grumble in public, my mother says it's silly, that it happens to everyone. But I'm really obsessed with it, I can't help it.

T. Is there any specific situation where it happens?

C. At first it only happened when I was very nervous, so what I did was not eat if I was going somewhere with people. And it worked. But for some time now, I'm scared of it happening in any situation and I'm no longer able to take the bus, go shopping or to the bank, in fact, I don't leave my house anymore. I went out today to come to therapy but I spent two weeks in my pajamas without going out.

2. *List of Symptoms*

A very important source of information to evaluate the patient's situation is the list of symptoms. These can give us a lot of information to allow us to make a diagnosis as well as a way to evaluate if there is improvement in the patient's condition throughout therapy.

It is important to make the patient explain to us in more or less detail the problems that bring him to consultation, and try to avoid closed yes/no type answers. It is much more convenient to indicate the intensity of the symptoms,

Table 10.1 List of categories of symptoms

Sleep Category	
Bruxism	Periodic limb movement
Difficulty falling asleep	Restless legs syndrome
Difficulty maintaining sleep	Restless sleep
Difficulty waking up	Sleep apnea
Dysregulated sleep cycle	Sleepwalking
Narcolepsy	Snoring
Night sweats	Talk during sleep
Night terrors	Nocturnal enuresis
Nightmares or vivid dreams	
Attention and Learning Category	
Difficulty completing tasks	Lack of alert
Difficulty making decisions	Lack of common sense
Problems with time management or personal space	Dirty and careless writing
Difficulty remembering names	Does not listen
Problems changing attentional focus	Poor concentration
Difficulty changing tasks	Poor drawing skills
Difficulty thinking clearly	Problems with math
Difficulty understanding conversations	Poor short-term memory
All too frequent distractions	Poor sustained attention
Reading problems	Poor verbal expression
Demotivation	Poor vocabulary
	Problems finding words
	Slow thinking
Sensory Category	
Auditory hypersensitivity	Tinnitus
Sensitivity to chemical substances	Vertigo
Kinetic dizziness	Visual deficits
Poor body awareness	Visual hypersensitivity
Somatosensory deficits	Tactile hypersensitivity
Behavioral Category	
Addictive behaviors	Manipulative behavior
Aggressive behavior	Motor or vocal tics
Anorexia	Nail biting
Binges and purges	Oppositional or defiant behavior
Compulsive behaviors	Poor eye contact
Compulsive intake	Poor self-care
Weeping	Poor social and emotional reciprocity
Excessive talking	Poor speech articulation
Hyperactivity	Fits of rage
Impulsivity	Self-destructive behavior
Inflexibility	Stuttering
Lack of appetite awareness	
Lack of sense of humor	
Lack of social interest	

(*Continued*)

Table 10.1 (Continued)

Sleep Category	
Emotional Category	
Agitation or anger	Lack of pleasure
Anxiety	Lack of social conscience
Depression	Low self-esteem
Difficulty calming down	Mania
Easily embarrassed, in which situations?	Mood swings
Emotional reactivity	Negative obsessive thoughts
Fears, of what? When?	Obsessive worrying
Sensations of derealization	Panic attacks
Flashbacks of trauma	Paranoia
Impatience	Suicidal ideations
	Irritability
	Lack of emotional awareness
Physical Category	
Allergies	Muscular weakness
Asthma	Nausea
Chronic constipation	Premenstrual symptoms
Clumsiness	Balance problems
Difficulty moving or walking	Poor fine motor coordination
Difficulty working	Poor gross motor coordination
Encopresis	Reflux
Fatigue	Epileptic crisis
Palpitations	Skin rash
Hypertension	Spasticity
Hot flushes	Stress urinary incontinence
Immune deficiency	Sweating
Irritable bowel	Tachycardia
Low muscle tone	Tremors
Muscle tension	Incontinence due to urinary urgency
Muscle contractions	
Pain Category	
Abdominal pain	Tension headaches
Chronic pain	Sciatica
Pain due to fibromyalgia	Headaches due to sinusitis
Mandibular pain	Stomachache
Joint pain	Trigeminal neuralgia
Migraine headaches	Muscle pain

for example from 0 to 10; when they started; and if they improve or worsen in different circumstances.

The way of explaining the symptoms, to insist on them or to disregard them; giving priority to the suffering of others instead of one's own; not taking into account the consequences that the burden of the illness brings to the family, etc. will also indicate much of the personality traits of the patient, which will greatly condition the therapeutic approach to help that person.

T. I'd like you to read the list I've just given you, and tell me what symptoms you have of those that appear in the list and to describe them a little so I can have an idea of what is happening to you. Read the list and mark the symptoms you most identify with.

C. I'm sure that when I read them, I'll have them all, my god, it's terrible. Let's see ... I most identify with difficulty thinking clearly, deregulated sleep cycle, demotivation. I hadn't told you before because I was ashamed but I also sometimes binge and vomit.

T. I thank you for your trust, is there anything else besides the fear of your stomach grumbling and what you've already told me?

C. I have very low self-esteem and obsessive negative thoughts about me making a fool of myself.

Table 10.2 Questions to assess the degree of anxiety

How often have you had the symptoms in the last two weeks?
If you have anxiety, how would you rate it on a scale of 0 to 10?
Intensity and duration of current symptoms
When did they first appear? How would you rate the intensity of the disorder on a scale from 0 to 10?
Experiences with anxiety
What do you consider are the causes of your anxiety?
Frequency, intensity and duration of symptoms in the past
In recent months, has the intensity and frequency of symptoms increased or decreased?
Avoided or feared current situations
What situations do you tend to avoid out of fear?
First event
When was the first time the anxiety or disorder started?
Were you using drugs at that stage? And now?
How was the family situation at that time?
Was there any personal, work, or academic element that stressed you at that stage?
Parent–child role reversal
Do you remember situations in which you took care of your parents because they were sick, sad, or depressed or disabled by alcohol or other substance abuse?
How often did it happen? How long did it last?
The most representative moment of the symptom
What was the strongest or most unpleasant moment of the disorder you had?
Most recent attack
What are the most recent problem you've had related to your problem?
Internal and external signs that precede the symptoms
Is there any conditioning factor that you know of that causes you more discomfort and worsens the disorder?

Table 10.3 Chart to learn about psychological and psychiatric backgrounds

Psychiatric treatment
Have you taken any type of medication in the past to treat a psychiatric problem?
Are you currently on any treatment?
Do you have any diagnosis?

Psychological treatments
Have you ever gone to a psychologist before? Why?
What did you like most about your previous psychologist?
What did you least like about your previous psychologist?
Why have you decided to not return or continue with him or her?
Were you given a diagnosis?

General medical issues
Is there a medical disorder that may be related to your pathology? Like irritable bowel, allergies, chronic pains, headaches, hyperthyroidism etc.
Have you ruled out that they are organic disorders?

Excessive concern with the disease
Have you ever feared that the anxiety is something more serious?
Are you afraid of being able to get serious illnesses because of all this?
Do you frequently visit the doctor or emergency rooms for fear of dying or having an undetected illness?

3. *History of the Disorder in the Past and Current Situation*

T. Do you have a memory of the first time this happened? (In many cases patients will not remember this, but we can use hypnosis techniques to help them connect to their memories).

C. A memorycomes to mind of when I was about 10 years old and we were watching a play the school had taken us to. It was morning and I had not had breakfast and my stomach started grumbling and I felt great shame. The kids were laughing quietly and I couldn't get up and leave because I was in the middle of the row of seats and would have drawn too much attention to myself. I still remember it now and it feels like it was yesterday.

T. Of course. And the sensation of impotence had to be terrible.

C. I was angry with the world, with my mother for not making breakfast because she'd overslept, with my classmates for laughing at me, and, above all, with myself for making a fool of me and being so dumb and embarrassing. Yes, above all, with myself.

4. *Previous and Current Psychological and Psychiatric Treatments*

We must inform ourselves about possible psychological or psychiatric disorders in the present and/or in the past and if they were diagnosed, as well as if there were psychological and/or psychiatric treatments and if they are currently taking medication.

In order to direct our therapy, it is very important to ask the patient if they have previous experience with other therapies and therapists. Asking what helped her most about her experience (= strengths) and what she least liked (= weaknesses) can advise us on how we can approach therapy. If, for example, a patient tells us that he went to a psychoanalytic therapist and that he felt bad because the therapist never spoke to him, we will know that he is a person who is going to need a lot of psychoeducation. Or, if he went to a cognitive-behavioral therapist and told us that the charts and exercises that he was given between sessions helped him a lot, this would indicate that we should use tools of this type during treatment.

T. Cadence, have you ever been to a psychologist or psychiatrist in search of help before coming to me?

C. Yes, I went to the psychiatrist a couple of times but they did not help much. They gave me pills that did not suit me very well, and above all, they did not help me solve my problem. I felt worse, as if I was to blame for not getting well.

T. Did you ever go to a psychologist?

C. Yes, I went to a woman who worked in the area where I live. I felt better at that stage, I made progress and started to lead an almost normal life. But she got a position somewhere else and left the practice.

T. What did you like most about her?

C. She did not judge me, she understood me. I felt she was almost like a friend. She would give me tasks to do between sessions and encouraged me very much when I made progress. Now I remember that I also went to a psychologist once but he did not speak.

T. I would like you to explain to me when you feel anxiety overwhelms you. Can you give me an example?

C. I have a terrible fear of my stomach grumbling in public, my mother says it's silly, that it happens to everyone. But I'm obsessed with it, I cannot help it.

T. Is there any particular situation where it happens?

C. At first it only happened when I was very nervous, so what I did was not eat if I was going somewhere with people and it worked. But for some time now, I'm scared of it happening in any situation and I'm no longer able to take the bus, go shopping or to the bank, in fact, I don't leave my house anymore. I've come out today to get to therapy but I spent two weeks in my pajamas without going out.

5. *Existence of Dissociative Disorders*

In disorders related to attachment and in post-traumatic stress disorders, we will often find traumatic dissociation. It is very important to assess this possibility because, if it exists, we will need special protocols to be able to work on it. In these cases, as I like to say to my patients, "we will arrive much sooner by going slowly."

According to Putnam (1997), dissociation is a process that produces an alteration in the thoughts, feelings, or actions of a person so that, during a period of time, certain information that comes to mind cannot be associated or integrated with other information as it would happen in normal conditions, due to the existence of a trauma. On the other hand, other authors (Steinberg & Schnall, 2003) comment that dissociative experiences are characterized above all by a "compartmentalization of consciousness." This expression refers to the fact that certain mental experiences that are normally expected to be processed together and at the same time (thoughts, emotions, sensations, memories, and the sense of identity), are functionally isolated from each other while in some cases remaining inaccessible to the conscience or to its voluntary amnesic recovery.

In order to explore the existence of dissociation, we can use Steinberg and Schnall's questionnaire (2003). Taking into account that it is a qualitative questionnaire, we are interested in the answers and comments given to us about the different items. This information will be very useful for assessing whether we should take special precautions throughout the treatment.

It has five sections with their corresponding items:

- Amnesia;
- Depersonalization;
- Derealization;
- Identity confusion;
- Identity alteration.

We can find the complete questionnaire here: https://trastornosdisociativos.files.wordpress.com/2012/06/cuestionarios-steinberg.pdf

6. Presence of Unresolved Grief in Childhood or Adulthood

In Chapter 6, I talked about the importance of ruptures in attachment and how, in severe cases, the panic/separation circuit is activated. If this is activated frequently in childhood, the person will be extremely sensitive throughout his life to any type of loss, be it real or imagined.

Anxiety in patients is frequently due to a traumatic or unresolved grief. Describing complicated grief, Payas (2012) recounts:

> When natural emotion loses its regulatory capacity of the real experience and becomes a rigid and maladaptive defense, it functions as a way to short-circuit

> the processing of experience and reduces the discomfort associated with loss, but at the expense of nullifying the possibility of elaboration of meanings and changes: fear becomes anxiety, panic or phobias.
>
> (p. 248)

As we can see in this text, the description of grief in adulthood does not differ at all from the descriptions we have made of the emotions a child has when he goes through an experience of attachment rupture with his caregivers. If these bereavements have been frequent or very intense in childhood, it is obvious to think that the amygdala will have developed hyperactivation in the face of possible attachment ruptures; these losses can be real or imagined. In people suffering from panic attacks, we should look for grief that has overwhelmed the alarm system, causing this pathology.

When gathering data, it is fundamental to ask:

> What losses were there throughout life? These can be real or imaginary. For example, feeling alone because a little brother was born or because the parents spent the day working will be treated as a rupture in attachment as well as if there is a death of a loved one. As always, the more involved the attachment figures were in the problem, the younger the age at which it occurred, and the more the fear circuit was activated, the greater the traumatic impact will be.

Table 10.4 Questions to learn about loss and grief

Has there been a death of a person or persons very dear to you throughout your life? Which ones? *(Obviously the younger the patient's age when the loss occurred and the closer the person was to the deceased, the more significant the trauma would have been.)*
Has there been any death of a significant person for you in the year prior to the first severe anxiety or panic attack?
(They can be family or friends.)
Has there been an important event that has forced you or someone very close to you to leave because of medical reasons (hospitalization), work, etc.?
(That is, some kind of distance that the patient could have perceived as grief.)
Has there been a time in your childhood that made you feel especially lonely or vulnerable?
(It is very common for patients to say that they do not remember or that their childhood was very happy. We must investigate and not get carried away by the avoidant responses of our patients.)

T. Cadence, forgive me for bombarding you with questions. But I need to get to know you better. Have you ever lost someone who was very close to you?

C. Yes, my grandmother. Actually, she was like a mother to me, she was the person who took care of me as a child because my mother was always working.

T. How old were you when she passed away?

C. 15. I miss her a lot.

The patient starts crying, and I keep a compassionate silence out of respect for her grief.

7. History of their Attachment Relationships the Past and Present

The type of attachment that each person develops in his childhood will determine how he relates to others (and himself) throughout life. Bretherton (1985) argues that models "as I think others see me and as I see myself" are interchangeable. For example, a child who experiences parental rejection is very likely to develop a negative model of himself or herself.

Feelings of unworthiness, perfectionism, blaming others for failures, the need to take care of everyone, and so on will be acquired during the first years of life as a form of interpersonal regulation. When these behaviors are insufficient or become ineffective, regulatory strategies will make their appearance which, if ineffective or defective, will lead to psychological disorders and the associated anxiety.

Bartholomew (1990) – based on Bowlby's work – argues that attachment patterns in adulthood reflect internal working models of oneself as that of the attachment figures in childhood. The models of oneself can be divided into positives (I think of myself that I deserve love) and negatives (I think of myself that I do not deserve love). In the same way, the models of others can be differentiated into positives (I think others are available and care about me) or negative (others are believed to reject me, are distant, or do not care about me). These models combine and give four different types of attachment (Feeney &Noller, 1996).

The CaMir model or adult attachment questionnaire in its reduced version by Balluerka et al. (2011), adapted in its content to the needs of this book, is a basic tool to assess the attachment type of patients who come to our practice. Once again, it is important to emphasize that the questionnaire should be carried out in the form of open questions to help patients to reflect on their past and current attachment history.

Determining the attachment relationships that occurred in childhood and what they are like as adults will provide us with valuable information to correct past experiences during treatment. It was the feeling of guilt and shame that led to regulatory strategies that allowed them to find a new balance that would

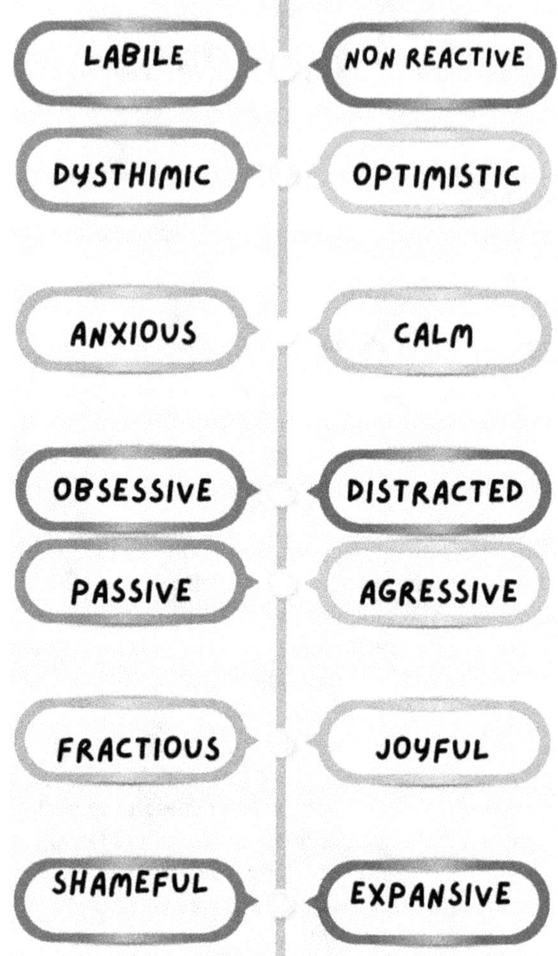

Figure 10.2 Type of attachment based on how they see themselves and how they believe others see them. Based on Feeney and Noller (1996).

reduce the discomfort. Our goal in therapy is to know what happened in those crucial early years and help eliminate the patient's feelings of guilt and shame.

> *When the patient is able to experience what happened through the eyes of the person he currently is, accompanied safely by the therapist, an emotion is produced that replaces the previous one. The guilt and shame associated with what happened are eliminated.*

Table 10.5 Reduced version of CaMir (adult attachment questionnaire)

1. In my family, the experiences that each member has outside the home are a source of conversation and enrichment for all.
2. As a child, I had few opportunities to experiment on my own.
3. The threats of separation, of relocation to another place, or of breaking family ties are part of my childhood memories.
4. In my family, everyone expresses their emotions without fearing the reactions of others.
5. My parents were incapable of having authority when necessary.
6. In case of need, I am sure that I can count on my loved ones to find comfort.
7. I wish my children were more autonomous than I have been.
8. In family life, respect for parents is very important.
9. As a child, I knew that I would always find comfort in my loved ones.
10. I think that I have been able to give back to my parents the love they have given me.
11. The relationships with my loved ones during my childhood seem to me, in general, positive.
12. I hate the feeling of being dependent on others.
13. Although it is difficult to admit, I feel a certain grudge against my parents.
14. I can only count on myself to solve my problems.
15. As a child, my loved ones were often impatient and irritable.
16. When I was a child, my parents had renounced their role as parents.
17. It is better to not feel too bad about a loss, or grief, in order to overcome it.
18. I often spend time talking with my loved ones.
19. My loved ones have always given me the best of themselves.
20. I cannot concentrate on anything else, knowing that some of my loved ones have problems.
21. As a child, I found enough love in my loved ones to not have to look elsewhere.
22. I am always worried about the grief I can cause my loved ones when I leave them.
23. As a child, they had a laissez-faire attitude.
24. Adults should control their emotions towards children, whether it be pleasure, love, or anger.
25. I like thinking about my childhood.
26. As a teenager, no one from my environment ever fully understood my concerns.
27. In my family, when one of us has a problem, the others feel involved.
28. Currently, I believe I understand the attitudes of my parents during my childhood.

Adapted from Balluerka et al. (2011)

Personality Patterns

It would be impossible to get up in the morning and have to relearn everything we have learned in the previous days and years of our lives. Our brain keeps memory of what has happened to be able to invest energy in different things. This is what we know as a system of "cognitive economy," that is, to maximize the performance of our brain with the lowest possible expense so that it can be used in other areas such as reproduction, raising children, or solving problems. This is the meaning of the "implicit procedural memory" (see Chapter 5).

The more we have performed a behavior or the earlier the age when we learned it, the more difficult it will be to change it later. The kindling phenomenon (Morrell, 1990) will make it more and more consolidated in the unconscious or implicit memory. In other words, the more often we do something, the more likely we are to repeat it, even if it is no longer effective or even if it is pathological. Changing that behavior, emotion, or thought will take a lot of effort for it to be modified.

Just as when we are born and we learn the language of our parents, we acquire many emotions and behaviors that we learn at a young age, with a tendency to repeat them again and again until we are unable to do them in a different way. This is what we call "schemes" or personality patterns. These are behaviors and/or emotions that are configured in childhood, are maintained and developed later on, and are imposed on the experiences of adult life even though they are no longer applicable (Young et al., 2013).

Many of these schemes will be created from the relationships we have had as children with our environment and the responses we have had to demands for care or attention. When the parents attend positively, children incorporate internal working models that will make them feel that they can have positive relationships with others, and if they have been negative, they will have a feeling of unworthiness, guilt, shame, and fear of being rejected in interpersonal relationships.

These patterns, recorded in the unconscious, tend to be repeated over and over again, being recorded as implicit memory, and we can only change them if we focus all our attention on them and, by making them explicit and conscious, we can act on them. I believe that a large part of our work as therapists is to detect these repetitive, unconscious, and pathological patterns and, by exposing them and making them conscious, helping our patients to change them for more adaptive ones. Many times these patterns will change spontaneously and sometimes corrective emotional experiences will be needed to allow new learning that, when reinforced, replace the previous ones that were dysfunctional.

In the case of people with panic attacks or excessive anxiety, pathological embarrassment, or excessive rumination, among other disorders, there are control or regulation strategies that have helped them to manage the discomfort at some time in the past but with the passage of time have become patterns that are pathological. During conceptualization, we must know which are the most frequent and help patients to make those patterns that are performed unconsciously conscious.

According to Young et al. (2013), maladaptive patterns are:

- Characterized by a broad and generalized pattern or theme;
- Made up of memories, emotions, cognitions, and bodily sensations;

- Relative to oneself and to the relationship with others;
- Developed during childhood and adolescence;
- Elaborated throughout life;
- Dysfunctional to a significant degree.

There are many classifications of personalities to evaluate the presence of personality patterns that govern the behaviors and emotions of individuals. In this section, I will highlight some of the "schema therapy" of Young et al. (2003). In Figure 10.8, we can see the seven dimensions of the emotional temperament that these authors defend.

The patterns of abandonment/instability and imperfection/shame will be more characteristic in people who inhibit their anger and annoyance, and have tendencies to be caregivers and perfectionists. The characteristics are:

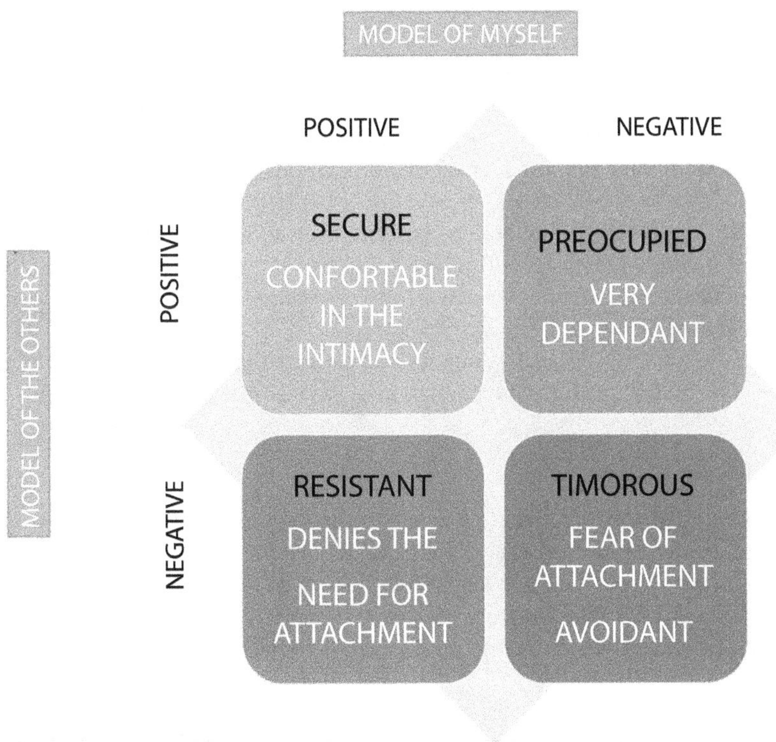

Figure 10.3 Dimensions of emotional temperament. According to Young et al. (2003), these have been identified by revising the scientific literature and their own observations.

Pattern of abandonment/instability: They have the feeling that the important people in their life will not be there because they are emotionally unpredictable, they are only there erratically, or they will die or leave the patient for someone better.

Pattern of imperfection/shame: Equivalent to the feeling that one is imperfect, bad, or undeserving and that, if exposed to others, they will not love them.

The patterns of grandiosity and insufficient self-control and self-discipline will be more characteristic of individuals with narcissistic features who project their anger outward, never feeling guilty for anything bad that happens to them.

Grandiosity pattern: These individuals feel special. They try to control others to meet their needs. They consider others inferior and useless. No one lives up to their expectations. They blame everyone else when things do not go as they think they deserve.

Pattern of insufficient self-control: They have problems controlling themselves and setting goals they can accomplish. They have no capacity to tolerate discipline, and are unable to contain their emotions and impulses. They tend to have antisocial behaviors and blame others for everything that does not go well; they look for short-term gratifications.

Obviously, we will not find these personality traits in all patients, nor in a pure way, but it will happen very often, and it will be very useful when we work on psychoeducation throughout therapy as well as with all the work related to the traumatic experiences of the past.

In Table 10.6, we find questions for our patients that help us to know what their most common patterns are in relation to the disorder that concerns us.

Conclusions

The conceptualization or gathering of the patient's history is crucial when dealing with any treatment and especially in anxiety and panic disorders. On many occasions, we can perform it in the first sessions in an orderly manner, but often, due to the discomfort or inability to give a coherent speech or the urgency to alleviate the symptoms that cause much suffering in the patient, this will not be possible. In these cases, we should start with psychoeducation and/or stabilization (see Chapters 11 and 13 respectively) before we can gather the history.

The gathering of information should include data on both the medical and psychological history of the disorder and the personal history of the patient, personality traits, attachment figures, and their relationship with them. In this way, we can get to know the patient and, above all, the patient can get to know himself. We will find data that will be narrated by the patient (explicit memory), but

Table 10.6 Some open-ended questions that we can ask to know the tendency of the person for some personality traits or others

Pleasing personalities, the "I'm sorry" syndrome
Do you worry too much about what others may think of you?
Do you worry too much about other people getting angry with you?
Do you avoid conflicts and arguments at any price?
Do you always put the needs of others ahead of your own?
Do you find it hard to say no, even when you realize that they are taking advantage of you?
Do you absorb the stress of others, and make too much effort and interest for others to be well?
Personalities with fear of loss/separation and conflict
Do you worry excessively about the safety and well-being of your family and loved ones?
Are you constantly worried about the possibility of separating yourself or losing one or some of your loved ones?
Do you worry too much about being alone or having a situation that you cannot face alone or getting sick?
Do you worry too much about your health, about death in general, or about dying yourself?
Personalities with emotional inhibition
Do you try to hide your emotions for fear of bothering or hurting others?
Do you minimize or conceal feelings of frustration, anger or resentment within yourself to avoid a confrontation?
Do you feel that you hide feelings of sadness or anger?
Do you think showing sadness or anger is a sign of weakness?
Is not being a bother or a burden one of your greatest characteristics as a person?
Narcissistic personalities
Do you feel that you are often wrong?
When was the last time you said someone was right and recognized that you had made a mistake?
What opinion do you hold of your family, colleagues, etc.?
How do you feel when you are not right?
Do you usually feel easily satisfied?
Do you usually interpret the comments of others as something personal?
Are you very sensitive to success and failure?
How do you think others see you?

we must also investigate gaps in the narration, contradictions, or inconsistencies that denote aspects contained in implicit memory (often forgotten or not considered relevant), which are crucial for understanding the origins of the disorder.

In any case, it is important to emphasize that the collecting of information will be present throughout the entire treatment. As we proceed, new data will appear that will be very relevant or different nuances of events already included in the history will emerge that will help the patient and the therapist to cast a new light on the history of the disorder.

It is important during this phase that the patient be able to ask everything he needs to know. Often when we advance in therapy, we will have to explain again many concepts or guidelines that help the patient to know himself better and to be able to change what is pathological.

References

Balluerka, N., Lacasa, F., Gorostiaga, A., Muela, A., & Pierrehumbert, B. (2011). Versión reducida del cuestionario CaMir (CaMir-R) para la evaluación del apego. *Psicothema, 23*(3), 486–494.

Bartholomew, K. (1990). Avoidance of intimacy: An attachment perspective. *Journal of Social and Personal Relationships*, *7*, 147–178.

Bretherton, R. (1985). Attachment theory: Retrospect and prospect. *Monographs of the Society for Research in Child Development*, *50*(1&2), 3–35.

Feeney, J., & Noller, P. (1996). *Adult attachment*. Sage Publications.

Leeds, A. (2012). *EMDR therapy basics and beyond*. Guilford Press.

Morrell, F. (1990). *Kindling and synaptic plasticity: The legacy of Graham Goddard*. Birkhauser.

Payas, A. (2012). *Las tareas del duelo. Psicoterapia del duelo desde un modelo integrativo-relacional*. Paidos.

Putnam, F. (1997). *Dissociation in children and adolescents. A developmental perspective*. The Guilford Press.

Rollnick, S., & Miller, W. R. (1995). *Motivational interviewing: Preparing people for change*. Guilford Press.

Steinberg, M. D., & Schnall, M. (2003). *The strange in the mirror. Dissociation the hidden epidemic*. Harper.

Young, J. E., Klosko, J. S., & Weishaar, M. E. (2003). *Schema therapy: A practitioner's guide*. Guilford Press.

11 Psychoeducation

Not having had a sense of control during childhood and the strategies that have been created to feel that one has it (or the need to not feel that there is no possibility of control) have been the pillars on which the psychological deterioration began to build. The therapist will try to give back that feeling of control over the emotions, behaviors and thoughts that lead to healing. Through psychoeducation – helping the patient to better know what was the origin of their problem and why it is maintained at present – we can get them to begin to understand what is happening to them and, therefore, feel that they can change it. It is a crucial part of the treatment that will have two main objectives:

1. Strengthen the therapeutic alliance; helping the patient to feel heard and cared for. People who suffer from emotional disorders have often had the feeling of being invisible, unattended, or even assaulted. Making our patients feel cared for throughout the treatment process will help them rectify those negative experiences that are the basis of the disorder.
2. Give patient a feeling of control. Patients who come to treatment with these disorders have the feeling that they have lost control over their body, their emotions, and their thoughts. Explaining how their brain and body works will help them to understand what is happening to them and they can create, with our help, strategies that allow them to begin to feel that their problem has a solution and that nothing strange is happening to them.

There are four aspects that are crucial in psychoeducation in order to explain what is happening to patients and help them understand their problems and start creating solutions:

- How are we going to work throughout treatment?
- What are emotional disorders?
- How does our childhood influence us throughout our life?
- What are dissociative disorders?

DOI: 10.4324/9781003646341-13

How Are We Going to Work Throughout Treatment?

As we have said before, it is impossible to exhaustively plan the treatment because, throughout it, hidden traumas may appear, situations that require immediate attention in the present, or symptoms that we will have to reduce in order to start doing deeper therapeutic work.

Throughout the book we will find how to work on each of the phases exhaustively, but our goal in this part of the therapy should be to create confidence in that the patients will feel better with the treatment and that they can trust us, yet without giving more information than necessary because we would only manage to overwhelm the patient and disorient him more. Let us not forget that patients need to believe that we are in control at all times. It is necessary to involve the patient in the process but only with what is strictly necessary to generate trust and a sense of control.

The therapist will have a map of the process that we will only share with the patient as it becomes strictly necessary, and the stages will vary according to the needs of the patient. As an example we may say:

> *I'm going to help you relax here in the session and explain techniques and give you audio recordings so you can relax at home (I have hypnosis recordings that I send to the client). If at any time you are very upset or feel that you need to tell me something or there are things you do not understand, it is very important that you tell me, so I can explain it to you as many times as necessary.*
>
> *I will explain in detail why your mind and body react as they do. Maybe you have the feeling that all this happens for no apparent reason, but in nature there are no coincidences and we have to understand why all this happens inside your mind.*
>
> *Throughout your life, things have occurred that, combined with genetic and biological aspects, have caused this disease that you suffer from now. I know that it is very important for you to reduce the symptoms that you have and I am going to help you do it. But for me as a therapist it is also very important to eliminate the causes that brought about this disorder to give you tools so that it won't happen again.*
>
> *I'm going to ask you questions to get to know you better. If any of them bother you or you do not remember, just tell me. Maybe, during treatment, new things may appear that are relevant and we will add them to our roadmap.*
>
> *If you find it comforting, I'll give you some forms to fill out either here or between sessions with different questions that will help us see what the symptoms are like and if there is improvement during the treatment.*
>
> *As I told you, we are going to work with the origin of the disease and to help you feel that you can regain control of your life. You will see that as I*

help you to know yourself better and you understand why your body and mind cause these symptoms, you will begin to control them and feel much better.

Finally, as it cannot be avoided, I will help you to face situations that scare you. You will see how many times you will succeed only as the therapy progresses as if the problem was diluted little by little and you feel that you need to do different things that you did not dare to do before. In other cases, I will have to help you to face them in a conscious way so that these fears become a thing of the past.

At the end of the therapy, when you are much or completely better, we will see each other occasionally (once a month at the beginning, afterwards every three months) to check if there has been any relapse or any problem that I can help you with. Know that you can contact me at any time you need to, the doors here are always open for you.

What Are Emotional Disorders?

We have talked about this topic previously in the first chapters of this book. Although in that part we elaborated in depth on the biological aspects that led to the emotional disorders, we will return to them in this section in a much more didactic way. We must be careful not to use any scientific jargon that our patients are unable to understand. It is very important to explain the biological aspects of the disorder with a language that patients can understand and thus assimilate everything we tell them. Depending on their cultural level or the patient's interests and academic training we can use a more metaphorical, technical, or exhaustive language in the explanations we offer.

I will use simple language in this section which is the one I use with my patients to explain to them the origin of their disease and the symptoms of the emotional disorders. To delve into these topics, please refer to Chapter 2 or the specialized bibliography.

Below is one explanation I usually give my patients. (This text is general for all types of emotional disorders and the therapist must adapt it to the patient's personal circumstances, be it an obsessive disorder, a social phobia, or anxiety disorders).

Our brain has evolved over millions of years, becoming increasingly complex. We have been acquiring characteristics throughout our evolution that we still share with the rest of the animals.

We share the most basic elements for survival with reptiles, such as breathing, reproducing, sleeping, eating, feeling pain ... this is the most primitive part of our brain and it is right at the point that unites our head with our back. This part of the brain reflects the most primitive emotions such as fear or sexual desire. It is responsible for the sensations that we feel in our body when, for example, we are hungry or something scares us.

We share emotions with monkeys and some mammals, such as taking care of our children or relatives, being in a group, feeling bad when someone suffers; it is a part of the brain that is much more related to emotions. It is the part that stores the memory of how our relationship with our parents, our brothers and grandparents or with our friends was. The organs in this part of the brain store a memory of traumas, for example, and it is the one that will store the memory of something that was dangerous in the past and will try to protect us, so that it does not hurt us again.

Human beings have a part of the brain that is not shared with any other living being; it is the part that allows us to produce language or make tools or recognize ourselves in a mirror. This part is responsible for thinking. It is the part that tells us what is logical or what we should do.

The two first parts of the brain that we share with the rest of the living beings are what we call "unconscious," because they handle situations that we cannot control. Imagine that you meet someone, you can like him or not – independent of your will – or that you cannot control being thirsty or sleepy or afraid. It is this part that is going to be the one that controls what things you are afraid of, even when they don't make any sense.

The third part of the brain that only we humans have is what we call "conscious" and it is the part that tells us what is logical or what we should not do. I'll give you an example: Imagine a smoker who the doctor has told to quit smoking. That person consciously knows that he spends money that he does not have, that he can get cancer, etc., but unconsciously he has an addiction and cannot quit. There is a struggle between what his conscious mind tells him and what his unconscious mind allows; and both are in the same head. So, it is very normal that the person does not quite understand what is happening to him.

The same thing happens with fears: I can be afraid of dogs or elevators or high places, and I consciously know that nothing will happen to me, but unconsciously I panic. At some point in my past, parts of my brain (maybe when I was very young) understood that some things were dangerous and no matter how long ago it was, those parts are going to continue believing that those things are dangerous.

*It is obvious that there are fears that are innate and others that are acquired over time (we're all scared of lions, but only some us are afraid of pigeons). So, when my unconscious brain perceives something that is dangerous for me, it will react to defend me, making my body go into flight or fight mode either to attack, run away or defend myself. The sensations of warning that I feel in my body is what we call "*anxiety,*" and, as we have all been able to confirm at some point, they can be extremely unpleasant.*

*This fear of situations or things that cause fear are what we call "*phobias*" and as they provoke very unpleasant sensations in us, we avoid anything that* *causes us a phobia. My unconscious brain will be alert and will try to protect me against anything or any situation that reminds me of that phobia. But, in addition, the thing gets a little more complicated because the human being, through thought, is the only animal that can have phobias to things that are real to us. For example, you may be afraid of things that could happen (for example, see black clouds and fear that a storm may come) or have phobias to things that are not particular to something real, which is what I call* "intangible phobias."

Human beings may be afraid to make a fool of themselves, afraid to love and not be reciprocated, not to be worthy. That is, there are many phobias in us that are related to guilt and especially to shame, which we do not share with any other being (can you imagine a zebra ashamed of being naked?), but which cause the same or worse discomfort as a phobia to something real. Since the suffering of the anxiety is added to the feeling of not knowing what is happening to them, it becomes clear why many people avoid places or activities where they have to relate to others.

In the case of a patient suffering from panic attacks, we could explain it like this: What happens if the alarm system that causes the anxiety has been activated for a long time by situations that I experienced in my past, such as depressions, my parents fighting, loss of loved ones? The alarm system explodes, and I start having very strong anxiety attacks that produce fear of having a heart attack or dying, and when I go to the hospital they tell me it is anxiety. So, added to the fear of dying is the fear of going crazy because I do not know what is happening to me. We call this "panic attacks" and they are very, very unpleasant.

People who suffer these attacks do not know why they have them or where they can have them, and begin to develop phobias for places where they think they may happen again. Some people even begin to be afraid of going out. We call this "agoraphobia." *Those who suffer these attacks are afraid of doing things alone for fear that something will happen to them. Since they cannot control the situation, they need to be surrounded by people they trust, to feel safe. What they do not realize is that the more they avoid these situations or let themselves be accompanied by other people, the more the unconscious brain reaffirms that there is a danger and as such will increase the fear and anxiety every time they do something.*

The symptoms that you have, although they are very unpleasant, are something natural produced by the warning reaction of your mind. The most common symptoms that occur when we have anxiety are heart palpitations, tremors, excessive sweating, dry mouth, suffocation, nausea and/or discomfort in the stomach, pressure/pain in the chest and/or heart, vertigo or dizziness and, in cases of panic attacks, fear of dying, fear of going crazy, and fear of fainting.

Another problem is that if the unconscious part of our brain does not find something specific to be afraid of, it begins to develop more and more fear of things. As a result, anxiety causes us to avoid more and more situations and may even cause fear that something bad will happen to our loved ones.

Can you better understand now why your body reacts like this to situations that cause you fear? It tries to help you avoid situations that you consider dangerous, even if you know consciously that they are not.

Little by little, throughout the therapy, we will help the unconscious part of your brain learn that these irrational fears are not necessary and, therefore, the anxiety will gradually disappear. The symptoms will improve as you understand the origin of your problem and how you have arrived at this situation, and we will also give you tools for you to act differently so that your brain stops perceiving danger where there is none.

How Does Our Childhood Influence Us Throughout Our Lives?

We have already elaborated exhaustively on the importance that attachment relationships have during childhood and adulthood in the etiology of the disorder. In this section, we will explain to the patient how the relationships we had with our caregivers in our childhood influence our way of living the world in the present.

It is very important to highlight that this part of psychoeducation must be done very carefully because, while attachment relationships will be vital in the origin of the disorder, it is also where we will find the most defenses when conducting the therapy (Leeds, 2012). We will find idealization of the caregivers, phobias of traumatic memories, fear of breaking the bonds, fear of being naughty for criticizing the parents, and so on. We will look at how to work with all this in detail in Chapter 15 on defenses.

During this phase, it is crucial to go at a pace that the patient can tolerate, because if we activate defenses, the only thing we will accomplish is breaking the therapeutic alliance and maybe even losing the patient. The stronger the bond, the more will we be able to deal with everything related to attachment, which, although it is the origin of the problem, is also the trickiest part of the treatment.

As in the previous section, we used more or less colloquial language depending on the needs of the patient. An example would be:

All human beings are born with basic emotions that are genetically programmed and that are unconscious. They include fear, the need to relate to others, or attachment to the people who care for us, among others. Can you imagine a 3-month-old zebra separating from the herd? How long could it survive without being hunted by an animal or starved? Very briefly, right? Almost everything related to our caregivers we share at brain level with most mammals and, therefore, for a human child it is vital to have physical and emotional contact with its parents.

Like the zebra that loses its mother in the herd, if a small child feels that he is not in physical or emotional contact with his caregivers, he will feel discomfort at first, fear later and, after a while, he will panic. There are many situations in which this rupture will occur (and are necessary for the child to learn to be alright on his own or to trust other people), but if these breaks are very frequent and/or last too long or caregivers mistreat the child, his brain will be hyperactivated by a constant feeling of fear.

This constant activation of the fear circuit during childhood will cause physiological alterations in the child that will be important throughout the rest of his life. I'd like to explain it using a metaphor: When there is an earthquake in Japan, there is hardly any material damage nor are there victims. The same earthquake in Nepal causes significant destruction and thousands of deaths. Why? Because of the houses' foundations. Our relationship with our caregivers during our childhood will be the pillars on which we will build the edification of our personality.

A child who has his cerebral circuit of fear hyperactivated during his childhood will most likely have alterations in his brain chemistry that will make him hypersensitive in his reactions to the problems of life, his relationships with others, and his fears and phobias.

*(*Attention*: the next part should be explained to the patient only when we are sure that the therapeutic alliance is very strong):*

Perhaps you can remember events in your childhood and adolescence such as being mistreated or abused, having lost a loved one or having been very sick, having felt alone or rejected. These experiences of the past can help you to understand much of the symptoms that you are having now and why your circuit of fear is hyperactivated and causes you anxiety.

But many times, it doesn't take something very serious to cause discomfort in your relationship with your parents or other caregivers: one of your parents may suffer from depression, or there might have been frequent fights at home, or a feeling that they do not love you or you feel less loved than some sibling, that your mother or your father or both have leaned too much on you, making you responsible for things for which you were not prepared at your age. All this can also cause alarm signals in our brain that permanently and insidiously make us unable to relax at any time, for fear of provoking the rejection of others or feeling alone. And when we are adults and we lose a loved one or someone rejects us, our alarm system, which was already quite overloaded, explodes without us being able to understand why and we can have extremely unpleasant symptoms, about which we do not know why they are produced or where they come from.

There are people who are afraid to make a fool of themselves in public (for example, when sweating too much or having a rumbling stomach) which may lead them to avoid relating to others or, even worse, to suffer very acute anxiety attacks or even panic attacks, making them feel that they are going to die and being afraid that something bad could happen to them or their loved ones.

Even if it seems absurd to you, your unconscious mind tries to defend you from something it considers dangerous even if you consciously feel that it makes no sense. Think that until about the age of 10 almost all of our learning is unconscious and that in the first 4 years of life, we learn 80% of what we will learn throughout our lives.

Your unconscious mind tries to help you in a way that hurts you and makes you suffer, and we have to make it act differently. In order to do that, the first thing is to know why it does things in a way that is so painful for you. One of the ways that your unconscious helps you during your childhood is by making you responsible for things that go wrong in relation to your parents. It is better to believe "I am defective" than to believe that "my parents are defective," because until adolescence the priority of your mind is to remain attached to your parents. That's why your mind makes you feel a lot of guilt and shame, because it was necessary as a child to do this, so you could maintain the bond.

A bit of guilt and shame are necessary and healthy to be able to live in society, but when they are excessive, they become pathological and make people suffer a lot because it makes them incapable of leading a normal life. We will be working to find out what your childhood and your relationship with your close family was like. If something really painful, serious, or traumatic happened during the first years of your life, we may find an explanation for the origin of your illness, and if nothing important has happened, it will help me to know you better in order to help you with your problem.

What Is Traumatic Dissociation?

The traumatic dissociation of the personality is very complex (Van der Hart et al., 2006), even for psychologists and health professionals. Although it is necessary to know how to deal with it when working with psychological traumas, it is also unknown to most people outside the world of psychology and can be confused with disorders such as psychosis. Therefore, we must be careful when explaining it.

It will be a fundamental pillar on which we will build much of the therapeutic work. We must devote all the time that is necessary to psychoeducation on this section. Explaining in a simple way what the parts of the personality are, the reason why these parts are created, the function they fulfill, and how we are going to work with them will make the work much easier during the intervention.

As always, we will use simple and accessible language, using more technical or colloquial language depending on the needs of the patient. When providing psychoeducation while working with the parts, we can use metaphors from the Internal Family Systems Model (Schwartz, 1995; Earley, 2012) which is very pedagogical and accessible for patients.

Each one of us, depending on our circumstances, develops different ways of behaving towards others, facing challenges, facing life. This is what we call personality. There are characteristics in each of us that will make us behave in one way or another in different circumstances. Of course, personality is something very personal that cannot be seen or touched, although surely for everyone who knows us, and even for ourselves, there is an image or certain expectations of how we are going to behave at different times.

Personality can change depending on what we are doing, who we are doing it with, or even where we are doing it. Human beings have the ability to adapt to their environment based on their characteristics. For example, I cannot behave the same here with you in consultation as I would if I were with some friends in a bar watching a football game of my favorite team.

As we grow older, our neurons form networks with each other to identify circumstances of events that occurred in the past in order to remember how we should act in response to that stimulus if it occurs again. For example, imagine a girl who got bit by a dog as a child. Her neurons store a memory that dogs are dangerous, and when she is an adult and sees a dog she will feel fear. In other words, you will have a "part of your personality" that will be phobic to dogs.

But imagine that there is a child who suffers bullying at school. When he is an adult, he may be afraid to be rejected and, depending on how serious the harassment has been, it may be very difficult for him to relate to others or speak in public, and he may even develop a social phobia.

The more intense the experience that we have had, the more neurons will be included in the memory and that part will be more present. If the experience has been very good, I will want to repeat it often, and if it has been very bad, I will want to avoid it at all costs.

If something has happened many times or has been very intense, this part can become a somewhat rigid part of my personality and becomes something that forces me to do things even though I know that I may regret it later. The more intense and the younger the age when this part was created, the more rigid and independent it will be.

So, I will be the one who is "the self" plus the different parts of my personality that will be activated or inhibited depending on the circumstances. Many of these parts I like very much and others will cause me a lot of displeasure and, although I have tried to change them many times, in the end they appear again, in fact very often; the more I try to banish them or ignore them, the stronger they become and the more often they appear. Maybe you have come to therapy because there are parts of your personality which, instead of helping you, are hurting you and you need to change them so that you can be happy or just lead a normal life.

I'm going to give you an example I think will help you:

Imagine a girl whose parents spend the day working and her grandmother has to take care of her. The girl loves her family very much but feels very lonely, and that loneliness causes her a lot of discomfort. When she feels bad, she looks for her grandmother to talk to or play with, and her grandmother, who loves her dearly, always gives her food and constantly insists she eat (it's her way of telling her she loves her). The girl is not hungry but she eats all the food because she feels that if she does not, her grandmother will be sad. When her parents get home, they are very tired and they ask the girl if she has studied and insist that she has to get very good grades so that she can go far in life and not have the life that they have had; they are sacrificing so much so she can have a better life than the ones they have had. The years go by and this girl has become a woman, and those parts that were created when she was little are still there, and maybe she has come far in life and is obsessed with her work, and when she gets home and feels lonely she eats much more than she knows is good for her. The adult woman does not know why she acts like that, but we know that as a child she created a part that was happy when she ate with her grandmother and that perhaps she has associated happiness with food and another part that needs to be very effective in satisfying others. That is to say, she feels useful when she fulfills her responsibilities in a strict manner, but there is a hidden and very frightened part that is very afraid of loneliness and another part that makes her eat to feel better.

I'd like to divide them into different types:

- *Public part: This is the part that we show to others. It is the one we like to show and the one we feel more secure with most of the time. They are usually parts which work, study, and relate to other people who are not close to us. It is a conscious part in the sense that we can handle it and show it at will.*
- *Impulsive parts: These are very energetic, and when they appear, they do so very hastily and without measuring the consequences of their actions – like a group of firefighters who are going to put out a fire and do everything possible to accomplish it, regardless of the collateral damage. They are what cause people to get into drugs, fall in love with people who harm them, or binge and then vomit. They will do anything so that the person does not suffer, even if the results are worse than those they try to avoid. If you recognize these parts inside, maybe you do not like them, but even if it seems like a lie, they want to help you; they do it in the only way they*

know how and you have to help them do it differently. Other psychologists call them Emotional Parts (EP) and, in this case, they would be focused on defending against pain and fear.

- *Controlling parts: These parts are executive; they are dedicated to the things of daily life. They are centered on studying, work, caring for children – in short, on fulfilling daily life. Another group of psychologists call it the Apparently Normal Part (ANP).*
- *Hurt parts: These are the parts that suffered the pain of fear or loneliness or rejection. The greater the damage that was done to the child, the more frightened these parts will be and the more active the firefighter parts will be to protect them. The priority of all parts will be to prevent the child from feeling the pain again, and no matter how many years it's been, the pain will still be there. We cannot forget that these unconscious parts live in an eternal present and do not grow or change with age. These parts will also be called EP but will focus on avoiding suffering and pain.*
- *Rejected parts: These are those parts that we try to hide from others and, most of the time, from ourselves. They represent everything that we do not like about us. Most of the time they coincide with what the people surrounding us when we were little did not like, or so we thought.*

Do you better understand now why many of your symptoms make you think that you are not in control of your life or why you are so afraid of some situations, or you can't stop doing something even though you feel it hurts you? They are different parts of your personality that take over depending on the circumstances. Can you imagine an orchestra that did not have a director? Each musician would play his instrument without taking the others into account and it would be chaos, similar to when the orchestra begins to tune their instruments. I will help you to be the director of your internal orchestra so that all your parts participate in an orderly way and you can create a delightful sound from your life.

Conclusions

Anxiety is a sign in our body that occurs when we are faced with a danger that we often do not know about. Psychoeducation is very important during the first phases of therapy in order to help patients know what is happening to them. By being able to understand it, they will begin to have a sense of control over what happens to them.

In this chapter, I have didactically developed four aspects that I think are very important: the origin of fear and how it influences our body; the importance of attachment in our lives; dissociation and how it sometimes causes us to act in a way that hurts us, but is unavoidable; and how the therapeutic model will be developed. During this phase, it is important that patients are given the chance to ask everything they need to ask. When we advance in therapy, we will often have to re-explain many concepts or guidelines that help patients get to know themselves better so as to be able to change what is pathological.

References

Earley, J. (2012). *Working with anger in internal family systems therapy*. Pattern System Books.

Leeds, A. (2012). *EMDR therapy basics and beyond*. Guilford Press.

Schwartz, R. C. (1995). *Internal family systems therapy*. Guilford Press.

Van der Hart, O., Nijenhuis, E. R. S., & Steele, K. (2006). *The haunted self: Structural dissociation and the treatment of chronic traumatization*. Norton & Company.

12 Dissociation and Working with Parts

Raskolnikov, the protagonist of Crime and Punishment, *suffers a life of misery and hardship. Forced to leave his studies because he is unable to pay for them, he turns to an old and greedy lender to loan him some money to survive. A part of him feels frustrated and believes that he deserves a great future comparable to that of Napoleon. Another part of his personality is angry because his sister is going to get married without having consulted him, and yet another incubates the idea of killing the old usurer and thus leaving his debt paid.*

At the end of the novel, prey to the chaos he feels inside, he accepts that he is a normal man and that he deserves to be punished according to his actions. Imprisoned in a labor camp in Siberia, he finds love and finally feels that he has a real goal in life and is true to himself.

In the novel, Dostoevsky masterfully describes the psychological struggle the character has with himself, trying to find something that gives meaning to his life: an inner struggle between the different parts of his personality that fight to give him that meaning.

Janet (2003) was the first to highlight the defensive function of the dissociation of the "unconscious" as a way to reduce anxiety and psychic conflict in the human mind. He proposed that dissociation serves defensive and adaptive purposes, including automation of behavior, efficiency and mental economy, resolution of conflicts that are unsolvable, isolation in catastrophic situations, cathartic discharge to certain emotions, and providing order and sense where only chaos is perceived (Putnam, 1997).

In everyday life, dissociation would be the ability to do two things at once, for example when we drive a car and have a conversation at the same time. If something dangerous happens on the road, all our attention will be focused on avoiding that danger. We all have the experience of not remembering whether we have forgotten something we had to do, or forgetting things that were important at the time but that we have stored in our memory over time.

In situations where there is a very strong emotional experience, our brain can create compartments (Putnam, 1997) wherein we store events or emotions in isolation that cause much pain when evoked. In some very serious cases, such as sexual abuse, they can remain amnesic. The compartmentalization allows us to

DOI: 10.4324/9781003646341-14

leave aside situations that have been very painful in the form of implicit memory. The younger the age and the greater the threat, the scarcer the emotional and cognitive tools will be to be able to respond to that situation and the greater the compartmentalization or dissociation will be.

Human beings have what we call "action systems" (Van der Hart et al., 2005) which are those elements that make up one's personality and are constituted by parts that are conscious (ANP) and others that are unconscious or emotional (EP). These action systems can be of two types:

- Action systems focused on gratification and daily life;
- Action systems focused on defense, mostly on avoiding and protecting against aversive stimuli.

Imagine we are returning home at night and have to go through a dangerous area. We decide to take a taxi to avoid risks. In this case, it would be the ANP that makes the decision to do something to avoid a danger. If, instead, we decide to walk and we see someone who threatens us and without thinking we run in the opposite direction, it would be an EP that has taken control, making us act impulsively and unconsciously.

We all have different action systems for different moments or activities. It is not the same to go to work at the office, to go hiking in the mountains, or to go out dancing and drinking at night. Each of these actions will require different behaviors, cognitions, and emotions, that is, different resources. In people with structural dissociation of the personality, the dissociated parts will tend to achieve their own objectives without taking into account the needs of the system as a whole. Each part will have its own age, memories, and priorities which differ from other parts of that same person. The greater the dissociation, the greater the autonomy of these parts will be and the less connected they will be. There may even be phobias between these parts.

The action systems are acquired and will become more sophisticated as we grow up. In the first years of our life, they will be closely related to our caregivers. If, in the first years of our life, there are traumatic situations, the systems will create a dysfunctional organization that can persist, even when as adults everything is normal in our lives (Van der Hart et al., 2005). According to these authors:

> Some action systems mediate mental and behavioral actions concerning daily life, and include exploration of the environment (including work and study), play, energy management (sleeping and eating), attachment, sociability, reproduction, and care taking (especially rearing children) (e.g., Cassidy, 2000; Panksepp, 2004). Other action systems are dedicated to defensive actions in response to threat (by another person) to the integrity of the body,

> social rejection, and attachment loss. This defensive action system, which human beings share with many animals, involves several subsystems: hypervigilance, freeze, flight, fight, total submission. In the case of trauma-related structural dissociation of the personality, the coordination and cohesion of action systems appear to be disrupted, so that survivors' actions are not well-adapted to prevailing circumstances.
>
> (p. 3)

When we are working in therapy and have access to those implicit memories that were dissociated, we can see reactions of fear, anger, crying, and pain which are identical to those experienced in the moment of trauma that could not be expressed. In many cases, our patients will tell us that they are surprised by their reaction because they thought they had overcome it or because they did not even remember it. When there is an emotional impact and the neurons become related to each other, what is known as an "engram" is created. Engrams are neural networks that store the memory of trauma so as to learn from the experience and to defend themselves if there is a similar threat. These engrams can be associated with phobias (tangible or intangible) or activities that prevent discomfort (e.g., addictions) or create personality traits that help regulate discomfort (e.g., taking care of others to feel useful and loved).

We have engrams at the cortical level that are conscious and drive our daily life. They are the ones that, for example, help us to know how to do a task or to decide when we should go to an appointment. At the unconscious level, they will be stored in procedural memory. They are the ones who help us do things without constantly checking how to do them, for example, driving a car. The parts that are focused on tasks of daily life will be called the Apparently Normal Part of the personality (ANP; Van der Hart et al., 2005).

At the subcortical level, we have engrams that are related to emotions such as fear, anger, guilt, or shame. We will call these parts the emotional parts (EP) of one's personality. They are beyond our will; they act impulsively and that is why we call them "unconscious" (Van der Hart et al., 2005). In Figure 12.1 you can see a vertical distinction between conscious parts that correspond to actions that we perform willingly and another unconscious part that is beyond our control.

The younger the age at which these parts were created, the more related they were to a threat, and the greater this was, as well as the closer the figure of attachment that caused the fear, the greater the structural dissociation of the personality.

In summary, according to the theory of structural dissociation of the personality, we will have parts (engrams) that will be associated with different action systems, which may be related to everyday life or to defense. The work in therapy will consist of working with them to achieve their integration (the opposite of dissociation). The sequence that we will follow when working with parts will be:

DISSOCIATIVE PARTS OF THE PERSONALITY

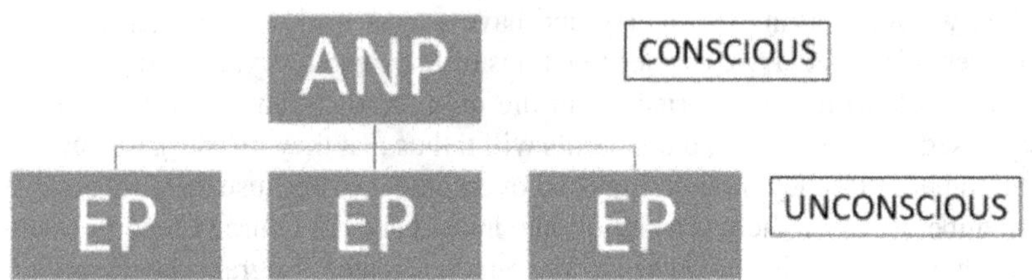

Figure 12.1 The parts of the personality may belong to its conscious or unconscious aspects

- Stabilization, function, and acknowledgment of the parts;
- Phobias among parts;
- Integration.

Stabilization and Acknowledgment of Parts

In order to work with parts, we must be clear that the following elements are present, although it is almost never possible for all of them to be given:

- Good emotional tolerance;
- Life environment as stable as possible;
- Willingness to undertake temporary discomfort to gain long-term relief;
- Good ego tolerance;
- Adequate social support;
- History of therapeutic compliance.

To know which parts are intervening and how they do this in the patient's mind, we can use models in which the parts are defined metaphorically (Schwartz, 1995; Earley, 2012). In order to better conceptualize the cases, I work with five types of parts, each with a different origin and a different function in the present:

- Public parts;
- Impulsive parts;
- Controlling parts;

- Hurt parts;
- Rejected parts.

In some cases, some parts may overlap with others. For example, a public part may be a rejected part at the same time, or an impulsive part may also be a controlling part. The model is proposed in order to better understand what parts exist within the system and, above all, what function they fulfill. To continue with the parallelism between the model of structural dissociation and another more metaphorical one to facilitate the work with these parts, we would obtain the following graph (Figure 12.2):

Public part or Self: This would be what the theory of structural dissociation calls ANP. It is the part from which the person interacts with the world and with other people. Due to traumatic experiences of the past, it has been very debilitated, and that can cause other internal parts to not see it as sufficiently strong and, as such, will not trust it. In a healthy and integrated person, the Self occupies a place of leadership and can control the different parts of the system. In a traumatized person, it has an observing role with the consequent feeling of ineffectiveness and impotence when relating to oneself or others.

COMPARISON OF STRUCTURAL MODEL AND METAPHORIC MODEL

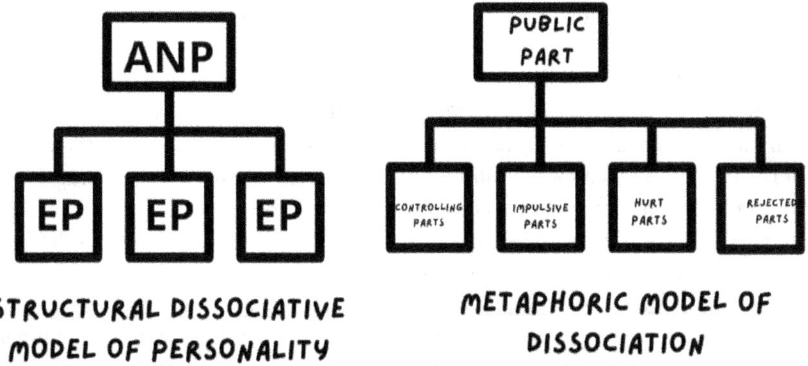

Figure 12.2 In these drawings, we can see the parallels between the structural dissociation model and metaphorical model of parts.

The goal of therapy would be to strengthen the Self so that the parts can trust it and the internal system can act in an effective and orderly manner. The parts want the Self to be strong, but as long as this does not happen, they will continue in their role for fear that the traumatic situation will repeat itself. As the therapy takes effect and the Self strengthens, the different parts will be integrated and coordinated, giving the patient a feeling of control.

A metaphor that can help to understand the role of this part and which can also be useful as psychoeducation would be the following: to work with this part we must reinforce and install resources in the patient, even if he believes he has none. We can even use the following:

> *Imagine an orchestra full of wind, string, and percussion musicians and that each one plays his instrument without coordinating with the others. It would be a chaos of noise. But what would happen if there was a conductor who would coordinate them? Then, beautiful music would sound. That is the role of the Self: to coordinate and direct the different parts of the system.*

T: You tell me you have no hope and that I'm your last resource. But it takes a lot of courage to come to therapy.

C: Yes, but I've come out of despair. I think I've hit rock bottom.

T. The good thing about hitting rock bottom is that you can only go up from there. What would your life be like if in three months the problem were to be solved?

Hurt parts: As children, we all had painful experiences of fear, guilt, or shame; these experiences are necessary to be able to live in society and know how to live with others. But if those experiences were very intense or traumatic, we would try to forget them or even hide them from our consciousness (dissociate them). These parts are like children who have been hurt, rejected, or abandoned. They are the parts we do not like about ourselves, and that is why the system rejects them.

The tendency of the other parts will be to remain hidden and not manifested so that they do not interfere with the rest of the system. The fear that these parts will suffer again is what leads to avoidance strategies. But these parts desperately need to be taken care of and loved. However, because they are fragile and afraid of suffering, they are rejected by the rest of the system. Bringing them to the present causes a strong feeling of discomfort and pain (anxiety) in the individual, so the system spends a lot of energy keeping them isolated.

As time passes, these parts will be carrying more and more pain. Whenever there are situations similar to the one that originated it (e.g., real or imaginary rejection) these parts carry more pain and, consequently, more expenditure of energy in preventing them from coming to light, leaving the patient too exhausted to perform their daily life tasks.

It is very important to know that two opposing forces exist in the internal system of the patient: a centrifugal one (from the inside out) of the rejected or wounded parts of discharging the pain and being listened to and cared for (having a corrective experience of the initial emotion); and a centripetal force (from the outside in) of the impulsive or controlling parts to avoid suffering the same pain again.

T. It seems like you had a very complicated situation at school with sensations of rejection and loneliness, right?
C. The truth is that I had never looked at it like that before, but it seems that I did.
T. Did you often feel that sensation during your childhood?
C. Well, now that you mention it, it's possible that I did as a child, because my parents worked all day and I was always with my grandmother.
T. I think about that child who feels lonely and I feel sorry for him, doesn't the same happen to you?
C. It's something I'd forgotten, and the truth is that I'd rather not remember it.

Controlling parts: They have protective tendencies as well as impulsive ones but they do so by trying to control uncertainty. They are very afraid that the rejected parts may come out or the injured parts will suffer again, or both.

These would be the parts responsible for personality schemes and can take on different roles in each person – usually those behaviors that the patient wants to change but cannot and does not know how.

- *Controlling parts*: They try to have the person be in control of everything that happens around him: relationships, work, activities, and so on. They are afraid that any loss of control may provoke the rejected parts to come out. They banish emotions, dealing only with the cognitive and the rational.
- *Inner critic part*: This is a part that does not allow for mistakes; it is the person's worst nightmare because he or she is afraid of doing something wrong and of the consequences this may have for others. This part cannot stand doing anything wrong and being rejected again.
- *Perfectionist part*: Everything has to be perfect, both in terms of physical appearance and behavior; this part thinks that in this way it will be accepted and will not be abandoned or damaged.
- *Passive-pessimist*: Tries to avoid intimacy or any activity in which it may fail, with excuses such as not being up to it, not having time, not liking the people it meets. It avoids risks of any kind; by doing nothing with anybody, it cannot go wrong.
- *Caregiver part*: This part believes that it will only be accepted and loved as long as it takes care of others. Its function is to be always useful in relation to others.

- *Worried part*: This part always doubts everything and is never sure of anything; this way it avoids the risk of doing something and making a mistake, with the dreaded consequences this involves.
- *Narcissist part*: This part avoids rejection by looking down on everyone; it is never wrong, and if something goes awry, it will always blame the mistakes on others.
- *Aggressive part*: This part is always on the defensive, always angry with everyone. It constantly looks for physical aggression.

The more dissociated other parts are, the more rigid the controlling parts will be. These must not only defend the individual from external threats, but also from internal threats. The longer they have been fulfilling their role, the more rigid and inflexible they will be. These parts, unlike the public part, are ego-dystonic; the patient perceives them as negative in order to be happy. In many cases in which there are personality disorders, the controlling parts will coincide with the public part.

Impulsive parts: These will appear when, despite the efforts of the controlling parts, there is something that can emerge and come to the surface, with all the associated pain. These parts are beyond the control of the patient and will do anything to prevent the injured or rejected parts from surfacing. Although the purpose of the impulsive parts is the same as that of the controlling ones, the way they achieve it is completely different. While the latter are rational and ego-syntonic, the rescuers are perceived as ego-dystonic, impulsive, and damaging.

The impulsive parts are those that cause the person to have obsessions or to compulsively get high or eat. That is, they are the parts responsible for the compulsions and addictions that bring the patient to therapy. However, as we saw in the chapter on defenses, they are protecting the rejected parts in a way that ends up doing more harm than they try to avoid.

This model is very useful to mentally organize what role the different parts of the patient's internal system fulfill. Therefore, we must recognize them and, above all, help the patient to recognize them within himself. We can use, as we saw in the chapter on psychoeducation, explanations, so that the patient can mentalize and know their internal system and what role is being fulfilled by each of the parts that appear.

T. It looks like there's been a relapse?
C. Yes, I deeply regret it. I was so happy.
T. What happened?
C. I got into a fight with my girlfriend and I left the home. I called a friend to meet up and get something to drink and ... I knew what was going to happen, but I did it anyway. I got drunk and took cocaine. You don't know how much I regret that.

T. What was the most painful part of the argument with your girlfriend?
C. When she told me she didn't love me anymore. That's when I left so I wouldn't yell and do something worse to her.
T. It seems as if you chose to drink and get high so you wouldn't do something worse? I do not want to justify you, but it seems that by drinking you could forget about the fight. I wonder whether you could have done it in another way that would not have hurt you.

Rejected parts: They are those parts that the patient hides either because he does not like them or because they have been severely punished when they appeared in the past. They are parts that may feel very embarrassed or guilty, and that carry a lot of anger or pain.

They are usually very childlike parts that have been rejected by caregivers and that sustain the core of the problem because they are seen as fragile, helpless, or dangerous by the individual.

An example would be the rejected part in a girl who was abused in childhood and whose memory is amnesiac. It is a part with rage that has been very repressed by her caregivers. When these parts come to light they are usually replaced by impulsive parts that lead to taking drugs or compulsive sex or any uncontrolled behavior that will be perceived with much guilt by the public part.

T: You're saying that for three days you were drinking alcohol and taking drugs and you could not stop?
C. Yes. I can't stand these behaviors anymore, they're ruining my life, but when they come I can't stop them.
T. Did something happen before you started drinking and using drugs? A few days before, I mean?
C. I don't think so. Last week was normal, I went to my parents' town and they argued with each other over some silly thing, but they don't care anymore, even if they haven't seen me for a month.
T. How did you feel when you saw them arguing again without them caring that they had not seen you for so long?
C. I don't care. They've been doing it since I was little.
T. What would happen if you told them that it is a lack of respect towards you?
C. I already tried it and it's no use. I get frustrated for nothing.
T. Don't you think that this behavior of drinking and using drugs can be a way of not letting out the anger and helplessness you feel from seeing your parents arguing without respecting you?
C. I don't think so, I don't know, don't see it. But the truth is that whenever I have these crises it is after returning from my parents' home.

Public part	This is the one we show others. We may like it or not.
Impulsive parts	These are very extreme and are perceived as negative by the individual.
Controlling parts	They are parts that seek to have control. They are highly phobic towards the rest.
Hurt parts	They are the ones that sustained the damage. They are very childish.
Rejected parts	They are the parts we don't like about ourselves. They may form an alliance with the impulsive or controlling parts and tend to coincide with the hurt parts.

Most Common Parts

Emotional disorders are mainly based on four emotions, which are guilt, shame, and fear, and, associated with this, anger. Therefore, we will have emotional parts that will be associated with these emotions. They are in many cases rejected parts, towards which the rest of the system will feel phobia, either because they endure a lot of pain or because they are inappropriate at a social or personal level when they appear. Let us see how these parts work and how to work with them.

Fear-Related Parts

These parts are the ones that shoulder anger and fear. They are EPs focused on defense, and they can do this in two different ways: either by avoiding the conflict or creating it by taking on a very aggressive role. For hormonal reasons (testosterone is more abundant in men), we will see the former more frequently in women and the latter more often in men.

These parts carry everything related to fear, anger, impotence, and frustration. They are rejected by the rest of the system, either because they cause problems within the family or within society (such as physical violence) or because of their intensity, which leads to suppression and the appearance of symptoms to mask them (Busch & Milrod, 2004).

Anger is a basic emotion in all human beings (Panksepp & Biven, 2012) and should be discharged naturally either through crying, protest, or any other discharging mechanism. If it cannot be discharged and goes inward, it can lead to certain pathologies, and if it goes outward, it can lead to others.

The parts that kept the pain associated with fear and anger could not discharge it at the time and continue to bear it. This can happen for several reasons; the main ones are:

- Fear of failure: When showing being upset or angry, the caregivers showed hostile behavior and even aggression. That part learned to hide the anger because showing it could be counterproductive and even dangerous. Examples would be "good kids don't cry," "if you continue like this I'll give you a reason to cry," or even physical aggression.
- Fear of causing pain: That part learned not to show being upset or angry because it believed that it saddened or negatively affected their caregivers. An example would be "when I cry my mother gets sad" when the caregiver says, "look how you've made me feel" or "if you keep on crying, I'm going to start crying myself."
- Fear of appearing weak: Anger cannot be displayed because it is socially unacceptable and can provoke criticism or ridicule in others. It is necessary to contain it in public for fear of suffering shame.
- Fear of letting down: The role of good child has been greatly reinforced by the caregivers, comparing the child to a brother or a friend, highlighting how well they behave. If he gets angry, he is reminded of how good the other one always is. The anger is dissociated as something to be ashamed of. This part accumulates all the pain so that the other parts can continue to be reinforced by others. The contained part may end up appearing in adulthood as anxiety.

In all cases, by being unable to show anger, it gets dissociated and can become independent of the system, having its own motivations. In turn, this anger can be of three types:

- Controlling anger: This is a constant rage that manifests itself publicly. It tries to protect other parts that have been hurt and that this part perceives as weak. Paradoxically, although the part appears to protect the others, there is usually a lot of phobia amongst them.
- Rejected anger: This is the dissociated anger that cannot be displayed for fear of hurting others. It is the characteristic anger of an individual with a caring personality – someone who feels that she takes care of everyone and nobody takes care of her. The frustration that is felt cannot be manifested for it is unacceptable and transforms into anxiety or even panic attacks.
- Impulsive anger: Anger fulfills a controlling function of a rejected part that contains the pain and shame of something that happened. It is characteristic of individuals with a passive-aggressive personality.

People seek control mechanisms such as compulsive, addictive, or violent activities or tight control to avoid allowing the rejected parts to feel pain again. In therapy, you should work first by reducing the discomfort and emphasizing the pain that these angry parts bear and introduce the work with the rejected parts little by little.

Shame-Related Parts

These are the parts that, chronologically speaking, appear first in life; they are preverbal (Schore, 2010) and appear in somatic form. There are different opinions about the origin of shame in human beings. According to some authors, it is something innate and does not have a social origin in relation to others; it is a way of responding to any situation in which there is a rupture in something interesting. Other authors argue that its origin is the internalized image of anger or disappointment of the mother which causes an immediate halt of any feeling of search or well-being and an activation of the inhibition state. Furthermore, other authors, as we saw, sustain that it is an activation of the sympathetic system which, by not being calmed by the caregivers, is not deactivated by the parasympathetic system (Cozolino, 2010).

According to Miller (1990):

> The child who is very stressed because of abuse or neglect at a very young age, once he becomes aware of himself, can make sense of those internal states of discomfort (mom does not love me, I'm unfriendly, I'm alone) in relation to himself. I do not deserve to be loved, I am bad or I am not worthy. The thoughts of self-criticism that are less global could develop and create different ones such as: I have big feet, I am lazy or I am stupid.
>
> (p. 31)

This explains why many of the people who are afraid of being rejected focus that fear on a part of their body or their physiology that they consider to be defective. For example: "I cannot show my legs," "I am afraid of sweating in public," or "I am ashamed of people seeing my ears."

In any case, shame is a universal emotion that is present in all human beings on the planet regardless of origin or culture (DeYoung, 2015). It fulfills a function that helps one to be *able* to interact with others and create social norms that allow achieving a common good that is above the private good. You can feel shame both in social situations and when failing at tasks that are carried out without the gaze of another. Then, the critical look is internalized. As shame grows, it becomes more automatic and more immersed in mental schemes and less dependent on external circumstances.

The feeling of shame in childhood is perceived as very painful, and many defenses are created to never feel that sensation again. Parts associated with dissociated discomfort are created in order to continue having a relationship with the caregivers and perceive that the situation can be improved and/or controlled. In our patients, the part that we will find more frequently is the part associated with rejection.

Rejection-Related Part

This is the part that suffered the rejection and coincides with the wound. It is the one that felt inferior. It is a part perceived with much fear by the rest of the system, which sees it as defective. This part is the most delicate and the most infantile. It is the one that is going to be the object of the therapy and probably will be one of the last ones that we should work with. This part is the one that hides all the pain.

The other parts (controlling and impulsive) will do everything possible so that it does not suffer pain again and, thus, suffer more. It is a part that is rejected not only by the outside world but also by the internal system. That is why there are many phobias among parts that we must work on with a lot of compassion before accessing it.

The symptoms that we see in our patients with excessive fear or shame of relating to others (and, therefore, of being rejected once again) are related to the need to protect this part. When we work with this part we will observe that patients feel it as something negative, dirty, or even scary.

In my therapeutic experience, when I ask patients to imagine the rejected part, it can be, among other things: the girl from The Exorcist, a clown with sharp teeth, a black cloud, or a crazy girl. They always imagine it as something that is scary or disgusting. After working with the hostile parts that protect her, we must validate this part a lot and tune into her feeling of loneliness and abandonment, and little by little it will be transformed into a sad little girl (Paulsen, 2009).

The way to work with this part (I insist that it must be in the final stages of therapy) is as follows:

- *It seems that this part is very scary for you: I wonder if you have ever considered that she contains all the fear of being rejected?*
- *What do you feel when you look at this part? What do you think she feels when she looks at you?*
- *It seems that that part must have felt very lonely to have to be so angry. I wonder what we could do to calm it down.*

Caregiving Parts

This is a controlling part and comes up in order to be accepted. The thinking that hides behind this part is "I'm not worthy" and, therefore, "no one can love me for who I am, so maybe they will love me for what I do."

It is a part that causes a lot of pain and anger in other parts of the system because it seeks to be taken care of by others, and when this does not happen it causes a lot of resentment and anger that must be dissociated so as not to cause rejection, which causes discomfort and a new vicious cycle of caring for others.

The personality scheme is ego-syntonic ("I am like this") and coincides with the public part. This part will be exhausted by carrying the full weight of the system so it can be worked on from the first sessions, teaching the patient self-care techniques.

For biological and cultural reasons, it will be much more common in women than in men and, in many cases, it will be the basis of the personality: "If I don't take care of others, I'm worthless."

This part can be accessed with questions such as:

- *It seems that you always take care of others, but I wonder ... who takes care of you?*
- *Since when do you remember being responsible for the well-being of others?* (If she answers, "since childhood," we must empathize with how hard it must have been for her).
- *Don't you sometimes feel that you should take care of yourself and think about yourself more? If you did that, how would others react?*

Narcissist Part: This part can appear either because the person received excessive care since childhood (Millon, 2011) or as an overcompensation for the feeling of shame. Its function would be not to allow the individual to be held responsible for anything and therefore be able to avoid any feeling of being defective or not being accepted.

The people in whom this part predominates are usually very reluctant to go to therapy because it would be like recognizing that they need help. They will only do it if the family forces them or the defense of narcissism is not enough and they feel a strong anxiety for which they do not know the reason.

Narcissism is a defense to protect the part that felt rejected and will be the last to be worked on in therapy. In the first sessions, you will have to validate its ego so as to, little by little, work on the origin of the shame.

Guilt-Related Parts

Guilt, according to Schore (2001), is verbal. It is usually characterized by constant negative ruminative thoughts about things we have done and/or about how others evaluate them. It appears at an age posterior to shame, where language exists, at approximately 2 years of age, and appears in the form of internal dialogues. While fear is a projection into the future, guilt is always related to the past. We may be afraid that something that happened in the past will happen again, but we cannot feel guilt about something that has not happened. All the information we have is from the past, and guilt helps us not to repeat the mistakes we have already made. Healthy guilt serves to remember what happened and will not allow it to happen again.

In many cases, the parts that contain guilt will be the introjections of the caregivers. Their role is to do what the caregivers expected them to do (or think or feel) and in doing so not disappoint them. The greater the fear of being rejected, the more present this introjected part is. These parts cause a lot of discomfort in the patients; explaining what function they fulfill will help a lot to deal with it. For this, it may be useful to ask:

- *It is clear that you are your worst judge. When you speak to yourself like this, does it remind you of someone you know?*
- *Where (or with whom) did you learn that things should be that way and could not be otherwise?*
- *If we assume that feeling guilty was a way to help you, what would be the good thing about feeling like that?*

The parts that are associated with guilt can be controlling, rejected, or sometimes impulsive; they always have a defensive function and were created to be able to find acceptance in others.

Perfectionist Part: This has a controlling nature; it is the part that had to be created so as not to disappoint others and not feel shame. It is often reinforced by caregivers in the form of constant reinforcement of attitudes and results. This part fulfills a very important role in the lives of individuals without them knowing when to apply it and when they should avoid it. It usually works in an all-or-nothing mode.

It is a very useful part, for example, in work or academic fields, but it is disastrous in personal relationships. For patients, it is very difficult to realize when they should leave the role and when they should not. Our main task as therapists is to explain and help them understand when it is adaptive and when it hurts them.

Impulsive Part: Many times, behind the cognitive or behavioral compulsions of our patients, we will find these parts that are always taking control as a way of helping not to reconnect with the pain of the traumatized and/or rejected parts. They can do so in the form of compulsive behavior, bingeing, addictions, and so on.

These parts try to avoid at all costs the patient feeling guilty again about something that happened long ago and cannot be forgiven, usually something unimportant. However, due to the person's age and not having had the tools to handle it, it remained as something dissociated, often amnesiac. They are usually events that patients reveal regarding something that happened a long time ago and that, from the perspective of the adult, has no importance, yet was traumatic for the child.

The more dissociated the memory, the more difficult it will be for the adult to realize the insignificance of the event. The work will consist of the patient being able to relive the event and work on it with the tools he has in the present.

Critical Part

This is an ally of the perfectionist part. Although it is behavioral in nature (it is the one that acts), the critical part is verbal; it is the ruminations that cause the patients so much suffering.

This part was created as a way to review everything that was done and not make mistakes in order not to feel the rejection of the caregivers again; it stays fixed as a controlling part that spends the day reviewing and criticizing everything the patient does. This part usually has the belief that if it is not critical with the individual, he will fall into complacency.

Recognition of the Parts

To recognize the parts, we can use the following techniques:

Interview: This is about explaining the model of the parts in the most educational way possible and asking the patient to recognize behaviors or emotions that may be related to parts of his internal system. It is very important to explain that in doing this we do not think he is crazy (they usually confuse the existence of dissociated parts with psychosis or schizophrenia), but that it is an exercise in introspection and self-knowledge. It helps a lot to explain that it is a hypnosis exercise.

Dolls: One of the ways to get closer to knowing the parts is through the use of dolls (I use Playmobil action figures). The patient picks up the dolls that remind him of the parts he recognizes inside himself. By visualizing those parts, he can recognize them and it will be easier to recognize phobias between parts and to which group each one belongs (Colondrón, 2010).

Drawings on paper or blackboard: Another way to know the internal system is to draw a circle on a piece of paper or on a blackboard. The patient draws all the parts she feels inside (it is important not to let her include outsiders) and sees which parts represent what, as well as the size they have. It is very useful, when we do this in different sequenced sessions, to observe the evolution of the patient's internal system.

Dissociative table: The dissociative table technique can be used in order to know and work with the parts (Forgash & Copeley, 2008). The goal, as in the other methods, is to get the different parts to begin to show themselves and know each other; the ultimate goal would be integration.

The dissociative table can be useful both for getting to know the different parts and for stabilization; the only limit is the imagination. If there is severe dissociation that requires careful work, we can imagine a house with different rooms: film projectors to see aspects of the past without any emotion, rooms with toys for child parts, rooms that lock from the inside so aggressive parts cannot have access, and so on (Paulsen, 2009).

Work with Phobias between the Parts

When the division of the personality takes place, there are parts linked to continuing normal life and others that are centered on defense and are anchored in the trauma; they are either suffering or trying to avoid suffering the trauma again. The dissociation is maintained by different types of phobias between the parts that prevent integration between them. During this phase of therapy, we will have to work on:

- *Preparation*: in which careful planning is carried out.
- *Synthesis*: the resolution of the dissociation regarding the components of traumatic memories, as well as the beginning of a narrative history that finally includes all parts of the personality. The synthesis of particular memories or pieces of memories is a planned event that occurs within a session or a series of sessions.
- Understanding, including increased levels of personification and presentification. This last stage is much more sequenced in processes and will happen over a period of time.

Van der Hart et al., 2006 quotes

> *It is often a crucial connection lost in the treatment of traumatic memories, given that some therapists see the "recovery" of memory as the end of the process, while in reality, it is merely the beginning of a difficult and longer course. It is of paramount importance to include ANPs in this work, although there may be occasional moments when the synthesis and several levels of understanding may appear first among the EPs (for example, when several defensive subsystems could be integrated before the work with the ANP on the understanding of trauma).*
>
> (p. 145)

Phobias between parts can be:

1. *Phobias of the internal world*: These can be phobias of the memories that remain isolated (rejected or wounded parts), which is why the patient avoids approaching what happened at any price (controlling and impulsive parts).

The earlier and the more intense the trauma, and the closer the people who caused it, the greater the dissociation and the more polarized the parts will be, as well as the more immersed in their role (Earley, 2012). The parts may have different and even incompatible goals. For example, one part may be focused on being loved and wanted, and another part may be focused on the fear of rejection. Obviously, the objectives are incompatible, which will lead to a lot of suffering for the patient, since no matter what he does, he will suffer – whether he approaches others and will suffer for fear of rejection or whether he leaves and will suffer for fear of loneliness. This will cause a phobia between these two parts that will produce a lot of anxiety in the patient.

2. *Phobia of traumatic memories*: For example, when the EP is strongly reactivated by stimuli that recall what happened, it can interfere with the ANP. The ANP will respond many times to intrusions with mental avoidance and avoidance reactions. This extreme avoidance reaction of the EP and related traumatic memories is called phobia of traumatic memory. First, the patient must be helped to be aware of their fears of the mental contents (rejected parts) and to work through them. The careful pace of work and the regulation of hyper- and hypo-activation will be crucial to success. The lower the integrating capacity of the patient, the slower we must work in this phase. Here, the work with the defenses, which we will look at in another chapter, is very important.

   T. It seems that abuse was the cause of much of what is happening to you now.

   C. Maybe. But I'd rather not talk about that now.

   T. Of course, it must be really hard for you just to remember it. We're not going to work on that just now. But it is very important for me that you are able to understand that what is happening to you hasn't come out of the blue.

   C. Yes, now I can understand why I can't help doing a lot of things that I regret later.

3. *Phobia between parts*. Many mental contents that generate rejection are usually guarded by certain parts of the personality that may even scare each other. More specifically, phobia of dissociated parts of the personality will develop (Van der Hart et al., 2006). These conditioned reactions on the part of the ANP interfere with the normal integrating tendencies of the mind and thus maintain the structural dissociation of the personality. One of the most important interventions is the gradual introduction of dissociated parts to one another (i.e., reducing avoidance and phobic dissociation between parts of the personality in regards to oneself).

4. *Phobia of attachment (and, perhaps, to the therapist)*. Human-induced trauma has the power to seriously affect the system of action of attachment. Some authors see disorganized attachment as basic in complex dissociative

disorders (Lyons-Ruth et al., 2006). Since attachment is experienced as dangerous when one has been constantly hurt by others that one knew and trusted, a probable phobia of attachment and intimacy can develop. Attachment phobia is often accompanied, paradoxically, by an equally intense phobia of attachment loss. That is, "I am afraid of the people who should take care of me but I am afraid that they will not take care of me." This phobia is worked on with self-care techniques and dismantling the idealizations, thus allowing the ANP to have more and more resources and the EP to rely more and more on it to take control. In other words, the EPs must recognize the ANP as a central figure of trust, protection, and attachment, and not continue to look for it in figures that are pathological.

This phobia can also affect the relationship with the therapist since the client can see him as a savior, as someone who is going to cure him. Subsequently, not getting the results as quickly and effectively as expected, he can feel discomfort or aggression towards the therapist. Once again, the work here is psychoeducation: that the patient is responsible for their improvement by participating actively in the therapy. It is very important that, when the therapist does something that bothers the patient or makes him uncomfortable, he will be able to keep calm and be able to explain why he acted like this and even apologize.

T. I get the feeling that you really want to have a partner but when you find one you sabotage the relationship.

C. I start really well, but quite soon I start being afraid that he will leave me or get tired of me. And I start asking for proof of everything, where he's been, with whom ... And we start arguing because I control him.

T. It seems that your fear of being left by him makes you unable to trust him and him to end up leaving you.

C. Yes. That's how it is.

5. *Phobias of the external world*: These could be fears of intimacy, daily life, normality, changes to the future, even the therapist. The person feels very afraid to experience closeness or affection because in the past the people he loved the most were those who hurt him the most. There may be a phobia of normality that is expressed in the inability to work or to take on the slightest responsibility.
6. *Phobia of improvement*. Given that there are more and more stimuli that become aversive, traumatized individuals can avoid an increasingly larger part of their lives. Thus, patients develop phobia of normal life. Since normal life involves at least a basic level of taking healthy risks and changes, these experiences of normal life are rigorously avoided, which leads to a vicious cycle of fear and avoidance.

   T. *Panic attacks must cause you a lot of discomfort so that you cannot go out alone to the street.*

   C. *You don't know the half of it. Only the one who suffers it can know.*

T. *But it seems that every time you avoid going out on the street, even accompanied, you avoid doing more and more things.*

C. *Yes, I'm stuck in a trap I don't know how to get out of.*

To achieve the synthesis of the parts, it is not enough to integrate the traumatic memory; it must become a memory that can be narrated. The ANP must be able to become gradually less phobic and more receptive towards the EP, fully owning past experiences and elaborating a narrative history of the traumatic experience.

The treatment begins with the parts that are intrusive and interfere with the therapy, that is, we begin by reducing the symptoms that most disturb the patient in the present. Only when the phobias have been significantly diminished between the parts that affect safety can the patient's traumatic memories be treated. A treatment motto is always "safety first." The abilities to diminish or eliminate self-destructive tendencies include the ability to tolerate and modulate emotions and physiological activation.

Integration of the Parts

In this part, working with defenses will be crucial (see Chapter 15). Integration will often happen spontaneously during therapy or between sessions, and sometimes, we will have to force it. This work should be done as many times as necessary, although it will often be the patients themselves who do it when they start to become familiar with the process. In extremely dissociated patients with very serious traumas, such as sexual abuse, this stage of therapy can take months or even years to complete.

It will be impossible to achieve the integration of the parts if there is still fear among them and they cannot work together in the common project of helping the patient, which is basically the initial objective of the appearance of those parts. For the treatment of these phobias, we will use different techniques that have been developed by González and Mosquera (2012).

Processing of the Phobia of Mental Actions

We can ask the patient to draw for us or explain what she feels inside. If she cannot perform the task, we are facing a phobia of mental actions.

Processing of the Phobia of the ANP towards the EP

As we commented previously, the ANP may feel rejection or even fear towards some EP. It is important to do a lot of psychoeducation on the role of this part and to help achieve reconciliation. For example, at the beginning this could be done by asking "What do you feel when you see it?" or "What do you want to do with it?" or "Could you touch it, for example, just with one finger?"

Processing of the Phobia between Two EPs

We can either have the patient look at the drawing she made of her internal system or observe what happens when two dolls that represent her parts approach each other or imagine that one emotional part approaches another. If there is any discomfort, the patient can be asked what has happened. Depending on the intensity of the phobia and the patient's capacity, work continues until there is cooperation or integration between the two.

Installation of an Integrative Meta-conscious Perspective

The final step is when we know that there are no phobias between the EP and the ANP. The patient is asked to observe if there is any discomfort when thinking of an integrated vision of the whole Self. If there is not, we must install this feeling.

To help the integration, we can use the Loving Eyes Technique (Knipe, 2014), which consists of approaching the child parts with affection and tenderness, understanding that they are not responsible for what happened, often achieving integration between the child part (EP) and the adult part (ANP).

Let us see an example of a real case to understand what the work process is like. In this case, we are going to work with a traumatic memory in which child parts are involved with moderate dissociation between the EP and the ANP. It is optional to use bilateral stimulation to activate the process, but for this we must have the proper training in EMDR or else we can overactivate and traumatize the patient.

T. Have you become obsessed with your physical appearance again?
C. I went to the gym and cycled again because I look too thin and weak.
T. You know that the rest of us don't see you like that?
C. My mother, my girlfriend, you too, tell me that I am very strong, but I cannot stop seeing myself as small.
T. When you think that you look small, where do you feel the sensation of discomfort in the body?
C. In my chest.
T. OK. Can you close your eyes and feel that feeling in your chest and think you're weak and go back in time to the first time you felt something like that?
C. Nothing comes up.
T. We have all felt weak at some point. Please try again.
C. When I was 7 years old there were some gypsy children in my neighborhood and they threatened to beat me.
T. Do you recall any time that you felt especially weak? Fearful?
C. Yes. One time, they stole my watch. I told my father that I had lost it because if not he would have scolded me for being a coward and not defending myself.

T. Can you imagine that child and see how he feels when his watch is taken?

C. With a lot of fear and even more fear of how I was going to tell my parents. It was a birthday gift.

T. Can you approach that child with your current knowledge and your adult appearance? When you do, ask him if he knows who you are.

C. He says he doesn't know.

T. Tell him that you are him who has grown up, that he is now an adult and that he is strong and can defend himself.

C. He doesn't believe me.

T. Tell him a secret that only you two know, something that nobody else knows.

C. He's very surprised!!! I'm not going crazy, right?

T. As I explained before, it's your imagination. They are parts of your mind that store memories of events that were important to you. Can you defend that child?

C. Yes, I am doing it. I have thrown the children out and given the watch back to him.

T. How does the child feel now?

C. Much better; he's calmer.

T. Very good. Where would you like to take him? To your current home? To a park? To your parents? Whatever you and him decide.

C. He says he wants to come with me to my house.

T. OK, show him your house, a room where he can be, you can give him toys ...

C. Yes, he's very well, very happy.

T. OK, say goodbye to him and tell him that whenever he needs it, you will be there to defend him. When you remember what happened that made you go back to cycling and overworking in the gym. What do you feel now?

C. I don't know, it's very weird. I remember it as something unimportant, I don't know why I had to react like that. I have the strength to face things.

T. Perfect. Maybe in the past you felt fragile and afraid and you needed to feel stronger, but now it does not make any sense. Intellectual tools are more important than physical ones.

C. Yes, now I see it differently. How interesting.

Conclusions

We are all born with a basic emotional programming; in short, this is what we know as "systems of action" which are indispensable to survive those of attachment (closeness to caregivers) and defense (related to well-being and survival).

Whenever there is a pleasant or unpleasant emotional activation, our mind will store an emotional memory of the event, creating what we know as emotional parts that will be focused on the relationships with others, and others that will be focused on the avoidance of discomfort. If the experiences are excessive for the capacity of the child or the adult, these parts will be dissociated, and in extreme cases they will have their own memories, sensations, and so on.

The dissociative model is a continuum that ranges from mild dissociation – where the person is aware of everything that happened and where the parts are oriented to the present – to very serious cases where the parts are completely autonomous and still live in trauma time. At a pedagogical level and to facilitate its identification, we can use metaphors and descriptions that can help to facilitate the recognition of these parts and the subsequent work with them.

Therapeutic work will consist of recognizing these parts and working with the phobias between them and with elements external to the person. The patient is allowed to gradually become aware of his internal world and, by having reparative experiences, he can achieve an integration of these parts into his personality, until all are oriented in the present and can have a feeling of control over their emotions.

References

Busch, F., & Milrod, B. (2004). Nature and treatment of panic disorder. In J. Panksepp (Ed.), *Textbook of biological psychiatry* (pp. 345–366). Wiley.

Cassidy, J. (2000). The complexity of the caregiving system: A perspective from attachment theory. *Psychological Inquiry*, *11*(2), 86–91.

Colondrón, M. (2010). *Muñecos, metáforas y soluciones: Constelaciones Familiares en sesión individual y otros usos terapéuticos Desclee de Brouwer.*

Cozolino, L. (2010). *The neuroscience of psychotherapy. Healing the social brain.* Norton.

DeYoung, P. (2015). *Understanding and treating chronic shame. A relational neurobiological approach.* Routledge.

Earley, J. (2012). *Working with anger in internal family systems therapy.* Pattern System Books.

Forgash, C., & Copeley, M. (Eds.). (2008). *Healing the heart of trauma and dissociation.* Springer.

González, A., & Mosquera, D. (2012). *EMDR Y Disociación. El Abordaje Progresivo.* Pleyades.

Janet, P. (2003). *Psicología de los sentimientos.* Fondo de Cultura Económica.

Knipe, J. (2014). *EMDR toolbox: Theory and treatment of complex PTSD and dissociation.* Springer.

Lyons-Ruth, K., Dutra, L., Schuder, M. R., & Bianchi, I. (2006). From infant attachment disorganization to adult dissociation: Relational adaptations or traumatic experiences? *The Psychiatric Clinics of North America, 29*(1), 63–68.

Miller, A. (1990). *The drama of the gifted child: The search for the true self.* Basic Books.

Millon, T. (2011). *Personality disorders in modern life.* Wiley.

Panksepp, J., & Biven, L. (2012). *The archeology of mind. Neuroevolutionary origins of humans emotions.* Norton.

Paulsen, S. (2009). *Looking through the eyes of trauma and dissociation: An illustrated guide for EMDR therapists and clients.* BookSurge Publishing.

Putnam, F. (1997). *Dissociation in children and adolescents. A developmental perspective*. The Guilford Press.
Schore, A. (2001). The effects of a secure attachment relationship on roght brain development, affect regulation & infant mental health. *Infant Mental Health Journal*, *22*, 7–66.
Schore, A. (2010). Relational trauma and the developing right brain. In T. Baradon (Ed.), *The neurobiology of broken attachment bonds. Psychoanalytic, attachment and neuropschological contributions to parent-infan psychotherapy*. Routledge.
Schwartz, R. C. (1995). *Internal family systems therapy*. Guilford Press.
Van der Hart, O., Nijenhuis, E. R., & Steele, K. (2005). Dissociation: An insufficiently recognized major feature of complex posttraumatic stress disorder. *Journal of Traumatic Stress*, *18*, 413–423.
Van der Hart, O., Nijenhuis, E. R. S., & Steele, K. (2006). *The haunted self: Structural dissociation and the treatment of chronic traumatization*. Norton & Company.

13 Stabilization and Relaxation Techniques

Schopenhauer, the great German philosopher, already raised questions in the nineteenth century that we began to apply in contemporary psychology in the twenty-first century. He stated that animals can only live in the present while humans can plan the future or remember the past at will. The philosopher says:

> *That gives to man that thoughtfulness which distinguishes his consciousness so entirely from that of his irrational fellow-creatures. He far surpasses them in power and also in suffering. They live in the present alone, he lives also in the future and the past. They satisfy the needs of the moment, he provides by the most ingenious preparations for the future, yea for days that he shall never see. They are entirely dependent on the impression of the moment, on the effect of the perceptible motive; he is determined by abstract conceptions independent of the present. Therefore he follows predetermined plans; he acts from maxims, without reference to his surroundings or the accidental impressions of the moment.*
>
> Schopenhauer (2013, p. 37)

The evolutionary features that distinguish human beings have allowed us to colonize the entire planet and yet, we have paid a price: anxiety. As I explained throughout the book, anxiety is a warning sign that our brain misinterprets, causing different reactions that produce much suffering and discomfort. During the therapeutic work, we evaluate and work towards helping the patient understand himself better, determine the origin of his problem, and discover how to change his thoughts and emotions.

It is very important to teach strategies that help stabilize and reduce discomfort; these techniques can be used from the start as tasks in the consultation or to work on in daily life. If the patient feels very unstable, it will be necessary to sufficiently reduce the anxiety so that he can begin to feel that he can control his emotions and thoughts and can apply what he has learned.

In this chapter, I will explain three techniques that I consider very useful when working with anxiety, as well as how to use the resources that the patient has in order to bolster their strengths and help them feel in control.

DOI: 10.4324/9781003646341-15

Mindfulness

Mindfulness or full awareness is a psychological technique taken from Eastern religions such as Taoism or Buddhism. It would exceed the content of this book to explain in detail everything related to this technique. It is a "state of consciousness that implies paying attention to the experience of the moment" (Didonna, 2009). This concept can be divided into several other concepts:

- Living in the present;
- Not judging;
- Acceptance;
- Removing the mental auto-pilot.

1. Living in the Present

This is the main cause of anxiety in human beings. Although our ability to remember the past at will and to think about the future in order to plan has taken us to the peak of evolution, applied in a negative way it becomes a source of pain and suffering. If we think about the future in a negative way, we will be afraid, and if we think about the past in a negative way, we will feel guilt.

Human beings can achieve abstract thinking thanks to the development of the cortical areas. However, as we saw in Chapter 2, the amygdala does not differentiate real danger from imaginary danger. When we think about the future or the past in a negative way, the brain circuits related to warning will be activated, and our body will feel anxiety with the subsequent associated discomfort. This is going to be one of the main sources of suffering for our patients: thinking obsessively about what happened and what might happen. When one thinks of the present exclusively, anxiety cannot exist (Sapolsky, 2004).

Mindfulness therapies and those of Acceptance and Commitment (Hayes et al., 2011) insist a lot (very correctly, in my opinion) on living and thinking only in the present. The problem is that if a person suffers trauma, his mind will be frozen in what happened and, no matter how hard he tries, he cannot stop suffering because of what happened and feel fear of it happening again (Herman, 2015). It is very important to resolve the traumas before applying the techniques for focusing on the present. In my opinion, the most effective technique to achieve this is EMDR. Once trauma is resolved, there will be no problem in being able to work on awareness in the present.

To achieve this, we can use techniques to stop thinking or use objects that help patients remember to focus on the present. An example would be:

Living in the present (once the patient is ready) is absolutely necessary in order to eliminate anxiety; once it is achieved, patients will feel that they regain control of their mind and their lives.

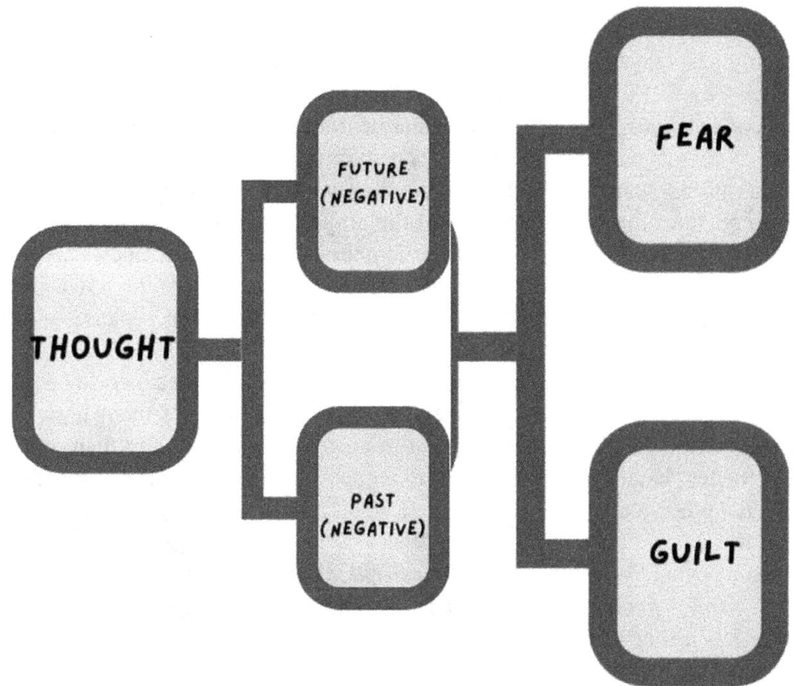

Figure 13.1 The human being is the only animal that can use thought to go to the future or to the past at will. When this is done in a negative way, it can be perceived as fear or guilt.

T. I know you can't stop worrying about things that could happen in the future. But I would like you to try to focus on the present, the here and now.

C. It's very hard.

T. I know it's difficult, but we're going to do it step by step. Every time a thought comes to you about something from the past or the future, stop your thinking and bring the mind back to the here and now. You can touch your skin or observe the clothes you are wearing. Anything that helps you return to the here and now.

C. But a lot of times I have to think about things of the future, like planning a vacation or remembering things I did in the past. How do I do it?

T. You can do it but in a positive way, without fear; plan your vacation and immediately return to the present.

C. OK, I get it now. Do I do it everyday?

T. Do it constantly. It will be hard at first, but it is mental gymnastics and, as you practice, you can end up doing it automatically.

2. Not Judging

Once again, due to our brain's architecture and physiology, human beings are the only animals capable of making value judgments and of acting according to decisions. In the words of Ortega y Gasset (1932), "man is an animal forced to make decisions." Decisions can either be right or wrong, with its consequent relief or contentment or with anxiety and suffering.

Making constant judgments about what we do or what others do leads to the increase of the warning levels of the amygdala (unconscious) and to the appearance of anxiety. Obviously, it is necessary to make value judgments and make decisions in order to be able to live, but once again I must insist that a pathology does not occur because of what is done but because of how it is done.

People who live with guilt and shame (and therefore with fear) do so because they are constantly judging themselves negatively. Showing them how they execute this process and helping them to change it can also help them to feel much better: having fewer negative thoughts, being emotionally more stable, and having less anxiety.

T. I don't know if you have noticed how critical you are with yourself. And I do not know if you are so with others as well?
C. No, I'm just critical of myself. I always judge myself very harshly.
T. And what do you gain by that?
C. Nothing. But I can't help it.
T. I wonder if someone in your past was that critical of you?
C. Yes, my mother. She never liked anything I did.
T. And you liked that?
C. No way. I hated it and still do.
T. Maybe you've learned to talk to yourself like your mother spoke to you. Don't you think the time has come to change it?
C. I'd love to. But I don't know how to do it.
T. Every time you hear that criticizing voice, stop it. Imagine that you spoke like this to another person. Experience how it would feel. At first it will be difficult, but little by little you will see how it becomes easier until you can change it completely.

3. Acceptance

Acceptance is the opposite of resignation. Acceptance means that if there is something I do not like, I put all my energy into trying to change it. Resigning means that if I do not like something, I put a lot of energy into getting angry and I will only have little left to change anything.

This is another of the issues in which we differentiate ourselves from animals; they can only accept. Obviously, there will be many things that happen to them that they do not like, but they learn to live with them and try to change them without getting frustrated.

Every time human beings get angry or frustrated, they make the emotional brain perceive an alert with the consequent mechanism of fear and anxiety activation. This does not mean that one must always be submissive or accommodating; it means that we must use all our energy to change it but without discomfort or anxiety. An old Chinese proverb says "If you cannot change it, why get angry? And if you can change it, why get angry?"

T. You seem frustrated and I imagine that this must cause you a lot of discomfort.
C. Yes, I'm sick of not achieving anything that I set out to do. I don't feel like doing anything.
T. Maybe if you put more energy into occupying yourself and less into worrying about things, things would go better.
C. Surely, yes. But I don't know how to do it.
T. You spend a lot of energy lamenting and complaining. Try to do the simplest thing first and, little by little, you will be able to do more complicated things. But above all, do not waste any energy in lamenting or getting angry.
C. OK, I'll try.
T. I recommend that you do not try, because there you have an implicit possible failure. Just do it.
C. OK, I'll do it.

4. Remove Automatic Pilot

We have seen how our brain tends to repeat thoughts, emotions, or actions as a way to make better use of resources and to have available energy to use in other matters. We call this unconscious memory implicit and more concretely "automatic or procedural," and it is very useful and necessary for survival. Sometimes, however, when it acts in a negative way, it can become our biggest enemy.

We will often have to stop the processes we carry out and reflect on the appropriateness of our actions, thoughts, or emotions; as we saw in Chapter 5, this is what we know as mentalization (Fonagy & Luyten, 2014).

This section is directly related to the other three; we have to learn to stop our usual automatic processes and learn to live in the present, to accept our reality to better be able to change it and to not make constant judgments. Some authors also call this *flow* (Csikszentmihalyi, 1990). It is the feeling of allowing ourselves to be carried away by the moment and by activities that give us a sense of well-being, achievement, and fulfillment.

Hypnosis and Relaxation

There are many relaxation techniques; the best known is the "Jacobson's progressive relaxation" which consists of successively tensing and relaxing the different muscles of the body one by one to achieve deep relaxation. In my opinion, it has the disadvantage that it is cumbersome and takes a long time to execute.

Another highly recommended technique is "meditation," which has shown multiple advantages on a physical and mental level (Didonna, 2009; Hayes et al., 2011). The drawback is that patients have a hard time leaving their minds blank, and when they try they are frequently assaulted by thoughts of discomfort and anxiety. Meditation is recommended only when patients have little to no anxiety; it is very useful (especially combined with yoga exercises) as maintenance to prevent relapse.

In my opinion, hypnosis (and self-hypnosis), guiding patients with suggestions about what they should think and how they should act or feel, makes it much more difficult for them to think about their problems. Furthermore, the state of relaxation is much deeper. *Important: You should not perform quick relaxation on people with high levels of anxiety. When trying to relax too fast, they may not control their breathing or their sensations and may suffer a panic attack.*

Self-hypnosis is a relaxation technique in which the patient is taught to relax as quickly as possible. There are many self-hypnosis techniques. Here, I am going to reproduce the one that I like most because of its effectiveness and ease. It must be said exactly as I reproduce it here:

> *Close your eyes and let your eyelids rest. Now, pretend you want to open your eyes and you cannot. That's it ... very good. Let them rest again and let that relaxing sensation sink down from your eyes all over your body, little by little, very slowly, until you reach the tips of your toes. Enjoy that feeling for 30 seconds and when you open your eyes again you will find yourself much more calm and rested.*

Once we have done it with our voice, we will teach the patient to do it alone until he can repeat it effortlessly. We will recommend doing it whenever he wants as a fast and simple way to relax.

Hypnosis is an ancestral relaxation technique in which the patient is relaxed as much as possible and suggestions are made that can help him change different aspects of his personality as well as reduce anxiety. There are mainly two types of hypnosis:

- Naturalistic or Ericksonian hypnosis: Does not use inductions, but uses the patient's non-verbal communication, metaphors, or symbols as a way to help the patient relax. The defenders of this technique uphold that the patient will use what he hears unconsciously to be able to change what he needs to change. An example of Ericksonian induction would be:

As you hear my voice and start feeling how your body adjusts to the position, I wonder if you have already decided if you prefer to do a deep relaxation or a light one (= double bind technique) or maybe you have decided not to relax at all (= confusion technique), but I'm sure your unconscious will already know what to do and is already making the necessary changes to help you change what you're worried about. Or maybe it's just allowing you to relax so you can imagine that you see yourself from the outside (= dissociation technique) and you will think what advice you would give to a friend who was going through a situation similar to yours (= distancing technique) and, if it turned out to be good advice, how good it would feel to see how much better he feels (future protocol technique).

- Classic hypnosis: This poses three differentiated phases when performing the relaxation.
  - Induction;
  - Deepening;
  - Suggestion;
  - Closure;
  - Induction is a standard technique that helps the patient to relax deeply. The one I like best is the "Elman induction."

Stare fixedly at my hand. Breathe as deeply as you can, hold your breath. Now let the air out slowly and start closing your eyes.

Now pay special attention to your eyelids. You can relax your eyelids so much that they will not want to open. Once you have done this, stay in that state of relaxation. Verify that your eyelids do not really want to open. Good, now relax more deeply.

Now, let that sensation that you feel in your eyelids run all over your body from the top of your head to the tips of your toes, as if wanting to reach a relaxation ten times deeper.

All right; now we will continue towards a deeper relaxation. I'm going to count backwards from three and, when I get to zero, I'll ask you to open your eyes and close them again. When you do, you'll be twice as relaxed as you are now. Once again. I'm going to count backwards from three and, when I get to zero, I'll ask you to open your eyes and close them again and when you do you'll relax twice as much than you've done so far.

I will raise your hand and then drop it. Do not help me lift it, just let me do it while you're still very relaxed. Let me do everything; good, now let's deepen this relaxation.

Now that we have relaxed your body, we will relax your mind. Allow your mind to relax, just as your body is relaxed. In a moment, I'm going to ask you to count slowly and calmly, starting with number one. After each number, let your mind duplicate the relaxation. After some numbers (which will not be many), you will be able to relax your mind in a more pleasant way so that the numbers will vanish, vanish, vanish until they disappear. If you want to, you can do it easily. When the numbers are gone, you will raise the index finger of the right hand, to let me know that they are gone ... (your patient says "one") gently ... (Your patient says "two"). Now double your mental relaxation. (Then say "three" and so on.) Now, let the numbers go away as your relaxation and your mind is (four) doubling your mental relaxation, until they vanish, vanish, vanish. When the numbers vanish, say "well done, go deeper."

- Deepening: Once the induction is completed, you can deepen the trance state using different techniques. The one I use most is the staircase, which goes as follows:

Now, while you remain deeply relaxed, imagine that you are at the top of a seven-step staircase. The staircase will lead you to a quiet and relaxed place. As you go down step by step, your state of drowsiness, of pleasant heaviness and relaxation, will intensify. Finally, when you get to the bottom, when you step on the last step, you will be more connected to your inner self; in a state of deeper, intense, and pleasant trance. Now visualize the steps of the staircase that you are going to descend while you remain more deeply relaxed and asleep. It is not necessary to visualize the whole staircase; it is enough that you see in your mind the step that you are about to tread. Imagine now that you raise your foot and now you step on step number seven. You immerse yourself in a deeper dream, you can feel the heaviness and drowsiness that extends through your body and through your mind. You raise your foot again and step on step six, a deeper and more intense dream. Each step takes you closer to your inner self and further away from the external reality that is unimportant, which is why you want to continue descending the staircase ...

- It would continue like this until the person reaches step number zero.
- Suggestion: This is the most important text. We will use scripts that we wrote before the session or use a standard one depending on the patient's problem. For the suggestions to have more effect it is important that the patient be as relaxed as possible. An example could be:

You are going to imagine a future in which the problem that has brought you here has been completely solved and you can imagine the surprised faces of the people you love upon knowing that you have become a new person. You could not imagine that moment would ever come nor how easy it would be for you. Gone are all the worries. All the troubles that you experienced have helped you better realize what you want. Everything that has happened is strange to you, as if it had happened to a different person, as if all that happened to someone else a long time ago. In fact, you will be able to enjoy this feeling of calm and control for the next minutes, hours, days so as to feel that everything works so much better.

- Closure: This is the final moment of hypnosis, which should be done slowly and little by little so that the patient adjusts to a rhythm that is more convenient for him. For example:

Now you are going to gradually move the parts of the body that you wish, and you are going to open your eyes when you please, and you are going to let all the suggestions you have heard be a part of your body, your mind, and your spirit.

In my therapeutic practice, I always record the sessions and later send them to the patient's cell phone so that he can hear them at home whenever he wants. With this, I have three objectives: a) he has a tool to relax outside the office; b) he feels accompanied and comforted by the voice of the hypnosis – it is as if the therapist continues to accompany him between sessions; c) it allows the messages that I want to transmit to be heard many times and can therefore penetrate deeper into his mind.

Stabilization Resources

To help patients feel better and to better tolerate discomfort and anxiety we can use stabilization techniques that help the patient get a sense of control over their emotions, thoughts, and feelings. Some of these are:

1. Control over Breathing

Breathing is the guide of our mind; this is known by all meditation and yoga practitioners around the world. If breathing is accelerated, the mind gets agitated, whereas when breathing is calm, the mind becomes calm.

When there is danger (and therefore anxiety) our brain sends orders to the body to get into fight-flight position (as we saw in Chapter 2, even though the danger is not real) and, among other things, hyperventilation may occur, in which case more oxygen is carried to the different body organs (Sapolsky, 2004).

Since there is no real demand for extra oxygen, this hyperventilation causes an increase in carbon dioxide in the blood, which is known as hypocapnia, with the consequent alkalosis of the blood. The symptoms that are caused when this occurs are:

- Tachycardias;
- Sensation of suffocation, lack of air;
- Sensation of dizziness;
- Sensation of dying from a heart attack or from suffocation;
- Sensation of going crazy.

The degree of discomfort will vary from mild (in the case of moderate anxiety) to extreme (in people suffering from panic attacks). In fact, individuals who have panic attacks usually end up in the emergency room because they think they have suffered a myocardial infarction. When this happens, the diagnosis is anxiety.

It is very important to explain this very clearly to the patients, so they know what is happening to them and that in no case, however unpleasant the symptoms, will they suffer a heart attack or die.

In order to help them control their breathing in case of an anxiety or panic attack, there is a very simple but extremely useful exercise. It has to be practiced with the patient several times during sessions before they can do it alone. The exercise goes like this:

> *As I have explained to you, by not being able to breathe properly you provoke the symptoms of suffocation. When you feel that you are short of breath, you will hold your breath for 5 seconds and then you will exhale very slowly through the mouth and briefly inhale through the nose and return to hold your breath for 5 seconds. Let's do it together: Breathe in through your nose, hold your breath. We count: One, two, three, four, and five. Very good. We exhale very slowly through the mouth and breathe in through the nose. We count: one, two, three, four, five.*

It is important to explain that this exercise will be very difficult to do when they are in a crisis and that it is important that they do so as soon as they begin to feel the symptoms of discomfort. It is very convenient to rehearse it several times during the day so as to be able to practice it with ease when there is discomfort. With this exercise, we will help patients to much better control their symptoms and to give them a feeling of control.

2. Light Stream

This technique can be useful for both physical and emotional pain. It is also an energy enhancer (Shapiro, 2010). If you feel upset, concentrate on those unpleasant emotions/sensations in your body. Ask yourself the following: If that sensation/emotion had a form, what would it be? If that sensation/emotion had size, what would it be? If that sensation/emotion had color, what would it be? Then think about your favorite color or what color you would associate with well-being. Imagine that a light of the chosen color enters through the top of your head and goes to that shape (unpleasant sensation) inside your body. That light does not end, it is continuous, like a beam of light. The light is directed towards the form, it vibrates in and around it. Imagine, what happens to the shape, its size, or its color.

3. Creating a Safe Place

This technique consists of creating a safe place which can be real or imaginary, and imagining that the patient is in it. It consists of trying to experience the associated feelings of well-being and calm with the greatest possible intensity. Once one can imagine it with ease, it can be done any time the person has anxiety in order to relax.

4. Paint Can

We can imagine a disturbing memory and imagine that we put it inside a can of paint. Once inside, we remove it and see how its color changes and therefore the associated sensations (Shapiro, 2010). We can also do it with bodily sensations or situations that we are currently experiencing. Similar techniques may be imagining that we see the traumatic memory on a movie screen and change the color or speed of the film.

5. Spiral of Emotions

This technique is used to be able to get accustomed to and work with unpleasant sensations. The patient is asked to imagine the sensation and explain where he feels it. He is asked, if that feeling were to turn, in which direction would it do so? When he answers, he is asked to imagine that it turns in the opposite direction. This exercise can be done as many times as necessary until it disappears or fades away. In this way, the patient can get accustomed to the sensations.

6. Memory Container

This technique is widely used in sessions where traumatic or annoying topics have been worked on and we do not want to destabilize the patient between sessions. He is asked to take all the work from that day and put it in a tight container and imagine that he throws it to the bottom of the sea and it will not reopen until the next session. It can also be said that the therapist can keep it in his office until the next visit. The most important thing is that the patient not reopen it between sessions.

Conclusions

In order to work safely, it is crucial to have stabilization resources so that they can be worked on both during the sessions and by the patient who can resort to them when the therapist is not present.

There are several techniques that we can use, such as mindfulness, which includes techniques to learn to center the mind in the present and accept what happens without resigning nor judging oneself. Hypnosis is also a very useful tool to help patients relax and at the same time to be able to give them suggestions that help to modify emotional aspects or thoughts that are harming them.

Hypnosis is a very useful resource to help patients relax and help them imagine a future in which they have new resources or where the problem is solved. Recording the hypnotic sessions is also very useful for the patient to continue the therapeutic work between sessions. There are several types of hypnosis that should be used depending on the therapeutic needs and the characteristics of the patient

I have also raised the possibility of using the patient's own resources, for example breathing, which is extremely important to everything related to anxiety, as well as techniques to regulate anxiety such as the "container of memories," the "safe place," or the "light stream."

References

Csikszentmihalyi, M. (1990). *Flow: The psychology of optimal experience*. Harper & Row.

Didonna, F. (2009). *Clinical handbook of mindfulness*. Springer.

Fonagy, P., & Luyten, P. (2014). Mentalising in attachment context. In P. Holmes & S. Farnfield (Eds.), *The routledge handbbok of attachment*. Routledge.

Hayes, S. C., Strosahl, K. D., & Wilson, K. G. (2011). *Acceptance and commitment therapy: The process and practice of mindful change*. Guilford Press.

Herman, J. (2015). *Trauma and recovery: The aftermath of violence–from domestic abuse to political terror*. Basic Books.

Ortega y Gasset, J. (1932). *The revolt of the masses*. Norton.

Sapolsky, R. M. (2004). *Why zebras don't get ulcers: The acclaimed guide to stress, stress-related diseases, and coping*. Holt Paperback.

Shapiro, R. (2010). *The trauma treatment handbook. Protocols across the spectrum*. Norton.

Shopenhauer, A. (2013). *El mundo como voluntad y representación*. Alianza.

14 Bodywork

The first connection between mother and child is purely physical. During his first years of life, the child is completely dependent upon his caregivers, and it is they who have to help him regulate himself, calming him when he is hyperactivated and stimulating him when the activation is too low. We have seen how attachment relationships with caregivers condition regulation strategies both for the internal and external world.

The influence of attachment is reflected not only in the child's mind but also in many aspects related to the physical sphere. Our body has an implicit memory as well. This memory, which we will not be conscious of in the future, remains in our brain in the form of neural network systems. In adult life, these systems can be triggered by a stimulus related to what happened in the first years of life and may come in the form of symptoms of somatic diseases such as headaches, muscle pain, or chronic fatigue. Our body stores memories of what happens throughout our lives (Van der Kolk, 2014).

Anxiety is a warning signal we feel in our body towards something that our nervous system perceives as dangerous. For a child, danger in the first years of his life may mean not being able to meet his physiological needs; attentive caregivers will ensure the child returns to a state of well-being. These experiences of small discomfort and subsequent calm are necessary for the child to learn to regulate small frustrations (Schore, 2003).

If the caregivers are not able to regulate the child or when they themselves are the source of discomfort, anxiety will be frequent and excessive and he will be much more likely to suffer in the future. We will always experience anxiety in the body, and the more often we feel it in childhood and adolescence, the more likely we will suffer it in adulthood.

As we saw in Chapter 2, humans may be triggered because of something real, like when we know that someone close to us has been diagnosed with an illness; or because of something imaginary, like the fear that a catastrophe will happen, or simply when making a decision. For centuries, medicine has been based on the fact that our mind and body are two completely separate entities without any relation to each other. Currently, medical science contemplates that body and mind are interrelated.

DOI: 10.4324/9781003646341-16

Today we know that the most primitive parts of our brain are connected to our body through the autonomic nervous system and through hormones. We have all had the experience of getting nervous or scared and feel our heart speed up; we start to sweat more, our mouth goes dry, we can even get dizzy, or our head or chest may hurt a lot.

When there is an aversive stimulus, the emotional parts of our brain activate the sympathetic system into fight-flight mode which provokes tension and alarm in our body. When there is a positive stimulus through the parasympathetic system, it will provoke sensations of well-being, smiles, open postures with relaxed shoulders, and facial expressions of tranquility, which are ways of interacting with others in a friendly way.

In cases of threat, the amygdala is activated in the central nervous system (CNS) and will stimulate the search for help through the sympathetic system. If this is not enough or an activation of the fight-flight mode does not appear and the threat is excessive, the dorsovagal branch of the autonomic nervous system (ANS) produces an immobilization response that can be very traumatic for the human being (Porges, 2011). This system is operative from childhood and can be activated for many reasons: from negligent and/or aggressive caregivers to hospitalization, loss of loved ones, and so on. The body will store a memory of the trauma, creating a somatic memory. Our body, just like our brain, will store information of what happened in order to remember and avoid the pain again in the future.

In Chapter 1, we talked about neuroception, a concept created by Porges (2011) to highlight the unconscious process that takes place to evaluate different stimuli and know if they are safe or dangerous. Depending on the assessment that our brain makes of the stimulus, one branch or another of the vagus nerve will be activated, which will produce a sense of alarm and fear or of calm and tranquility. A child who suffers constant frustrations or abuse will have a greater tendency in adulthood to evaluate all the stimuli as negative, which will constantly make him feel sensations of discomfort in his body, maybe going on to develop somatic illnesses such as chronic pain, intestinal problems (irritable colon), allergies, diabetes, or heart problems (Sapolsky, 2004).

The somatic memory remembers what happened to avoid dangers in the future and thus have resources to be able to face the threat (Van der Kolk, 2014; Seijo, 2015). If, for example, we felt shame when we were 4 years old because our mother scolded us and our body felt a discomfort in the belly, every time we are ashamed, our body will feel it in the same place. As I will later expand on, the implications that this will have on the therapeutic work are immense.

Emotions and Our Body

Emotions would be the valuation we make of an external or internal stimulus. They can be pleasant such as, for example, joy; or painful, such as anger or

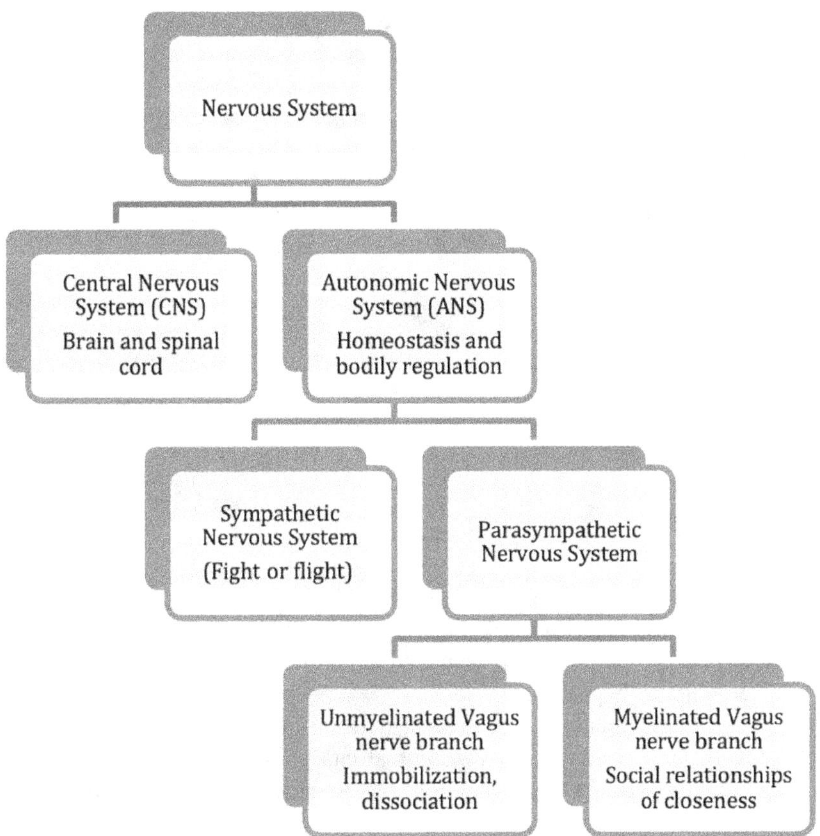

Figure 14.1 Hierarchy of the different systems of both the CNS and the ANS. They become sequentially activated when faced with internal or external stimuli.

sadness. They are classified as basic or innate, for example fear, and secondary when they are socially acquired and are characteristic only of human beings, such as guilt or shame (Aguado, 2010).

Sensations are our body reactions to an internal or external stimulus, which obviously can only be felt inside our body. They can be pleasant or unpleasant and help the amygdala to assess how to react to different situations, either by looking for them or by avoiding them.

According to Damasio (1994), being able to feel the emotions in our body would have a great evolutionary importance for animals to assess whether a stimulus is positive or dangerous. That way they can react instinctively in a matter of milliseconds and do not have to waste time on a conscious assessment that would take time away from a dangerous situation that could endanger life. This would be one more trait that humans share with other animals and has been acquired evolutionarily.

Damasio called these sensations we feel in the body regarding different stimuli "somatic markers" (Damasio, 1994):

> What does the somatic marker achieve? It forces attention on the negative outcome to which a given function may lead, and functions as an automated alarm signal which says: Beware of danger ahead if you choose the option which leads to this outcome. The signal may lead you to reject, immediately, the negative course of action and thus make you choose among other alternatives. The automated signal protects you against future losses, without further ado, and then allows you to choose from among fewer alternatives.
>
> (p. 172)

According to this model, somatic markers can be generated from two types of events: primary and secondary inductors (Damasio, 1994):

- The primary inductors are stimuli that have innately or through learning been associated with pleasurable or aversive states. When one of these stimuli is present in the immediate environment, an emotional response is necessarily and automatically generated.
- The secondary inductors are generated from the memory of an emotional event, that is, imagining a situation that can produce pleasure or aversion. They do not occur in a real situation. Just imagining something can activate them.

As we have seen, the somatic marker can be pleasant in the case of positive stimuli, or unpleasant in the case of negative stimuli. To test this hypothesis right now in your body, can you think of a recent situation that causes you discomfort or something that may arise in the future that scares you? How does your body feel? Do you notice any discomfort? Now take a deep breath and imagine that you are reunited with someone you love very much and who you miss. How does your body feel now? Is there any part of your body that feels fulfilled? Observe how different the feelings of imagining something annoying or pleasant are.

In light of a stimulus, there is a neuroception that goes through the thalamus and the amygdala. This organ will decide if the stimulus is dangerous or pleasant, and through the ANS we will have uncomfortable or pleasant bodily sensations that will condition our subsequent response. These sensations will return to our brain through the insula which, by reaching the cortical areas, will provide information about the associated emotional assessment.

If the intensity of the alarm is low, a rational approach/avoidance/submission decision can be made. However, if the stimulus is perceived as very dangerous, it will not pass through the cortex and there will be an unconscious reaction of panic and, in extreme cases, of immobilization.

Damasio (1994) raises another very important matter for psychotherapy and everything related to working with the body. Sometimes our brain, to save energy and have even more immediate responses, does not perform the stimulus-mind-body-mind cycle but reacts directly without evaluating the bodily sensations in what he calls the "as-if loop." In this case, the brain would completely bypass the body. The CNS acts automatically regardless of whether the assessments, when the stimulus is perceived, are negative or positive. This could explain the existence of somatic memory (Rodríguez et al., 2005).

This would explain why many patients permanently experience fear when there is no real threat. If, during childhood, there have been many aversive stimuli, they will continue to live with a sense of constant danger as adults. Although there is no real danger, the brain will act automatically without waiting for the body's reaction. There will be a strong anxiety without them knowing what produced it. This is what happens to people with panic attacks who feel a sense of imminent death without there being anything to cause fear. This is also the basis of many somatic diseases that do not obey any organic reason.

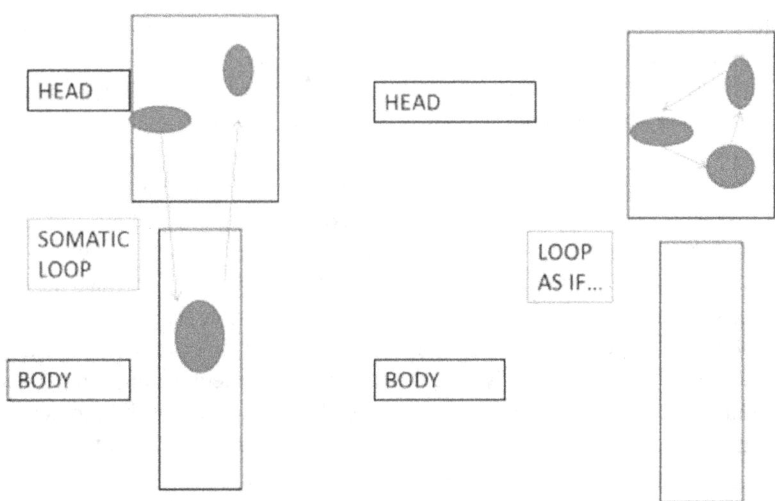

Figure 14.2 In normal conditions, there is reciprocal information flowing between body sensations and the CNS assessment. Occasionally, alert circuits in the brain may become activated without sensory stimulus. This is known as the "as-if loop." Damasio (1994)

Alfonso is a 30-year-old patient who comes to consultation suffering from ulcerative colitis that causes much discomfort as well as from digestive problems that begin to affect his relationship with his partner. When the anamnesis is done, it is observed that he is an extremely perfectionistic and self-demanding person. His mother was a very demanding person who was never satisfied and who demanded that he study at all times. When he is asked to close his eyes and feel the sensation and bring back an image, what comes up is the fear when he hears the keys opening the door and the fear that his mother will scold him for something he has done wrong.

In this case the danger no longer exists, but Alfonso continues to live as if it were still happening, and his body reacts in the same way as it did then. This example also gives us other important information on how to work with somatic sensations. We can think of something and observe the reactions of our body (top-down processing) but we can also feel the sensations and observe if any memory, image, or any associated sensation comes to mind (bottom-up processing) (Van der Kolk, 2014). Our body keeps a somatic memory of everything that happened even though we do not have verbal memory or images of what happened, that is, although there is no explicit memory.

In many cases there will be no memory of any traumatic event and there will be no explanation for what happens at the somatic level. Almost no one has memories from before 3 or 4 years of age because the hippocampus and language areas have not developed and, therefore, there cannot be semantic memory, a narrative sense of the self. But from the first months of life, already in the womb, our body is subjected to different sensations that are evaluated and remembered so it will know how to react in the future.

Basically, we can find three situations in which there is a feeling of discomfort in the body without knowing the origin.

1. The fact that there are no conscious memories of something does not mean that it has not happened; nobody can remember their birth, but if one can read this, one necessarily had to be born at some time. Our body keeps memory of what happened from the first months of life, ever since we began to exist in the maternal womb. Some authors even argue that constant anxiety often originates in a mother who was anxious during pregnancy (O'Shea, 2009). We know the influence that our somatic memory has since before our birth from Polyvagal Theory (Porges, 2011). We call the moments of negative emotions that have been lived before having access to language (approximately before 4 years of age) *preverbal traumas*.
2. In cases of very serious trauma (regardless of the age at which it happened), there could be an absence of sensations. In cases of very serious threats, the body releases many opiates that prevent the feeling of discomfort in

order to survive the trauma, and it is not true that there were no sensations but that the impact was so severe that the body became paralyzed and the mind dissociated as a way to protect us. The body and mind were frozen at that moment and they spend a lot of energy so that the frozen pain does not appear again in, what is known as *somatic dissociation* (Scaer, 2014).

3. People in whom the cortical areas of the brain predominate tend to intellectualize everything and not feel anything. As we saw in the chapter on defenses, this is a way of not feeling the discomfort associated with what happened. This is often enhanced by avoidance behaviors, especially physical ones such as bodybuilding or extreme sports,also with an intellectualization or excessive rigidity that helps to avoid the sensations associated with the pain caused in the past by negative emotions.

With patients who have feelings of discomfort and do not know their origin, we must take extreme precautions because we may find ourselves in a situation of preverbal trauma or dissociation. With people who have difficulty feeling what is going on inside their bodies, we must use a lot of psychoeducation and start out working in an intellectual way so that the patient can reduce their defenses and begin to face the dissociated sensations.

In other cases, we will find the opposite situation: individuals who are overwhelmed by emotions and feelings of discomfort that cause them much suffering. The demand will be that we alleviate their discomfort as soon as possible.

Table 14.1 Hierarchy of the different systems of both the CNS and the ANS. They become sequentially activated when faced with internal or external stimuli.

Origin of Lack of Sensations	*Explanations*	*Ways of Avoiding Pain*
Preverbal traumas	That happened when I was very young, I don't remember it.	It happened a long time ago, there's no way I'll remember.
Traumatic dissociation	What happened must have been very painful, but I'm over it; I don't feel anything when I remember it. I didn't feel anything back then; it's like I'd seen it in a movie when I was watching it.	That happened a long time ago, it doesn't bother me anymore but I'd rather not think about it. It's impossible it'll affect me.
Body–mind dissociation	I don't have a trauma anymore, I never feel anything in my body. This exercise isn't for me, I don't feel anything when I think about upsetting or unpleasant things.	Intellectualization Obsessions Sports that demand a lot of effort In eating disorders, anorexia may be a way of not feeling the body

Symptoms may be headaches, muscle contractures, chest or stomach pains, sore throat, and so on. The therapist always has to make a good assessment before starting somatic work. If we start too early or too intensely, we can overwhelm the patient's capacities and they will abandon therapy or, what is worse, we will retraumatize them.

In cases where the sensations are very strong and overwhelm the patient, we will have to use relaxation techniques to help him regulate himself before beginning to work with the sensations. A very common error when it comes to the approach taken with these patients is to perform intense meditation or relaxation techniques from the start as a way to help them calm down. If the sensations are rather intense or the patient is quite dissociated, we may find that the person begins to have a panic attack. *We should never relax a patient who is overactivated or dissociated too quickly.* When they notice their sensations, there will be a rebound effect that can make them hyperventilate and become emotionally overexcited, and, in some cases, suffer a panic attack.

Another very common mistake is to recommend meditation or self-hypnosis techniques to extremely anxious patients. It is quite difficult, nearly impossible, for these patients to leave their mind blank, and being unable to achieve it gives them more anxiety. It is much more advisable in the first stages of therapy to give audios of hypnosis or to teach them to distract themselves and not focus on the bodily sensations until they can learn to self-regulate (see Chapter 13).

Working with the Body

Every person is different in the way they feel their body, in their sensations. There will be patients who, even if they try to feel something, will tell us over and over again that they do not feel anything, and others who will feel excessively and who will even be afraid of their sensations, such as people suffering from panic attacks.

None of these states are useful when working with sensations. So, in therapy we will work within what we call the *window of tolerance*: a zone between the two extremes in which the patient can work with what he feels in his body without disconnecting and without overly stimulating himself.

In patients with anxiety and panic attacks we will find that they step outside the window too easily. Therefore, we will have to do a very delicate job of keeping them within an activation spectrum that is therapeutic for the patient or we risk retraumatizing them. At other times, they can become hypoactivated and not feel anything in the body, which can lead us to the error of believing that there are no sensations, and it may so happen that they are so intense that they overwhelm and collapse the patient. Work with bodily sensations can be very activating in some people so we should always work within the limits that the individual can tolerate. It is just as serious that they have abreactions that

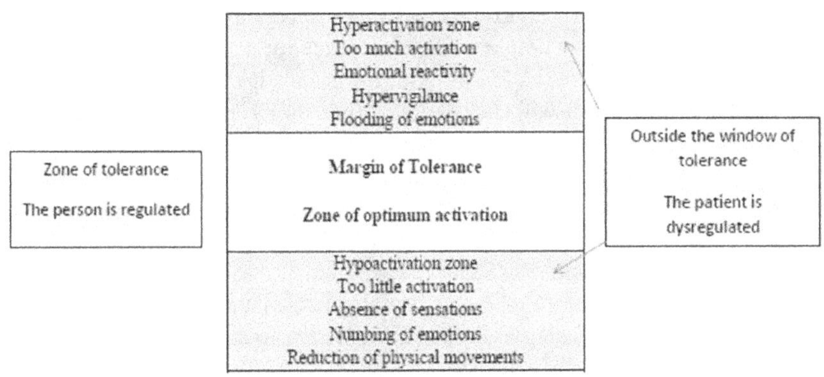

Figure 14.3 The Window of Tolerance.

hyperactivate them as it is that they collapse; this would be an excess of emotional charge that leads to dissociation.

Regarding what time we should introduce the work with the sensations, this will depend on the type of attachment and how they are handled. In all cases it is advisable to do so when the therapeutic alliance has been consolidated and to introduce the work little by little. In individuals with anxious or disorganized attachment, they will first need to be stabilized, while in those individuals with avoidant attachment, a more cognitive work of psychoeducation must be done first; then the therapist must get them closer to the sensations very slowly so that they learn to know and tolerate them. People with tension anxiety due to excessive control will find that their way of protecting themselves in the past was to not connect with their body. We must have patience because this type of patient will tend to get frustrated easily when they find this work unhelpful and difficult. Once again, I must insist that we are the ones who have to adapt to the needs of the patients and never the other way around. We need to be careful and always keep in mind, whatever our professional approach may be, that we must work within the patient's window of tolerance.

Techniques for Working with Sensations

There are many therapeutic techniques for working with the body: focusing (Gendlin, 1982), sensory-motor therapy (Ogden & Minton, 2000; Ogden & Fisher, 2015) or somatic experience (Levine, 2010). I will briefly develop the latter.

Scaer (2014) proposes dissociation from a somatic point of view. He states that all animals have a capacity to discharge anger or frustration but that human beings have lost this capacity. When a lion cannot hunt a gazelle, it will have a surplus of energy (stress) that it will eliminate from its body through tremors or continuous movements. The gazelle that has survived will also have felt a lot of fear and will also need to eliminate all the accumulated stress; it will do so in the same way that the lion would. If a bird hits a window, it will be immobilized for a few seconds and then it will shake and continue to fly. However, if we grab it and prevent those tremors, it will move in a disoriented way; it will be unable to fly and, in a few hours, it will die (Levine, 2010). All living beings have natural mechanisms of discharge of the energy associated with the event so that there is no trace of the trauma in the body.

According to some authors (Scaer, 2014), humans, with the acquisition of a highly developed prefrontal lobe and lateralization of the brain, have lost this capacity. It is as if by being able to reflect, we no longer need to unload the traumas in that way and we can do it by verbalizing or mentalizing them. In many cases, the body, by keeping a somatic memory of the trauma, will react with symptoms of pain or anxiety when there is a stimulus that reminds us of it.

A very basic explanation is the following: the work with the technique of "somatic experiencing" consists of facilitating the controlled discharge of the blocked energy with the completion of the unfinished movement at the moment of the traumatic event, even if this is done through imagination. To achieve this, we must always work within our patient's window of tolerance, making him observe with curiosity the sensations he has when he remembers the traumatic event. Curiosity and fear are incompatible (one emotion generates dopamine and the other noradrenaline in our brain). There will be an activation of the sensations and, immediately, a relaxation of these, in what is known as "pendulum," helping to discharge the energy that remained (Levine, 2010).

We will find that some patients will have a wider window of tolerance and will be able to work with a greater pendulum, and others will have a narrower one. In these cases, with this work we can help them feel the sensations that tend to be avoided and slowly widen the window of tolerance by accepting a greater activation of the sensations each time.

A phenomenon to highlight is kindling, which consists of a perpetuation of pain stimuli (apparently affecting the thalamus) which could explain many diseases with chronic pain, such as fibromyalgia or chronic fatigue. It would be a delayed somatic expression of trauma (Rodríguez et al., 2005). It is a situation in which the nervous system continues to register pain when in reality there is no cause that produces it anymore.

Relating sensations with emotions will help discharge the energy that was blocked during the traumatic event with the help of the reassuring presence of the therapist, substituting the attachment figures who were not available at the time, either because they were not there physically or emotionally or because they were not helpful. According to the polyvagal theory model, in the first phase we seek social help and, if it is not available or insufficient, our body and mind are placed in fight-flight mode and later in collapse-dissociation mode. The presence of the therapist replaces the figure of attachment who was not there when it happened and helps focus on the here and now, the only situation in which homeostasis can be recovered.

Aurore is a 26-year-old patient who comes to the clinic because she is afraid of upsetting her mother, and this causes her many problems with her partner because she always has to ask her mother's permission for everything, even for the smallest things, such as what clothes to buy her daughters or where to go on holiday.

T. Aurore, I want you to imagine that you do something without asking your mother. Where do you feel the sensation of discomfort in your body?
C. In the pit of my stomach.
T. I would like you to imagine if you had to give it a color and a shape, what would you give it?
C. It would be like a round, black ball.
T. Very good. I would like you to observe it and see how you feel observing it.
C. I feel really bad, it makes me want to cry.
T. Crying is not a bad thing, but I do not want you to feel bad and get overwhelmed. Can you remember the nice sensation you felt earlier when you hugged your daughters? Do you remember where you felt it?
C. Yes, in my chest, in my heart.
T. Very well, feel it now. When you feel better observe the two sensations. How different they are.
C. Yes. One is very heavy and the other very light.
T. That's really good. Feel the black ball in your stomach again.
C. It's become more diffused, a little less heavy.
T. Very good, keep feeling it.
C. I see myself as a child with my mother and as a mother with my daughters.
T. How is the sensation now?
C. The pleasant sensation in the chest predominates. I notice how I breathe better. I do not have to do what my mother wants. I am an adult woman, and I am a mother now. I am no longer a child.
T. Feel the sensation again. Has it changed? Has it moved?
C. It's barely there. It's almost completely disappeared.
T. Imagine doing something without asking your mother or doing something that she doesn't find right. How do you feel?
C. Very good. Much better. I don't know why I've acted like this all this time.

By practicing these exercises over and over again we can connect the fragmented parts of the trauma on a physical, mental, and emotional level. Being able to narrate the experience and/or experience it in a corrective way makes the body change the somatic memory of what happened. People with EMDR training can accompany these exercises with bilateral stimulation. However, due to the activation that it causes, it is necessary to be properly trained to be able to apply this technique to the somatic work.

We can also work with the body not as a way to solve a specific traumatic event but as a way to change the way we face the world. Procedural memory is one that causes us to repeat actions, emotions, or sensations in a repetitive and unconscious way. If we felt displaced during our childhood, we would tend to close our shoulders, and if we did not want to stand out we would tend to avoid looking into people's eyes. With the passage of time, all these gestures will be part of our repertoire of unconscious behaviors (Ogden & Fisher, 2015).

By changing our sensations and postures, due to bottom-up processing, we can change how we feel about ourselves and others. You can do the experiment of smiling a few seconds and you will see how you will feel much happier. During therapy, we can explain to our patients behaviors of the body that we observe and that changing them can help them change their cognitions and emotions as well. The therapeutic work consists of going in a little and leaving. Going in to a degree that the patient sees that he can come out of easily is a way to empower the patient; this is always done within their window of tolerance.

Seijo (2015) states that these bodily attitudes are somatic defenses that arose in situations of emotional activation and that may reappear during the therapeutic work; when reliving emotions or memories from the past, the body will respond in the same way as it did then. The work with these defenses (see Chapter 15) must be very carefully done because they play a role in the protection system, which should be respected.

According to Seijo (2015), some somatic defenses that we will find during therapeutic work are as follows:

- The tension shown in different parts of the body reflects the repression of an emotion that wants to leave but that is blocked, usually rage (e.g., clenching the jaw, fists, legs, etc.);
- Lifting the shoulders is a gesture of protection; the emotion that usually accompanies it is fear;
- Biting the lip usually means controlling sadness;
- Forward inclination of the body in the chair shows protection and defense against emotions that the person avoids showing;
- Sitting in the corner of the chair shows discomfort and a desire to get out of the situation;
- Withdrawing eye contact or interrupting it at any specific moment shows the avoidance of not wanting to receive something from the therapist, of not being seen, or of fear of being exposed;
- Speaking in the third person means not taking charge;

- Blockage in the chest prevents fluid breathing; it is a way of getting blocked or of not letting go;
- Tension in the neck is an attempt to control what happens in the process; it is related to the feeling of losing control;
- Tension in the throat usually means the prelude to crying, what was not said, or what was not spoken about, representing a communication blockage;
- Stress in the jaw means unexpressed or contained anger, and is related to those with a tendency to be "chewers";
- Appearances of sleepiness during the processing speaks of the person having exceeded his threshold of tolerance to what is being released. It is a way to show that the processing is too intense;
- Headaches during the processing represent traumatic material that the person is reluctant to let out. It may be a sign that there is some dissociative part that is making an appearance;
- A sensation of fogginess shows that some part is protecting what is coming out or wants to show itself. It is usually common when people try to talk about their childhood and is a part protects contact with that information;
- Sensation of the ears ringing as if the person could not hear, or numbness in the hands, are clear signs of dissociation during reprocessing;
- A curious sensation is the one where the patient is on the verge of anger: it is situated over one of the eyebrows, usually the right one, and is usually the prelude to a containment of blocked anger;
- Stress in the back and weight in the shoulders usually signifies the burden and responsibility that the person feels in his life;
- Moving the foot constantly during consultation is a way to release the tension that is felt.

Conclusions

From the first months of life in the maternal womb, long before we can think, our body has sensations and interacts with the environment. Starting at birth, the relationship with caregivers will allow the child to have either a normal or a pathological development at mental level but also a somatic one.

If in childhood there have been many situations of discomfort, the body will remember what happened in the form of somatic defenses. The brain uses the body in order to know if the stimuli that occur in the environment as well as on the inside are either positive or threatening. If there have been many situations of discomfort in the past, the body may respond negatively to any stimulus, causing strong anxiety. In other people, the defense will be to not feel anything as a way to avoid the pain suffered in the past.

In therapy, we offer the space and the occasion to be able to discharge the energy that was collapsed. In a corrective way, the body can feel the negative experiences of the past which can be processed. As a result, the body will discharge the residual energy that prevented the resolution of the trauma. Somatic work is also important in order to promote non-verbal communication that will help to recognize the emotional states of the patient.

Regardless of the treatment protocol we follow to work with anxiety, work with the body is fundamental: not only does it allow the patients to manage their discomfort but it is also quite useful when trying to better understand the emotions and sensations of our patients.

References

Aguado, L. (2010). *Emoción, afecto y motivación.* Alianza editorial.

Damasio, A. R. (1994). *Descartes' error: Emotion, reason, and the human brain.* G.P. Putnam's Sons.

Gendlin, E. T. (1982). *Focusing*. Bantam Books.

Levine, P. A. (2010). *In an unspoken voice: How the body releases trauma and restores goodness*. North Atlantic Books.

Ogden, P., & Minton, K. (2000). *Trauma and the body: A sensorimotor approach to psychotherapy*. Norton & Company.

Ogden, P., & Fisher, J. (2015). *Sensorimotor psychotherapy: Interventions for trauma and attachment*. Norton & Company.

O´Shea, K. (2009). The EMDR early trauma protocol. In R. Shapiro (Ed.), *EMDR solutions II. For depression, eating disorders perfomace and more*. Norton.

Porges, S. (2011). *The polyvagal theory. Neurophysiological foundations of emotions*. Norton.

Rodríguez, B., Fernández, A., & Bayón, C. (2005). Trauma, disociación y somatización. *Anuario de psicología clínica y de la salud, 1*, 27–38.

Sapolsky, R. M. (2004). *Why zebras don't get ulcers: The acclaimed guide to stress, stress-related diseases, and coping*. Holt Paperback.

Scaer, R. (2014). *The body bears the burden: Trauma, dissociation, and disease*. Routledge.

Schore, A. (2003). *Affect dysregulation and disorders of the self.* Norton.

Seijo, N. (2015). *Máster de Psicoterapia con EMDR. Módulo 6. Tema 2. Defensas Somáticas*. Universidad Nacional de Educación a Distancia (UNED).

Van der Kolk, B. (2014). *The body keeps the score: Brain, mind, and body in the healing of trauma*. Penguin Group.

15 Psychological Defenses

All living beings have an innate mechanism to avoid circumstances that are upsetting or dangerous; from the most primitive beings to the most evolved, they all tend to avoid painful stimuli and seek the pleasant ones. Fear is an innate circuit of all vertebrates' brains (Panksepp & Biven, 2012) and associated with this there are always defense mechanisms to avoid or to minimize threats. They can be, in the case of human beings, physical (e.g., running away) or psychological (e.g., denying something that is obvious).

The defense mechanisms that we will discuss in this chapter are processes to protect people from excessive anxiety or any other negative emotion (Cramer, 2009). These are automatic psychological processes that protect the individual against anxiety and threats of internal or external origin. From a psychodynamic point of view, defense mechanisms enable self-protection by reducing the awareness of thoughts, desires, or fears due to internal conflicts. From a cognitive-behavioral point of view, these would be protective psychological processes that allow the individual to deal with externalized threats as well as internalized stressors that create conflicts (Sharon & Hentschel, 2013). From a neurobiological perspective, defenses are neuronal associations that give a conditioned response to a stimulus that is perceived as dangerous or upsetting; the more often similar stimuli are produced to which the same response is given, the greater the probability that these neurons (with all the consequent hormonal responses) are fired together, leaving the defense more associated with the threat. As always, these threats can be real, for example "they will make a fool of me or assault me," or imaginary, for example, "I do not deserve to be loved." Once again, we defend the need to integrate different therapeutic approaches, which is why in this chapter we will work by integrating the three approaches, using one or the other depending on the needs of the patient.

The defense mechanisms (just like memory) may be implicit or explicit:

- Explicit: Voluntary and mediated by the cortical areas that process thought. For example, when a friend asks us for money and we do not want to give it to him, we can invent an excuse to not have to do it;
- Implicit: These are controlled by the subcortical areas and are, therefore, not mediated by any reasoning. They arise without us being aware of them; they

DOI: 10.4324/9781003646341-17

appear spontaneously. They are not always appropriate or adequate. They can, in turn, be of two types.

- Innate: They are those that are encoded in our genome and show themselves when there is a danger. E.g., idealizing parents as a way to continue to love them despite the abuse;
- Acquired: They are those that worked in our childhood and that are repeated in our behavior without being able to avoid them. E.g., lying in order to achieve something we want.

As children, we lack the cognitive and emotional tools to defend ourselves from many of the painful situations that are going to happen to us. Our parents play a vital role in order to defend us until we can do it ourselves. When those people who had to defend us could not or did not know how to, or when they themselves were the source of the threat, the child was forced to find ways, however basic and/or ineffective, to tolerate and overcome uncertainty. By force of repetition, these defense mechanisms will be strengthened at the neuronal level and will end up becoming behavioral patterns that are part of our personality, even though at present they might be totally maladaptive or even pathological.

The emotional wounds and the defenses used to defend ourselves are consolidated as implicit memory in an associated way, so that, when I am an adult and I perceive danger, the amygdala (LeDoux, 1994) will have associated the threat with the response regardless of age and context, thus creating an automatic and unconscious response that escapes the will of the person. Many of the problems for which our patients seek psychological help are defenses that have become maladaptive. Our therapeutic work cannot begin by eliminating the symptom (that is, the defense that has been created) but by making the patient see that there is no longer any threat. The defenses can be seen as a brain–mind mechanism used as a way to survive and to achieve a balance that neither hurts the external nor internal world (Ginot, 2015). As they are repeated they become more rigid and may cause bigger problems than the ones they try to solve.

Rachel is a 24-year-old woman who comes to consultation because she is afraid that her guts (intestines) will rumble in public and this prevents her more and more often from undertaking activities such as shopping, riding a bus, or even having fun. She is afraid of her bowel growling in public and of making a fool of herself.

In this case, the noise of the intestines is involuntary and causes much suffering. However, the fear response to make a fool of oneself depends on the patient's assessment of the reactions of the environment. In this case, we could work on helping her realize the irrationality of her thoughts and emotions, but the patient already knows this. It is much more useful to work on the fear of ridicule or rejection until she can acknowledge that her fear of a rumbling stomach and the subsequent reactions of others is excessive.

As we grow up, the defenses will increase in complexity and shape. The first defenses are acquired in relation to our caregivers and, later, as we mature, from friends and teachers. In adolescence, when sexuality begins to awaken and we start to compare ourselves with our classmates, trying to be attractive or accepted, and later in adulthood, most of these defense mechanisms are already a part of our implicit memory and appear spontaneously before any stimulus reminds us of any previous real or imaginary threat.

The greater the threat, the earlier the age when the threat occurred and the closer the attachment figure that caused the damage was, the more necessary the defensive mechanism and the stronger the connection between similar threats and defense responses will be. Although these could be very effective at the time as a way to reduce discomfort and anxiety, since they act unconsciously and outside of our will, they can become increasingly unsuitable even to the point where they become pathological.

It is important to note that defense mechanisms do not solve the source of anxiety; they only reduce it when they work well (Sharon & Hentschel, 2013). The conflict will continue to exist under similar or different conditions. We will often find that the pathology that brings our patients to the consultation is the mechanism that was created to be able to obviate or bear the conflict. The defenses are necessary, for example, after a trauma so as to be able to return to normality little by little. However, when quantity exceeds quality, or when the defenses are outside of what is considered healthy with respect to what happened, they have become a greater disorder than the one they wanted to avoid. This would be considered pathological.

In many cases we will find defenses that are much less complex and not quite so pathological. At other times, they will be much more insidious. Some authors defend that the structural dissociation of the personality is an extreme defense mechanism created to withstand uncertainty in the face of threat (González, 2015; Van der Hart et al., 2006). This is what we call "dissociative defenses." We know that through the autonomic nervous system, our body will also keep memory of the trauma – the so-called "somatic defenses" (Seijo, 2015).

Types of Defense Mechanisms

Although the defense mechanisms are not covered in the latest manual of psychopathology DSM-5 (APA, 1994), they did appear in the previous one, the DSM-4 (2002). These defense mechanisms have been divided conceptually and empirically into groups called defense levels. I literally transcribe the definitions taken from the manual. I will detail only the most important ones for the disorders we are working on.

1. High-Adaptive Level

This level of defensive functioning results in optimal adaptation in the handling of stressors. These defenses usually maximize gratification and allow the conscious awareness of feelings, ideas, and their consequences.

They also promote an optimum balance among conflicting motives. Examples of defenses at this level are:

- Affiliation: The individual deals with emotional conflict or internal or external stressors by turning to others for help or support. This involves sharing problems with others but does not imply trying to make someone else responsible for them.

As we saw in Chapter 2, this is part of the innate mechanisms of behavior against threats facing human beings. In people with anxiety, it will constantly be there as a way to withstand the discomfort. It becomes pathological when we cannot do anything without the company of people we consider safe.

- Altruism: The individual deals with emotional conflict or with internal or external stressors by dedicating himself to meeting the needs of others. Unlike the self-sacrifice, sometimes characteristic of reaction formation, the individual receives gratification either vicariously or from the response of others.

In its pathological part, the person cannot devote any attention or care to himself; he can only think about the welfare of others. It is an immature defense of the type "when my mother is well, I can be well." As we saw in previous chapters, this generates a lot of anger that, when unable to be expressed in a healthy way, will cause anxiety and/or panic attacks.

- Anticipation: The individual deals with emotional conflict or internal or external stressors by having emotional reactions in advance of, or by anticipating the consequences of, possible future events and will realistically consider alternative responses or solutions.

There is another universal defense in all human beings, which allows us to learn from the past to be able to plan in the future. However, when it becomes pathological it creates a repeated anticipation for different future scenarios (often catastrophic), which make the amygdala perceive a danger where there is none. This causes a stronger reaction of anxiety which, in turn, causes more anticipation. The vicious cycle is evident.

- Humor: The individual deals with emotional conflict or with internal or external stressors by emphasizing the amusing or ironic aspects of the conflict or stressors. We find this in many patients who use humor as a way to reduce conflict. In many cases, they do so as a way to seem happy while hiding their suffering inside.

- Sublimation: The individual deals with emotional conflict or with internal or external stressors by channeling potentially maladaptive feelings or impulses into socially acceptable behavior (e.g., doing contact sports to channel angry impulses).

We will see this mechanism very often in pathologies associated with emotional disorders, especially in relation to the emotion of anger (anger, frustration, feeling of helplessness). By not being able to express it openly, the patient will look for alternative mechanisms to mitigate it.

- Suppression: The individual deals with emotional conflict or with internal or external stressors by intentionally avoiding thinking about disturbing problems, wishes, feelings, or experiences.

This defense is vital in the therapeutic process because we will often find phobias towards the traumatic memories that will hinder treatment. We must be especially careful with this defense because it will help us to know at what pace we can work and what the core beliefs are that sustain the conflict.

2. *Mental Inhibition (Compromise Formation) Level*

Defensive functioning at this level keeps potentially threatening ideas, feelings, memories, wishes, or fears away from the patient's awareness. Examples are:

Isolation of affect: The individual deals with emotional conflict or with internal or external stressors by separating ideas from the feelings they were originally associated with. The individual loses touch with the feelings associated with a given idea (e.g., a traumatic event) while remaining aware of the cognitive elements of it (e.g., descriptive details).

We will often find this in patients who reveal something (that should be) painful without emotion. Although it may seem normal and adaptive shortly after the trauma, it may become pathological when time passes. It is a subtype of denial or suppression.

- *Dissociation*: The individual deals with emotional conflict or with internal or external stressors by means of having a temporary alteration in the usually integrated functions of consciousness, memory, perception of self or the environment, or sensory-motor behavior. We dedicate a complete chapter to this mechanism which, due to its importance and complexity, requires a special section.

- *Reaction formation*: The individual deals with emotional conflict or with internal or external stressors by substituting behavior, thoughts, or feelings that are diametrically opposed to their own unacceptable thoughts or feelings (this usually occurs simultaneously with their repression). We will constantly see it in disorders that involve thoughts or actions of a self-punitive nature. The aggressiveness that cannot be shown outwardly turns towards the individual himself.
- *Intellectualization*: The individual deals with emotional conflict or with internal or external stressors through excessive use of abstract thinking or by making generalizations to control or minimize disturbing feelings. Although we will hardly find it in this type of disorder, it is important to keep in mind: it gives priority to the cortical areas for fear of the emotions that lie within the individual. It changes feeling for thinking.
- *Repression*: The individual deals with emotional conflict or with internal or external stressors by expelling disturbing wishes, thoughts, or experiences from conscious awareness. The feeling component may remain conscious, detached from its associated ideas. This is a type of dissociation in which things are hidden voluntarily (dissociation is involuntary), for instance, for fear of the effects they could have if they were carried out. Patients spend a lot of energy in containing them, most of the time with little success.

3. Minor Image-distorting Level

This level is characterized by distortions in the image of the self, body, or others that may be employed to regulate self-esteem. Examples are:

- *Devaluation*: The individual deals with emotional conflict or with internal or external stressors by attributing exaggerated negative qualities to self or others. This is at the core of social phobias, panic disorders, and anxiety disorders. Individuals who have felt rejected by their loved ones in their childhood will internalize a fear of rejection that will make them feel devaluated in order to avoid being evaluated and therefore rejected again.
- *Idealization*: The individual deals with emotional conflict or with internal or external stressors by attributing exaggerated positive qualities to others. We will find this in many patients with complicated childhoods. Idealization allows the person to keep in touch with loved ones even if these are the source of the conflict. The problem with this mechanism is that it will often cause the idealization of others and the devaluation of oneself as a way to overcome the incongruity. It is a very complex mechanism to treat and should be done with great care since eliminating it can give patients a very strong sense of loneliness. In narcissistic disorders, we will find an idealization of the self that allows the person to not connect with his lack of resources or self-esteem.

4. Action Level

This level is characterized by defensive mechanisms that face internal or external stressors by means of action or withdrawal. Examples are:

- *Passive aggressive behavior*: The individual faces emotional conflicts and threats of internal or external origin showing aggressiveness towards others indirectly and not assertively. There is an external mask of open submission to others, behind which resistance, resentment, and hostility actually hide. People who use this defense either sabotage relationships with others or explode without any relation to what happened because they store a memory of each of the outrages they have suffered.
- *Impulsive behavior* (acting out)**:** The individual faces emotional conflicts and threats of internal or external origin through action rather than through reflections or feelings. The concept of defensive acting-out is not synonymous with bad behavior, since it relates to emotional conflicts. It would commonly be what we know as an "escape from oneself," that is, to perform acts or activities in a compulsive way so that we do not have to feel any emotion. Examples of this are workaholics or extreme athletes.
- *Complaints and rejection of help*: The individual faces emotional conflicts and threats of internal or external origin through complaints or requests for help that conceal hidden feelings of hostility or resentment towards others which are then expressed in the form of rejection of any suggestion, advice or offer of help. Complaints or demands may refer to physical or psychological symptoms or problems of daily life. This defense is quite similar to the passive-aggressive one. "I need and use others asking them for help or using them, which causes me discomfort. Yet, for fear of losing them, I hide my anger by showing it indirectly."

Working with Defenses

Defenses, as the name suggests, have arisen for some reason although at present we do not know why they arose and why they have become pathological over time. We must be very careful when working with them because we could leave the client "defenseless." In all cases we must use maxims that oblige us to be very respectful with the patient (McCullough, 1997):

- Maintain therapeutic alliance;
- Teach the patient to recognize which defenses he uses and if they are ego-syntonic or ego-dystonic;
- Regulate anxiety by teaching the patient not to be critical of himself. Encourage self-compassion. Identify conflicts (anxiety, guilt, shame or anger) that make the defense necessary;

- Work on strengths (resources) while working with defenses;
- Identify the emotions, phobias, and schemes that are hidden behind the defense;
- Generate a working hypothesis about the patient's patterns and confront them.

Maintain Therapeutic Alliance

We must never forget that defenses fulfill a protective function and that they are the result of pain. The therapist must work with care at all times so that the patient does not feel intimidated or forced to do a job that he does not want or is unable to do. The defenses, although they may be a reason for suffering, play a role, and the patient will only be able to eliminate them if he feels that we are not going to judge or hurt him again.

In these moments, more than in any other of the therapy, we must be very careful with the transference and the countertransference in the therapeutic process. Observing if the patient is prepared so that he can work with the nuclear material that caused the trauma is fundamental. Sometimes the therapist may be afraid of eliminating the defense, either because he does not know if he will be able to handle the patient's reaction or because he recognizes that defense inside himself. In the latter case, the therapist must seek supervision to be able to work on this topic.

When questioning the defenses, we must use Socratic language that prevents the client from feeling intimidated or judged. For that we can use expressions like: "Correct me if I'm wrong but …" In this way, we will give the patient the opportunity to continue when he is prepared to face the defense. If he denies the problem we will know that the patient is not ready.

Ask as if in doubt: "I don't understand … You are telling me that a 5-year-old girl can provoke …" or "You mean that of what happened, you were the only one responsible …" or "Maybe at that moment you did what you could with the tools you had …"

Teach the Patient the Defenses He Uses

The defenses the patient may use are (McCullough et al., 2003):

- *Ego-syntonic*: They are those defenses the patient agrees with. They are part of his Self and he does not want to change them. All avoidance or idealization defenses belong to this group. They are behaviors or thoughts that the patient perceives as something positive about himself but that hinders therapeutic work and prevents the resolution of the trauma.

An example would be a person afflicted with an irritable colon. When making the conceptualization, we observe that the patient is invariably anticipating problems, worrying about making everything perfect, and so on – in other words, under constant tension. As we have seen, this behavior can be performed as a control strategy so as not to feel emotions. When we point this out to the patient, he will tell us that he likes to be a "responsible" person.

- *Ego-dystonic*: These are the defenses that the patient does not want to maintain. They will often be symptoms that the patient has come to therapy for to improve. Most of the time, patients do not see them as defenses but as the source of their problems. This could be, for example, the case with addictions and obsessions that fulfill a function of evasion or distraction from trauma. Patients can come with a request to go out on the street without fear of having loose stools, for example, but we know that this is the defense that protects them from relating to others and from being rejected.

In these cases, we must be very pedagogical and have a well-established therapeutic relationship before we can explain it and work on it. Obviously, this type of defense will be dismantled as the therapy comes to an end. First, we will work on the trauma and then on the defense.

Obviously, the more ego-syntonic the defenses, the more difficult it will be to change them and work with them. In order to work with defenses, patients must see them as something that they must change. We must go from ego-syntonic defenses ("I am like that") to ego-dystonic defenses ("I do not want to keep doing this") (McCullough et al., 2003).

Regulate anxiety. Teach the patient not to be critical of himself. Encourage self-compassion. Identify conflicts: anxiety, guilt, shame or anger that make the defense necessary.

When the defenses are ego-dystonic (or when they stop being ego-syntonic), the patient will feel a lot of guilt and shame. It is very important to be very pedagogical and explain the function the defenses fulfill, and how they are secondary gain. There may be parts that cause the symptom in order to defend themselves against pain, but this may cause rejection by the other parts of the patient who want to lead a normal life (Van der Hart et al., 2006).

It is very important to teach relaxation and acceptance techniques (see Chapter 13) to help the patient manage the anxiety associated with those behaviors, thoughts, or emotions that he experiences as intrusive.

Another very important point is to work on the grief when the defenses begin to change. There may be a lot of guilt over having maintained them for so long (or for not having done anything to change them before).

It is essential that if the defense is impulsive, such as taking drugs or fighting to release aggressiveness, we must install self-control strategies while working on the origin of the defense. In cases where the defense is causing many problems in the present (self-harm, suicidal behavior, drug abuse, violence), we must work to reduce it because if not, it is impossible to work with whatever is hidden behind it.

Working on Strengths (Resources) while Working with Defenses

We have to keep the balance at all times between gradually working on eliminating the defense and working on what is hidden behind it as well as facilitating resources that allow the patient to be in control at all times. The defense fulfills a protective function, and we cannot leave the patient unprotected.

In some cases, neither the therapist nor the patient may find any resources. Still, we can use expressions of validation such as "you must be very brave to submit to this process, many people would not dare" or "you have to be very brave to be honest with a person you hardly know …" or "I admire how you have been able to face your fears, most people would not dare to do so …"

If we find more complex resources in the patient, we will use them; for example, "You say that you are unable to see yourself as someone useful but it seems that your children do not see you that way," "How do you think you would feel if the problem did not exist, what would be different?", "If you had to give advice to a friend who's going through this, what would you say?", and "What prevents you from saying it to yourself?"

Obviously, as more resources become available, the defense is less necessary. Ideally, patients should spontaneously express these resources, but if we see that there is fear or uncertainty, we should install the resources ourselves.

An important point is that in many cases during the therapeutic process the patients will doubt if they are doing well, thinking they are bad patients unable of doing therapy. In these cases, we must evaluate if we are going too fast and that maybe the patients are not ready to eliminate the defense yet. We must reinforce the alliance or we must validate them and install more resources.

Identify Emotions, Phobias, and the Schemes that Hide Behind the Defense

The most frequent emotions that we will find behind the defenses are fear (anger, impotence), guilt, and shame. Let's see how we can work with them in detail.

It is important to keep in mind that in narcissistic personalities, these defenses are concealed behind an ego that hides them so as not to feel pain of failure or humiliation. In these cases we must first validate the person's actions (thoughts, emotions) and then, little by little, work with what is hidden behind them.

Fear: We can use many synonyms when validating the emotion of fear. The terms that can help are *anger*, *impotence*, *frustration*, and *rage*. The way to defend against fear is to avoid it; this is what is known as a "phobia." We will find many intangible phobias in the work we do.

We can ask different questions to work with this defense:

- *What would scare you the most about saying what you think?*
- *What's the worst that could happen if ...?*
- *How would your mother (or father or brother) react if you told her how you felt?*

What would be the worst that could happen if you did what you want to do?

Guilt: A rather frequent defense is guilt, because it avoids confrontation and therefore makes the patient re-experience the feeling of rejection or failure. It usually takes the form of ruminative thoughts that exhaust the patient.

We can use the following questions to work with this defense:

- *It seems that you are your worst enemy. I wonder if you are reminded of someone in your family when you speak to yourself like that.*
- *If that sensation (thought, impulse) was trying to help you – I know it's hard to believe – how would it do so?*
- I wonder when you will feel that you have paid your due for what happened.
- *Where did you learn to feel (think, behave) like this? Surely it was necessary then but it seems that it's not helping you now, right?*

Do you think that sensations (thoughts, actions) are helping or hurting you? What's stopping you from changing it now?

Shame: If the previous defense is pain facing Self, shame is expressed facing others. It is a form of alarm so as not to feel rejection. Shame inhibits us in front of others.

We can ask different questions to work on this defense:

- *How do you think I feel or think when I look at you?*
- *What would you see if you looked in the mirror? What do you think others see?*
- *What would your mother (father, brother, partner) see if she were looking at you now?*
- *Do you think that avoiding that behavior is helping or hurting you?*
- *What's the worst thing that could happen if others knew what your problem is?*

Rejection is really tough but it seems that the loneliness is becoming unbearable, right?
The number of questions we can ask are almost infinite, and each therapist can create their own to be able to dismantle, step by step, the defense that sustains the problem. Whenever the patient is reluctant to work with a defense, we should consider that the client may not be prepared. In these cases, we can use phrases like "it's OK. We will arrive much earlier going very slowly," "This is your space and here you can and should express anything you need," "I thank you very much for your sincerity because I know that it is hard for you to tell me that and I assure you I'll take it into account."

Generate a Working Hypothesis about the Patient's Patterns and Confront Them

Finally, once the defense is ego-dystonic and the patient is ready to dismantle it, we can get to the point where he learned it and what function it has fulfilled all this time.

We can explain how, as time went on, that behavior (emotion, thought) has become stronger and therefore more difficult to avoid.

Explaining what our hypothesis about the function of the defense is can help the patient increase the connection between the different parts of his personality and encourage mentalization.

Once again, if the patient does not share the hypothesis or if what we say gives him anxiety, we should consider the fact that he is not prepared and we should review to what point we should return until he is able to accept it.

Working hypotheses are only inferences that we make; they can easily be wrong, and hence we should never try to impose our criteria on the patient. Many times, we will find that our hypothesis was not correct and we could do irreversible damage.

The brain, like any other organ in our body, has a capacity for self-healing, and once the defense stops being useful, the patient will find the best way to find another behavior (thought, emotion) that is more adaptive. We can act as the patient's travel companion, but if we impose our criteria we can produce more damage than the one we intended to avoid. Of course, we cannot let the patient feel unattended.

C. I wonder what I should do. Do you think I should tell my mother what happened?
T. I'd love to tell you that that is what I'd do. But then you'd be living my life instead of yours. What do you feel like doing?
C. I'm not ready to do that right now.
T. I'm sure that when the time comes, you'll know and will do what's best.

To finish the work with a defense, we can validate its need during all this time but deem it unnecessary now. It is important to highlight the possibility of relapses. The patterns that are deeply rooted may return. We need to explain that getting angry with himself will cause him to fall back into a vicious cycle which will be very difficult to abandon; it is much better to explore what function that defense tries to fulfill and calmly look for more adaptive strategies.

T. *Now I understand why you needed to think that (feel that, act like this) for a while. It is clear that it has been useful to allow you to move forward in life. But it seems that by helping you it was hurting you? Don't you think?*

C. *Yes. It's true that I could not stop doing it; it was beyond me. The funny thing is that now that I think about it I do not understand why I could not change it.*

T. *Sure, now you see it as if it had happened to someone else. But I wanted to tell you that if that defense has been with you for a long time, there are moments in which it may try to come back.*

C. *Oh, don't tell me that. I don't want to go back to that.*

T. *Of course, but that defense tries to help you and is very useful to indicate that you are straying from the correct path. You can use it as an indicator that there are things you should change in your life.*

C. *Sure, that's true. What do I do if it comes back?*

T. *You can thank it for warning you and change that which hurts you. And if you need it, you can come and see me and we'll work on it together. What do you think?*

C. *Perfect.*

The disappearance of one defense can cause another one to appear. Therefore, we must continue the therapeutic work until we reach the core of the trauma. The deeper and older the defense, the greater the precautions we must take. Another very useful way to work with defenses is through the EMDR approach, especially when they are related to trauma.

Working with Defenses from the EMDR Model

Within the EMDR model, several ways of working have been proposed, and we can help patients reduce defenses in order to reduce the conflicts that underlie them. These same proposals can be made without having to do any bilateral stimulation, but I think the results are far from being as effective. (I insist that this technique cannot be used without proper training.)

Knipe (2014) has created two models which allow us to continue working when there are blockages at the time of performing the therapeutic work due to the existence of defenses:

What's good about it? This technique is used when the patient has some behavior, thought, or emotion that he believes is harming him and which he cannot change. Consciously, the patient already knows all the inconveniences of the behavior. Still, there are unconscious motivations that sustain it. When asked "what is good about continuing to do or think or feel ...?" and by processing with bilateral stimulation, we force the person to see the problem from a different point of view, which will urge him to resolve the uncertainty. As we have seen, the brain has a capacity for self-healing, so the answer to the aforementioned question will help him to better understand the problem and will almost certainly go towards something more adaptive than what happened in the past. Find an example below, a technique that I use a lot in my sessions to help people quit smoking:

T. What's good about continuing to smoke? Think about the answer (bilateral stimulation).
C. There's really nothing good about it.
T. There must be something good if you've been smoking for 20 years, right? Think about that (bilateral stimulation).
C. It helps me relax. When I smoke, I stop what I'm doing and I relax.

Often when we continue stimulation, the person will end up saying that he has to change it or that he has spent too much time doing it.

Another technique by the same author (Knipe, 2014) is when there is resistance to continue going deeper with the treatment. It is useful when working with defenses that try to avoid reliving the trauma (phobia of traumatic memories) or to be critical of loved ones (idealization), or any other moment in which the patient resists working on a painful topic. It is very important to bear in mind that this technique can only be used if we feel that the patient is ready to remove the defense; if we do it too early, the only thing we will achieve is to retraumatize him.

The technique is to tell the patient: "0 being 'I do not have any problem in continuing working on this topic' and 10 'I do not want to talk about this in any way,' what number would you be at now?" And we process this with bilateral stimulation. An example:

C. I don't want to continue with this issue, I don't want to brood over the subject of abuse.
T. "0 being 'I don't have a problem continuing to work on this topic' and 10 'there is no way I want to talk about this,' what number would you be on now?
C. I don't know. Maybe a 5. I'm tired of going on and on about this subject.
T. Please, think about that (bilateral stimulation).

C. It's just more of the same. It's like reliving it again.
T. Please, think about that (bilateral stimulation).
C. I also realize that I have been carrying this for too long. I have to face my fears and end this now.
T. Please, think about that (bilateral stimulation).
C. I have to face my fears and end them definitively. I can't keep living like this. I think I'm ready to do something about it.

We continue doing bilateral stimulation until the discomfort is 0, which would mean that the defense has disappeared. It is a very elegant and simple way to help patients overcome their fears.

Shapiro (2005) uses the two-hand interweave technique. It is a very useful technique for blockages when choosing between two aspects and the patient asks us for help to decide. Obviously, we cannot decide for them, but we must help them decide for themselves. In these cases, defenses are hidden to support their decision against other people's opinions, fear of facing the future, and so on.

To use this technique, we tell the patient to put one of the decisions in one hand and put the other decision in the other. Once this is done, we begin to do bilateral stimulation until the person is clear about which decision is the best. An example:

T. You're asking me to help you decide whether to stay with your girlfriend or to dump her? But I think that is a decision you alone should make.
C. Yeah. But I'm going insane with the anxiety of making the right choice. I can't sleep just thinking about it.
T. I'd like you to place on one hand the decision of leaving her and on the other the decision of staying together (bilateral stimulation).
C. The truth is, I'm really upset because of what she did to me, it hurt me a lot. I wasn't expecting it.
T. Please, think about that (bilateral stimulation).
C. I don't want to leave her because deep down I love her but she's just hurt me really bad.
T. Please, think about that (bilateral stimulation).
C. She's explained why she did it and I haven't wanted to listen to her. I think I've been blinded by the hurt. Maybe I should give her a chance. I haven't behaved too well towards her either.

We continue stimulation until the person reaches a decision that is satisfactory. We must bear in mind that most patients come to consultation with the decision already made, and what they need most of the time is that we help them defend their decision. In this way, they can reach their own conclusions without us conditioning them.

Conclusions

Psychological defenses, like any other protective system of our organism, play a role, but sometimes, as in autoimmune diseases, the defensive system can become our worst enemy. There are two types: ego-dystonic defenses, which the patient perceives as intrusive and negative; and ego-syntonic ones, in which case they are perceived as a trait of his personality, even as something positive.

There are many types of defenses; these will vary in complexity depending on the patient's age (they will be stronger as age increases) and on the intensity of the pain suffered. Identifying them is necessary to be able to work with them in a sequential and therapeutic way.

The main thing is to keep in mind that if we eliminate a defense we will leave the patient "helpless" and we will do more harm than good. Defenses related to shame will require a very strong therapist–patient alliance, since the therapist becomes the object of transition with respect to the attachment figures who did not fulfill their function.

As we dismantle the defenses, we must install resources that reinforce the patient's safety until he can do without them. We should never try to impose our criteria because we can precipitate events for which the patient is not prepared or, even worse, worsen the pathology.

A very useful approach when working with defenses is the EMDR technique; however, only qualified therapists can and should do this. Bilateral stimulation acts as an enzyme that accelerates the processes of emotional connection and recovery, helping the brain to find behaviors (affect, sensations, thoughts) which are much more adaptive.

Working with defenses is continuous throughout the therapeutic process because under one defense there is often another more primitive and complex one hidden that will require a new process of analysis and disassembly.

References

Cramer, P. (2009). *Seven Pillars of defense mechanism theory*. Annual Meeting of the Rapaport-Klein Study Group. www.psychomedia.it/rapaport-klein

American Psychiatric Association. (1994). *Diagnostic and statistical manual of mental disorders* (4th ed.). APA.

Ginot, E. (2015). *The neuropsychology of the unconscious*. Norton.

González, A. D. (2015). *Trastorno de identidad disociativo o personalidad múltiple*. Sintesis.

Knipe, J. (2014). *EMDR toolbox: Theory and treatment of complex PTSD and dissociation*. Springer.

Le Doux, J. (1994). *The emotional brain*. Phoenix (2004).

Mccullough, L. (1997). *Changing caracther*. Basic Books.

Mccullough, L., Khun, N., & Stewar, A. (2003). *Treating affect Phobia: A manual for short-term dynamic psychotherapy*. Guilford Press.

Panksepp, J., & Biven, L. (2012). *The archeology of mind. Neuroevolutionary origins of humans emotions*. Norton.

Seijo, N. (2015). *Máster de Psicoterapia con EMDR. Módulo 6. Tema 2. Defensas Somáticas*. Universidad Nacional de Educación a Distancia (UNED).

Sharon, G., & Hentschel, U. (2013). El uso de los mecanismos de defensa como herramientas para el afrontamiento por veteranos isralies deprimidos y con TEPT. *Subjetividad y procesos cognitivos*, 17(1), 118–133. ISSN: 1666-244X Universidad de Ciencias empresariales y Sociales.

Van der Hart, O., Nijenhuis, E. R. S., & Steele, K. (2006). *The haunted self: Structural dissociation and the treatment of chronic traumatization*. Norton & Company.

16 Exposure to Feared Situations or Sensations

In Chapter 2 we saw how our brain activates different alarm mechanisms when there is danger and how it produces a fight-flight state that prepares us for defense or attack. If neither of the two situations is possible, immobilization will occur, with the consequent mental and somatic dissociation.

When we live an emotionally intense, threatening, or traumatic situation, certain neural networks will keep a memory of the event in order to avoid it in the future. In the same way, our body will keep a somatic memory of the trauma (Scaer, 2014). Both the mind and the body will keep memories of discomfort.

Our mind will activate the circuits of fear when faced with the element that produces the fear. The fear can either be real (tangible) or imaginary (intangible). The brain will send an alarm signal to the body, which is what we know as anxiety. In many cases, these sensations will be incapacitating, completely blocking the person to the point of disenabling them.

In all cases, the common bond will be anxiety (discomfort), fear either because of something known or unknown, and the need to avoid thoughts or situations that are associated with discomfort. We can find several types of avoidance.

1. *Pathological confrontation*: Attempts to solve the situation through aggressive or potentially risky actions. We can include four types of behavior here:

    - *Risky or potentially harmful behavior*: This includes activities such as extreme or dangerous sports in which the body and mind are taken to extremes so as not to feel anything. They tend to be characteristic of extremely cerebral people who are overly worried about having control. They become obsessed with achievements, demanding more and more, endangering their health and sometimes their life.

      A subtype of this behavior is seen especially in men obsessed with their body and their muscularity. This behavior is usually associated with an inferiority complex, of looking weak. Having a muscular body makes them feel strong and unafraid of others.
    - *Aggressive behavior*: Seen in individuals who use aggressiveness as a way to release anger. They constantly seek confrontation, which puts them in many risky situations.

DOI: 10.4324/9781003646341-18

Andrew comes to consultation because he is having more and more problems at work due to having fits of anger that become uncontrollable and scare his colleagues. He has already been warned that if he continues to act like this they will have to let him go. When we explored the reason, it seemed related to a huge frustration every time he felt ignored, something that happened to him as a child.

- *Self-control*: Efforts to control the emotions and sensations associated with discomfort. This may be an attempt to control sensations or thoughts. In both cases, there is a paradoxical effect that the more one tries to control them, the stronger they become.
- *Observing sensations and provoking them further*: This is known as a self-fulfilling prophecy. If I had an unpleasant sensation in the past I may be afraid of it happening again, and I will try to avoid it at all costs by watching my body constantly. This may lead to hypochondric behavior causing fear of contracting a disease. Simply having that feeling may cause a lot of anxiety or result in a panic attack.

In many cases people can be medicated to avoid the sensations with the aggravating circumstance. However, after a while the pills may provoke tolerance, and higher doses will be needed to withstand the discomfort, not mentioning the danger of creating a pharmacological dependency.

> *Anthony is a 30-year-old patient who used to suffer from panic attacks and has improved a lot in recent months. He comes to the session worried that he has had a new attack which makes him afraid to relapse. When we evaluate the stressful events that may have occurred in the last week we do not find any. When I ask him what he was doing when the attack happened, he told me that he had gone to a town with some friends and they decided to go up to a chapel that was at the top of a steep slope. When climbing, he began to notice that he was short of breath and began to be afraid of having an attack until he had one.*

In this case there was no stressor to provoke the attack; it was the physical sensations of sweat, suffocation, and tachycardia which activated the alarms. What most people would experience as fatigue, he confused with a panic attack. The fear of having it again was what caused him to have it. The paradox is that the need to avoid these sensations led him to think about them over and over again.

2. *Escape-avoidance*: Use of thoughts or feelings with unproductive or even pathological actions as a way to avoid the emotions and sensations that cause discomfort. These can be:

- *Search for external elements to attenuate discomfort*: This is the case with everything related to elements that help avoid feelings of discomfort: food, gambling, drugs, and so on.

  Sensations of anxiety become intolerable and ways of emotional control are sought through objects and/or activities that may result in some amount of well-being, in anesthesia, or even in a sensation of trance, albeit momentarily.

Jesus, a 25-year-old patient, comes to consultation because he abuses cocaine. He tells me that at certain moments something inside him stirs that drives him to use drugs and look for prostitutes. These attacks can last up to two or three days. When they finish, he swears he will not do it again because his mother cares a lot about him and he is upsetting her terribly. He tells me that he lives with his mother, who's been a widow since he was little and that he is an only child. When what happened before he took drugs and went to see prostitutes is evaluated, there always seems to be a fight with the mother. As she treats him as a small child, he gets extremely frustrated and this causes a lot of anger toward his mother. When he comes back from those "attacks," he cannot help but agree with her.

In this case we can see how the anger caused by his mother's attitude and his helplessness to express it or get it to change leads him to lose control. He feels important for a couple of days, after which he returns with a submissive and guilty attitude that perpetuates the problem.

- *Avoiding situations or objects associated to the discomfort*

  Another frequent form of avoidance is to avoid neutral elements that are related to some traumatic element. We know from operant conditioning that when there is an aversive stimulus next to a neutral stimulus, it is also contaminated by the sensation of fear that is associated with the negative stimulus. In many cases, the phobia will be related to something that caused the trauma, for example fear of driving after a traffic accident. In other cases, it could be a superstitious association, for example fear of driving because of the fear of having an anxiety attack while driving. We find this constantly in people with panic attacks: they avoid places where they are afraid of having an attack as well as being alone and/or making a fool of themselves.

Manolo comes to consultation because of an uncontrollable fear of driving the car on the freeway. When asked since when he has had it, he tells me that it started one night when he had an anxiety attack on the freeway and had to stop the car. A tow truck took the car, and he was taken to hospital by ambulance. When I asked him if something traumatic was happening in his life at that time, he told me that he was getting a divorce because of his partner's infidelity.

- *Avoiding situations where fear of judgement or assessment from others exists*
  This would include social phobias in which there is fear of being judged or examined. The sensations are related to a feeling of shame and low self-esteem which could be discovered when exposed to another person or to several people. It has to do with everything that is related to others: speaking in public or playing an instrument in public, among others. In some cases it can be confused with an obsessive-compulsive disorder (OCD) (Hernandez, 2022) because the avoidance is achieved through irrational fears that avoid relating to others, for example, having to go to the bathroom and others knowing about it, fear of sweating and others being aware of it, or fear of blushing.

Marina is a 22-year-old patient who is afraid of going out, having to go to the bathroom urgently and not being able to find one on time. Also, the fear of having an accident terrifies her. She has performed rituals such as not eating, vomiting, or taking laxatives before leaving home. When she is told that she can go to a bar, she says that she would not be relaxed because she needs them to be very clean. Upon further exploration, she says that she is afraid of a friend who, when she was young, laughed at her because she made a fool of herself. Living in a small town, she is afraid of meeting that friend. The fear of not being able to control the sphincters disappears when she comes to Malaga where nobody knows her.

- *Obsessive thoughts different from the real problem*
  Another way to avoid disturbing sensations is having an obsession. An obsession fulfills the function of avoiding thinking about something that worries and/or affects us. Obsessive people prefer to avoid suffering rather than face it (Hernandez, 2022). Fear of feelings of anxiety will lead to obsessive thoughts that, in turn, paradoxically, cause more anxiety.

Ida is a patient who cannot stop thinking about something that her husband told her 20 years ago about a previous relationship. For three months, since she discovered that he did not tell her the whole truth, she has not been able to stop obsessing about what really happened. She does not stop questioning him about all the details. When I asked her if there had been any traumatic event in her life, she told me that her father died in hospital. When he told her that he was sick, she had not given any importance to him and when she took him to hospital after he got worse, it was too late. Before my comment that it is better to obsess over something that happened more than 20 years ago than to think that she is to blame for her father's death, she began to cry inconsolably.

> In order to avoid thoughts of guilt with the consequent emotions and sensations, the mind chooses to think obsessively of something innocuous that obviously does not allow us to think about anything else.

What all these examples have in common is the need to avoid feelings of discomfort and/or anxiety. The problem is that avoiding the sensations without really facing them causes a vicious circle of anxiety–avoidance–anxiety. When we avoid a situation, the amygdala, where anxiety originates, reinforces the relationship between the phobic element and the fear (Cozolino, 2016). To use a metaphor, it is as if the amygdala said: "We have avoided that and nothing has happened. So, in the future it is safest to avoid it again." reinforcing the neural networks that associate the stimulus to the fear.

When to Face Feared Situations?

My experience tells me that people face their fears when they are ready; in most cases it is the people who decide to do it at their own pace. Do not forget that the brain, like any other organ, has an innate mechanism of healing that has been interrupted due to trauma. Once we begin to resolve it, the person tends to recover the psychological balance in a natural way with everything that comes with overcoming fears. In other cases, we will need to set objectives with the patients so that they can face them. Whatever the therapeutic model that we apply, in the end we will have to face situations, people, or sensations that provoke that fear.

There are two types of traumas (Shapiro, 2010, p.), 1) the capital T traumas that are due to situations in adulthood that coincide with PTSD; and 2) traumas related to attachment that comes from childhood. There are two ways to proceed:

- In cases of post-traumatic stress disorder, EMDR is a tremendously effective and efficient therapy. In a few sessions we can reprocess the memory associated with the trauma, and the person will have no fear of facing their fears. Here we can include everything related to PTSD and simple phobias.
- In cases where the avoidance comes from a fear stemming from childhood or related in one way or another to something that was experienced with the caregivers, we would be talking about a complex trauma whose solution is more complicated, and we would resort to the contents described in the book. These would be complex trauma situations such as panic attacks, obsessions, social phobias, and so on.

In the words of Barlow et al. (2011):

> It is important for patients to understand that the use of avoidance can contribute to maintaining current patterns of emotional response. Although patients may find avoidance strategies useful on some occasions, since they tend to inhibit the short-term experience of intense emotions, they rarely work well in the long term. First, avoidance prevents habituation, or reduction of response intensity through repeated presentation of the feared stimulus. Second and most importantly, avoidance interferes with the process of extinction or diminished response. Finally, facing that which is feared causes patients to feel a sense of control over what they fear.
>
> (pp. 119–120)

It is clear that the end of any therapy will be to face the feared situations again in order to habituate to what was feared and recover a sense of control. When there is no fear or warning, there will be no anxiety. The risk is that if the patient is not well prepared because the neural network associated with the traumatic memory is still very active or because the patient's coping rhythm does not coincide with the one we are trying to impose on him, it is very likely that we will only retraumatize him. I insist that in the vast majority of cases it will be enough to work with the situation that caused the fear so that the patient does it spontaneously at the pace that he decides he can take on.

In many cases the memory of the trauma will be known, and in many other cases it will not. In both cases, the work will consist of establishing a therapeutic relationship that strengthens the patient's resources, helping him to face his fears.

Coping strategies may be real or imaginary. We may highlight:

1. Situational Exposure

In this section, we refer to the patient's fear of external elements, which can be places, people, or situations. The fear of the sensations that accompany these stimuli will make the person avoid them at all costs. With the passage of time, an anticipatory anxiety is developed which, just by imagining that the situation could happen, causes fear. It is what we know as "fear of fear."

The idea would be to have the patient confront the stimuli in a prolonged and controlled manner until the associated fear diminishes significantly or disappears altogether (Brown et al., 2016). In all cases there is a fear of feeling emotions associated with going crazy, of making a fool of oneself, or even of dying; in all cases the patient is afraid of losing control. In order to face the feared situations, you can adhere to the following steps (Barlow, 2011):

a) Identify and make a list of places or situations that cause discomfort. A hierarchy of fears will be made, and coping will start with situations that cause less discomfort;
b) Agree with the patient on an approach and exposure method. You also have to agree on possibilities to be able to leave the situation momentarily to recover and then start again. The approach can be gradual or intense (= flooding technique);
c) Patients are encouraged to do the activities in a way that makes them fully responsible for the success of the situation. If the patient is not prepared, the approach can be done with a person they trust yet making it clear that later they should do it alone;
d) Feedback is given on what happened and the sensations that have been felt are evaluated: has the success been partial or total; has there been a failure; what happened, and how can it be done again to ensure success?

2. Exposure to Feared Sensations

Often patients are not aware that the real fear is not the situation or the object but the sensation associated with it. Other times, they are conscious that the fear is directly caused by the sensations. As we saw in the previous section, the fear of sensations is so great that the individual can provoke them himself.

When patients feel these sensations, the tendency is to avoid them which, as we have seen, is a way to make them more dangerous: the job will be to help the patient to feel and tolerate them.

This can be done gradually during consultation, after which the patient can apply it little by little in his daily life. It is also important to explain that the sensations are alarm signals of their bodies which can be used as a way to heal with the techniques we saw in the chapter on working with the body.

3. Worst Fear Technique

This technique has a paradoxical intention (Nardone, 2012). The tendency of patients towards fear is to avoid any situation or thought related to it. What patients are asked to do is to force themselves to think every day for a while about what causes them fear. The intention is that they stop avoiding phobic stimuli and room is created in which they are allowed to face them. The instructions of the task could be:

I'm going to ask you that every day at the same time you take five minutes (you can use a stopwatch) not a second more or less, and think about that situation or object that causes you so much fear. Your mind may resist or go to other issues but you must force yourself to think about it. When the five minutes are up, you continue with your normal life until the next day when you do it again.

This technique can be very useful in advanced phases of therapy; however, when done prematurely, the patient can be retraumatized.

4. Hypnosis

We are not going to make an exhaustive description of the hypnosis process for which manuals already exist which detail on how to work with this technique (Pérez et al., 2012). However, we will affirm that it constitutes a very effective tool in working with feared situations since the hypnotherapist is able to make them imaginary so that they can be overcome with success.

The personality of the person we have as a patient will determine the type of hypnosis we should give. Basically, we can find two situations:

A. Clients who have a great need of control: These clients will find it difficult to relax and let themselves be carried away by hypnotic suggestions. In these cases, I recommend using naturalistic or Ericksonian suggestions. Although these techniques tend to provoke a more superficial trance, they are very useful when it comes to negotiating the resistance of the clients. Suggestions can be used as metaphors that are related to the patient's problem, letting anyone create their own interpretations.

A long time ago when I was traveling through an exotic country they told me that there was a wise man who spoke my language and knew how to find the solution to the problems of other human beings. It takes a long time to find him. When I faced him, I realized that he knew the solution to my problems. He looked me in the eyes and said: Look inside yourself and notice how your fears do not belong to you; they belong to someone else. When I left I felt a tranquility as I had never felt before and I could not stop thinking about that phrase. I ask myself how you would use it when you find yourself in a situation that causes you fear.

B. Clients who are very impressionable: People with a more emotional profile or with dissociative disorders will be very impressionable and therefore very good subjects for hypnosis. In these cases, it is advisable to use classical inductions (e.g., the Elman induction, see Chapter 13) which will allow a deep relaxation; the suggestions can be direct and related to the patient's problem.

Now that you are totally calm and relaxed you are going to imagine that you are totally at ease and decide to face a situation that causes you a lot of fear. You are surprised at how calm you are and you are able to remain so. You approach slowly, totally calm and you realize you are in front of all those people talking very slowly, everyone observes you but you do not worry at all because you are totally calm.

5. Exposure to Traumatic Memories

On many occasions, we will find anxiety disorders, obsessions, or other types of disorders associated with a traumatic event such as the loss of a loved one, an accident, a serious illness, and so on. These disorders are usually due to traumatic losses such as the loss of a person or the loss of a job, a partner or the loss of health.

As I explained throughout the book, the individual, by trying to control himself, can acquire habits that are pathological. In these cases, it is necessary to deal with the trauma so that once the person has overcome this trauma, they can develop normal grief. On working with the traumatic memory, the person will begin to control himself in a healthy way. In some cases, however, additional help may be necessary.

6. Work with Phobia between Parts

As we saw in the chapter devoted to the structural dissociation of personality (see Chapter 12), there may also be phobias in the internal system between different parts of the personality. That is, there may be aspects of the personality of the individual that are being avoided and that cause anxiety.

These are aspects of the Self that are not integrated as part of the personality, and much energy is spent in keeping them from becoming conscious. It is a phobia for different parts of the personality. I like to tell my patients "if there is a fight inside you, whoever wins, you will always lose."

To work on the exposure to the parts of the internal system, mentalization is used, that is to say an exposure to those parts of oneself that are rejected, so that little by little they can be accepted and finally become integrated.

To do this work we can ask questions that oblige the patient to face them. As in all cases this work should be done gradually and only when the patient is prepared.

The questions can be:

- *Imagine that the part of you that you don't like is in front of you. What would you say to it? How could it help you?*
- *If your father (or mother or partner) were here in front of you, what would they see?*
- *If you looked in a mirror, what would you see?*
- *What would you say to that part of yourself that you feel is weak?*

I know you feel very guilty about what happened. But I can't understand how an 8-year-old girl can be blamed for something that I see belongs to children? What do you think of it now as an adult?

Conclusions

Fear is a primordial emotion for survival, but when it becomes excessive it can turn a person's life into a real hell. There are many fears and phobias, but what they all have in common is that the person who suffers them tries to avoid the situation or the feared object. This only aggravates the problem, creating a vicious circle of fear and avoidance that feed off each other.

Fear can be directed toward real objects or situations, or they can be imaginary fears. Both share a common physiology, and the reactions of fear and anxiety are identical. A fundamental part of the treatment regardless of the therapeutic approach is to face the fear.

This can be to other people, to objects, to the person's own sensations, to traumatic memories, and even to different parts of the personality. In order to overcome it and face it, "in vivo" techniques, such as hypnosis or facing the worst fear, can be used either during consultation or in daily or imaginary life. This allows for a progressive approach to the space of the aversive stimulus.

We can only say that the fear has disappeared when our body does not pick up any discomfort when we live it "in situ."

References

Barlow, D. H., Farchione, T. M., Fairholme, C. P., Ellard, K. K., Boisseau, C. L., Allen, L. B., & Ehrenreich-May, J. (2011). *Unified protocol for transdiagnostic treatment of emotional disorders: Therapist guide and patient guide*. Oxford University Press.

Brown, D. P., & Elliott, D. S. (2016). *Attachment disturbances in adults. Treatments for comprehensive repairs*. Norton.

Cozolino, L. (2016). *Why therapy works. Using our minds to change our brains*. Norton.

Hernandez, M. (2022). *Las obsesiones y el trastorno obsesivo-compulsivo. Una adicción al pensamiento. Entenderlos y superarlos con el modelo PARCUVE*. Desclee de Brouwer.

Nardone, G. (2012). *Miedo, pánico y fobias La terapia breve estratégica*. Herder.

Pérez, I., Cuadros, J., & Nieto, C. (Coord.). (2012). *Hipnosis en la práctica clínica. Vol. I Técnicas generales*. EOS.

Scaer, R. (2014). *The body bears the burden: Trauma, dissociation, and disease*. Routledge.

Shapiro, R. (2010). *The trauma treatment handbook. Protocols across the spectrum*. Norton.

17 Attachment-Related Treatments and Pathologies

Faust devoted his entire life to learning and knowledge. As the end of his life approached, he discovered he had never been entirely happy. To feel complete, he lacked something fundamental: love. The devil (Mephistopheles), who had studied human beings from their very beginnings, knew men were weak and needed relationships with others to feel happy. Mephistopheles knew that Faust would pay anything to love and be loved. The devil was sure he would sell his eternal soul for love. The price Faust paid for being happy killed Margarita and his son, which plunged him into a profound sense of guilt and shame. He discovered that happiness had a higher price than he had expected.

When I studied biology in the 1990s, I was taught that gene expression was direct, that is, genes were expressed and not influenced by the environment. We are still far from understanding how genetic inheritance affects the psychological disorders described in this book. Even though everything that takes place in the brain and affects the mind has an organic basis, it is also true that, nowadays, we are aware of the mutual influence between environment and gene expression, which is known as epigenetics. The occurrences in the person's surrounding environment regulate gene expression, and our gene pool conditions our actions. We cannot understand human beings without this relationship between the organic and the environmental. When considering the pathologies described in this chapter, I do take into account the multiple hereditary factors that influence psychological illnesses. In fact, I take them for granted and also understand they can often be modified as the environmental conditions change.

Neurobiology teaches us that, in infancy, children who were unable to regulate themselves emotionally with their caregivers and lacked secure attachment had to look for alternative mechanisms that offered them a sense of comfort. This was achieved by adapting their behavior to that of their caregivers. This will sometimes occur through the activation of the parasympathetic system, inhibiting contact with others and fulfilling other people's expectations, which will result in an *avoidant attachment* style. It may also take place through the activation of the sympathetic nervous system, making constant efforts to connect emotionally with caregivers through complaints or behaviors that make them stand out and be seen. This is what we know as *anxious attachment*. If the

DOI: 10.4324/9781003646341-19

attachment figures that should care for and protect the child are, at the same time, the source of alertness and fear, the activation of the dorsovagal branch of the parasympathetic system will make the child freeze, leading to what we know as *disorganized attachment*. In these cases, both the sympathetic and parasympathetic branches become ineffective in achieving a balance that allows self-regulation and other-regulation (Katehakis, 2016; Hill, 2015; Schore, 2001). In any case, genetics, social systems, and families interact in many ways and explain the appearance of pathologies. This chapter tries to be a guideline that may help to focus the treatment.

The emotional dysregulation of the early years will lead both the central nervous system (CNS) and the autonomic nervous system (ANS) to regulate themselves in an alternative, non-healthy, but adaptive way. Children will unconsciously seek out elements other than their caregivers that generate a sense of safety and control. As can be seen in Figure 17.1, an arch of possibilities exists, based on whether the sympathetic or parasympathetic system is predominantly activated. The sense of comfort emerges at the balance point between these two poles.

Figure 17.1 Sequencing the process for clients with avoidant attachment. Our work will imply interchanging stages or devoting more time to one stage and not others, depending on the intensity of the therapeutic alliance. Clients with avoidant attachment need to admire the therapist since they function at a cortical level.

Attachment disruptions without healthy repairs will lead to a feeling of fear and anger, followed by guilt and shame. If this anger is inhibited (= cold rage), the parasympathetic branch will become predominant, whereas if anger is expressed, it will lead to an activation of the sympathetic branch. If neither possibility can take place, there will be an activation of the dorsovagal nerve and subsequent freezing.

Treatment Sequence

People who spent their childhood searching for emotional and cognitive balance, and whose caregivers failed to regulate them in a healthy way, tend to have "secondary regulation strategies." Some people's expressions of stress become hyperactivated (anxious attachment) in situations where they sense a lack of closeness or abandonment, so they try to establish very close relationships with physical and emotional intimacy. On the contrary, individuals who deactivate their closeness-seeking system (avoidance attachment) spend their energy searching for elements (thoughts, actions, or substances) that allow them not to feel the discomfort associated with attachment disruptions, thus avoiding emotional intimacy (Mikulincer & Shaver, 2007). In the disorganized attachment, both strategies will take place incorrectly.

As we saw in Chapter 7, concerning the therapeutic alliance, childhood attachment relationships will determine how the client relates to the therapist, and consequently how the therapeutic process will develop. When approaching the different phases of treatment, it is necessary to take into account the regulation strategies developed by the client to deal with their feelings of discomfort. We cannot apply the same treatment format for everyone without taking into account their idiosyncrasies. We can establish some general rules on how treatment should be approached based on the type of attachment underlying the pathology.

To be confident about the client's type of attachment, and therefore the strategies they've used to regulate themselves, we may use tools – such as Mary Main's Adult Attachment Interview – which are beyond the scope of this book. I recommend using these indications as a flexible guideline based on the therapist's intuition.

1. Avoidant Attachment

Cortical areas are predominant in these individuals who doubt everything and everyone. They will be distrustful of the therapist, needing to feel that he or she has a firm grip on their problem. They will show very little access to traumatic memories, which will be denied or even not remembered. With this type of patient, psychoeducation is strongly recommended as a way to promote therapeutic alliance during the initial sessions before being able to analyze their problems in detail. Avoidant individuals are very reluctant to comment on personal situations, as they may suspect that the therapist will judge and disapprove of them.

Establishing a trustworthy therapeutic relationship will be the therapist's primary goal and challenge during the initial sessions. Individuals with avoidant attachment have trouble identifying their bodily sensations, and usually experience non-manifested and suppressed (inhibited) rage. Somatic work will be of great help once they can begin to recognize their physical sensations.

Cognitive defenses – such as trying to control the therapy or discussing the therapist's approach and opinions, while being very sensitive to any misunderstanding – seem to be predominant. Patients have a hard time expressing their discomfort, and they may often drop out of therapy without prior notice due to some misunderstanding they are unable to clarify since they prefer to avoid confrontation. Not showing any discomfort, adjusting to what they believed their caregivers preferred, and hiding their real needs was the way in which they learned to regulate themselves throughout their childhood.

Regarding the sequence of the different stages, Figure 17.2 illustrates how psychoeducation must be primordial in earlier stages. These patients like having

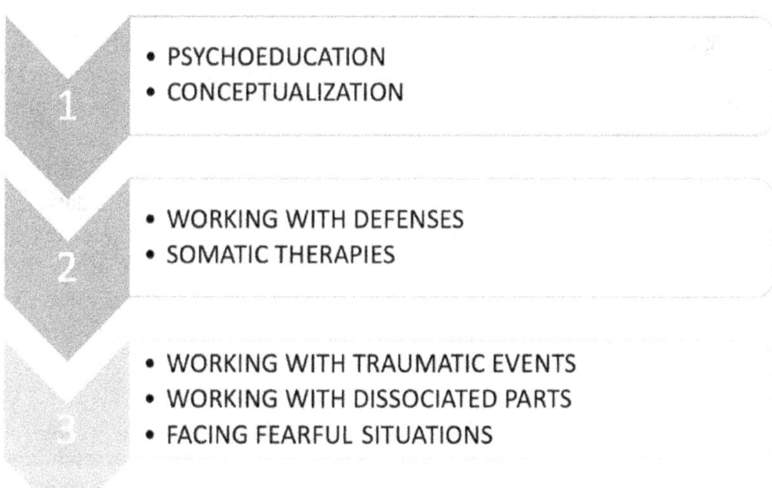

Figure 17.2 Sequence of the process with patients with anxious attachment. The stages may be more or less flexible depending on the degree to which patients are able to tolerate discomfort. Individuals with anxious attachment need to feel protected by the therapist, as the feeling of not being seen was what prompted the anxious regulation.

data and information on both what is happening to them and the development of the therapy. This part of the treatment can be used to gather relevant information on the patient's history, always using open-ended questions such as: "I wonder if you've ever felt like the example. Have you ever noticed your body reacting in that way?" Needless to say, these questions should relate to what is being discussed during the psychoeducational process.

Working with the body will be very complicated and will be associated with many defenses. The client learned to survive by avoiding feelings and emotions, so we help them reconnect with these in a very subtle and slow manner. Only when the client can trust us and feel that we can help can we begin to work with traumatic events and their associated parts.

The last part of the treatment will include coping with being able to have intimacy with other people and learning to regulate themselves and empathize with one's own as well as other people's emotions, thus substituting the initial regulation strategy for a much healthier and adaptive one.

2. *Anxious or Coercive Attachment*

Subcortical areas are predominant in patients with anxious or coercive attachment. Clients are searching for someone to save them from their discomfort, so they tend to overestimate the therapist and see them as someone who has the solution to all their problems. During the initial sessions, the focus should be on teaching clients to cope with body sensations and on them learning stabilization techniques to contain the emotional overflow so as to be able to reflect. Clients tend to exaggerate when assessing their traumatic experiences, even though there may be some amnesia, and will present and try to solve their issues with too much impetus.

Patients with anxious attachment long for greater emotional contact with the therapist and wish to continue the relationship beyond the boundaries of the treatment. Establishing boundaries in the therapeutic relationship is very important, so patients can learn to regulate themselves in the absence of the therapist as well as learn to fend for themselves. Modulating anger (frustration or helplessness) and learning to channel it will provide them with containment and assertiveness strategies to relate to others.

Emotional defenses such as "nobody understands me," "others don't understand my suffering," or "I know I'll never be well" are predominant. These defenses are not based on logical arguments and do not usually coincide with reality. Magnifying the discomfort and complaining to their caregivers was the way they learned to regulate themselves in childhood.

Figure 17.3 shows the sequence of steps to be followed with people with anxious attachment. It is possible to work simultaneously on gathering the client's history and offering emotional regulation techniques and psychoeducation about their disorder. Physical sensations will be quite intense and may be rather

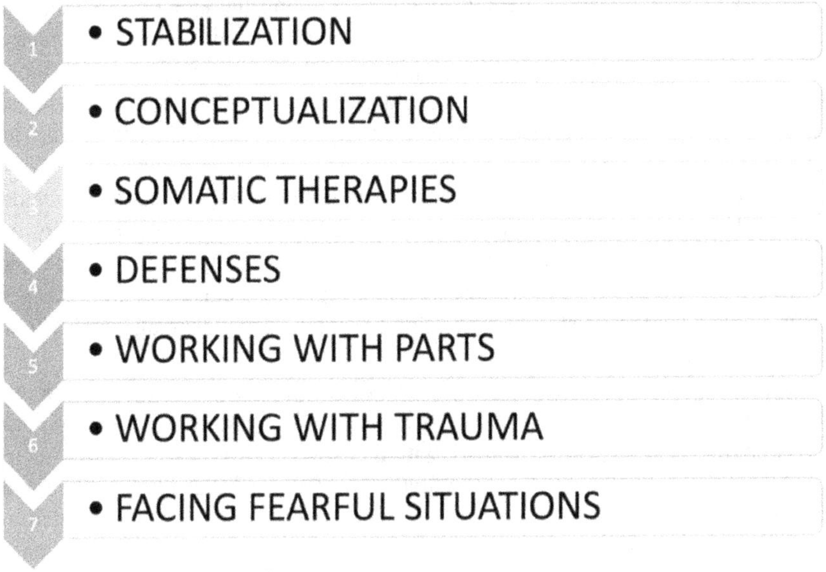

- STABILIZATION
- CONCEPTUALIZATION
- SOMATIC THERAPIES
- DEFENSES
- WORKING WITH PARTS
- WORKING WITH TRAUMA
- FACING FEARFUL SITUATIONS

Figure 17.3 The sequencing process for patients with disorganized attachment. The stages will need to be clearly defined due to the fragility of the patient's internal system. It can easily overwhelm the patient's ability to tolerate the therapeutic work and bring him out of the window of tolerance, which could retraumatize him.

useful in accessing traumatic memories and possible defenses. It is at this stage when dissociated parts of the personality may appear, which can be integrated by applying different techniques, as explained in Chapter 12. Once this work has been done and patients are capable of mentalizing, they will be able to face their fear of loneliness or distance themselves from people who act as attachment figures.

1. Disorganized Attachment

Individuals with disorganized attachment usually have a diagnosis associated with a borderline personality disorder; their therapeutic work requires specific protocols. In their childhood, there was no emotional regulation, and they did not learn to self-regulate or co-regulate. There is not a healthy predominance of some areas over others; instead, they become activated in maladaptive circumstances. When it comes to relating to others or to the therapist, they are afraid both of potentially dangerous emotional closeness and possible real or imagined abandonment.

These patients do not trust the therapist and at the same time consider him their last hope for healing. Establishment of a strong therapeutic alliance and containment will be the primary objectives during the initial sessions. In many cases, self-harm, substance abuse, complicated couple and family relationships, and so on are present. These issues should be approached gently to help clients develop healthy regulation habits before starting to work with other aspects of the disease.

The therapist should establish clear boundaries regarding contact outside therapy hours, whether it is telephone calls, messages, or unscheduled visits, as well as policies regarding appointment cancellation and payment. Setting clear and concise boundaries helps these patients regulate themselves and will get them to trust the therapist. Of course, this should never be done aggressively or coercively (Hernandez, 2020).

Dissociation and the existence of parts will be crucial, and there will be all kinds of defenses that must be carefully handled. The better the therapeutic relationship, the easier it will be to work with the patient.

As we can see in Figure 17.4, the first step will be stabilizing the patient and establishing a good therapeutic alliance that creates a safe basis from which to begin the work later. Data gathering, if possible, should be performed simultaneously to the previous phases, taking into account that there will be many dissociated situations that may appear unexpectedly during treatment.

Once the patient is stabilized and has adequate containment resources, we can begin the progressive work with the body sensations and possible defenses that arise. Working with both the parts associated with the body sensations and with certain traumatic moments may offer the patient significant symptom relief and a sense of control over the illness. This work should take as much time as is needed to achieve the maximum integration possible of the dissociated parts.

The processing of the parts should have advanced properly before starting to work with traumatic memories, which is always done in reverse chronological order. First, we work with the most recent traumatic events, and later we will start with childhood traumas and attachment issues.

We have reached the end of the therapeutic work when the patient is able to mentalize and face those previously dysregulating fears and situations.

It is well known that borderline personality disorder is related to disorganized attachment (Liotti, 2004), and while it is true that there is a strong correlation between insecure attachment and pathology, there are no studies that directly correlate anxious and avoidant attachment with any particular pathology. For example, individuals with high anxiety or panic attacks are associated with anxious attachment, but if there is substance abuse or any type of addiction, they are associated with avoidant attachment.

In the words of Mikulincer and Shaver (2007):

> From our point of view, mental disorders are produced by multiple processes, such as attachment problems or traumatic situations that occur in life, or other pathogenic situations that reduce the individual's psychological and social resources and weaken their capacity for resilience ... Although insecure attachment may contribute to psychological problems, mental issues may also exacerbate problems in attachment relationships, leading to a dysfunctional relational system.

In the following sections, I will describe how, based on how the CNS and ANS have been activated, different pathologies either associated with symptoms (DSM-5 Axis I) or with personality disorders (DSM-5 Axis II) will be present. I certainly do not mean to suggest that there is a direct relationship between attachment type and disease. I believe that both childhood experiences and the regulation strategies used to obtain a sense of comfort and control offer valuable clues that may help to explain many factors that have led to the disease, but obviously not all.

Axis I Disorders (Symptoms)

The descriptions in this section will be related to different aspects of emotional regulation mechanisms, either external or internal, that are or have been useful in the past to achieve a sense of comfort for the patient. These elements can lead to symptoms that cause substantial discomfort in the individual but, in most cases, they feel unable to avoid or control them. The emotions of fear, anger, guilt, and shame will be included in all the disorders outlined below (see Chapter 6). It is important to note that one disease does not exclude others, since comorbidity is prevalent. There are many disorders, but in this section, I would like to highlight the most common ones in our practice:

- Obsessive disorders: Thinking is used obsessively and may be accompanied by actions (compulsions) that attempt to alleviate the discomfort associated with that thought. Obsessions serve as a way to avoid other types of thoughts that are painful. Most of the time, the underlying belief is "I am not worthy," and all the obsessive rituals will be aimed at avoiding any thoughts related to this belief. Obsessions can be related to jealousy, hypochondria, fear of harming themselves or others, or cleanliness and order.

Individuals with this disorder have an avoidant attachment style and take refuge in the cognitive realm as a way of emotional regulation. They are those people who we call "controllers" because their obsession is to be in control of everything. Obsessive thinking helps them not to contact their emotions and feelings, which were painful in the past, and in doing so achieve a sense of control.

Most obsessive disorders are related to some incident that has made the individual feel guilty. Any traumatic event coinciding with the onset of the disorder should be explored. These events could be any of the following:

- Death of someone close to whom the client feels in debt (e.g., the death of a parent or an abortion);
- Feeling of guilt for having been bad or not good enough in taking care of loved ones (e.g., parents or siblings with an illness, where the individual feels responsible);
- Feeling of guilt and shame due to certain family situations that the person could not control, so thoughts become a way of avoiding (e.g., parents arguing or divorcing);
- Eating disorders: Food is used as a means of achieving emotional regulation, either by overeating (bingeing), eating and vomiting (bulimia), or not eating (anorexia.) In the case of compulsive food intake, though the disorder is based on food, it would be best to treat it as an addiction disorder (Katehakis, 2016).

Regarding the other two pathologies:

- Anorexia: This illness is related to a lack of food intake and becoming obsessed with extreme thinness. People with this pathology have an avoidant profile and are obsessed with control. They feel controlled and unable to control anything in their lives except their own body. The sensation of euphoria associated with the first moment that they reached the weight they considered ideal was connected with great pleasure, which – as we saw in Chapter 3 – is associated with a dopamine increase. The anger in these patients is directed towards themselves and is associated with the parasympathetic nervous system. The disorder implies regaining that same feeling of power, pleasure, and control. This illness can be accompanied by vomiting and, in that case, we speak of "purgative anorexia."
- Bulimia: This disorder consists of compulsive ingestions – inducing a state of trance – and later, vomiting – leading to a deep sense of guilt and shame. The onset is usually associated with diets they are unable to maintain, followed by bingeing and vomiting to compensate for the food intake. These patients are typically impulsive, with an anxious attachment style and a high activation of the sympathetic system. Anger that cannot be expressed is vomited along with the food. In some cases, "psychogenic vomiting" may be present, in which case the patient vomits but does so involuntarily and spontaneously. These purges are unconsciously used as emotional regulators.
- Addictions: The search for substances, people, or actions that are dangerous to a person's health, finances, or physical integrity. Addictions range from drugs to gambling, to other people, to food, or to sex, to name a few. The

symptom is the type of substance, behavior, or person that is used as a way to avoid feelings of emptiness. Addicts look for external elements that make them feel well and euphoric, preventing them from feeling any sensation associated with pain and anxiety.

In addictions not related to substances, the search for the gratification associated with an increase in dopamine in the CNS is often more important than satisfying the impulse – usually associated with a time in the past when the person or the substance provided a sensation of pleasure, control, or power.

Individuals who suffer from addictions mostly have an avoidant attachment style and constantly flee from emotions and sensations, which they perceive as intrusive and annoying. Addictions are almost omnipresent in patients who suffered disorganized attachment in childhood.

Some people may direct their anger inwards (cold rage) and others may lash out and be very aggressive (hot rage). In many cases, when an addiction disappears, it is typically replaced by another one. Therefore, it is especially important to work on the feeling of guilt and/or shame associated with the disorder and not only on the symptom.

- Somatization: These disorders occur at the physical level but do not have an organic explanation. They can show up as pain, contractures, gastrointestinal problems, allergies, sleep issues, or sexual problems, among others. There are clear indications that attachment trauma predicts somatic illnesses in adults. Brown and Elliott (2016) indicate that negative conversion symptoms such as loss of sensation or motor problems are related to an avoidant attachment style, while positive symptoms such as exaggeration of symptoms (e.g., astasia-abasia, coinciding with what was formerly known as hysteria) are related to an anxious attachment. In addition, disorders such as fibromyalgia are closely related to disorganized attachment.

Disorders related to high stress situations, such as respiratory and intestinal problems, contractures, and immune system deficiencies (Sapolsky, 2004), can occur in all types of attachment, stemming in all cases from poor anger management (helplessness). In some cases, it is due to the frustration of never reaching their own high expectations (avoidance); in other cases, for not achieving the emotional contact that is demanded (anxious attachment) of them; or because both of these are felt at once (disorganized attachment).

- Emotional deterioration: These disorders are due to emotion dysregulation leading to situations of high discomfort, stress, or panic, without there being any danger to the physical integrity of the individual. It can range from moderate anxiety to panic attacks and depression. This anxiety may be accompanied by symptoms of the previous groups (somatization disorders). I would like to highlight depression, generalized anxiety disorder, and panic attacks.

- Depression: Bowlby (1983, 1985, 1993) described that there are three situations in childhood that can be predictors of depression in adulthood:

1. When one of the parents or both die and the child perceives that he has no control;
2. When the child (after many attempts) is unable to create a healthy affective bond with his caregivers;
3. When the child receives the message that he does not deserve love or is not worthy and internalizes these schemes as part of his personality.

Depression can be reactive, that is, it occurs after a certain traumatic event appeared. It supposes a normal stage within the period of subsequent adaptation or a feeling of exhaustion when perceiving a lack of control over certain events, along the lines of the concept of "learned helplessness" (Dozier et al., 2008).

Dozier et al. emphasize that there is a lot of evidence that supports the idea that there is a relationship between suffering depression in adulthood and having had insecure attachment in childhood. In all cases, anger is a feeling of helplessness and frustration for which the person blames himself; it is a rage directed towards himself.

- Generalized anxiety disorder. According to Bowlby (1983), all forms of anxiety (with the exception of phobias to animals) are related to the lack of availability of attachment figures in childhood. Anxiety consists of a feeling of alertness and fear that is the opposite of a feeling of calm and security. It is produced by an activation of the amygdala in the CNS and of the sympathetic system in the ANS; it is common to all insecure attachment types.

In many cases, this warning system is hypersensitized and requires specific treatments (medication, neurofeedback, mindfulness) to reduce the alert to events that occurred a long time ago before being able to start therapeutic treatment and work with the causes of the disorder. In most cases, we will find that there is no recent reason of sufficient importance that can explain the discomfort, unless the motive lies in childhood experiences or ruptures in attachment relationships in adolescence and adulthood.

- Panic attacks: When the panic/separation circuit is too frequently activated during childhood, it becomes more sensitive and can be easily activated during adulthood (Panksepp & Biven, 2012), giving rise to what we know as panic attacks.

Individuals who suffer from them have acute anxiety attacks that make them afraid of dying, or of going crazy, or both. In many cases, secondary phobias develop, such as phobias to open spaces, closed spaces, places far from home, and bodily sensations, that is to say, fear of any sensation, situation, or place that they believe they have no control over.

People who suffer from this pathology are compulsive caregivers (avoidant according to Crittenden's adult attachment classification, 2015) who are always more worried about other people's needs over their own. In many cases, parentification has occurred in their childhood, and they were given far more responsibility than they could bear. Anger is highly contained and directed inward and explodes virulently in the form of panic attacks when they feel the sensation of not being in control; hence the main objective of therapy will be to enable them to express their discomfort without fear of being bad or that the therapist might judge them or their relatives.

Axis II Disorders (Personality)

Probably strongly influenced by genetics, certain personality traits can appear as a form of regulation that serves as a sense of control in relation to caregivers. These can vary in adolescence when attachment relationships are established with peers, or they may be strengthened, depending on the experiences one has.

Personality disorders are defined as permanent patterns of behavior that include an intrapersonal component (lack of control of impulses, affectivity, and stress), an interpersonal one (patterns of dysfunctional relationships) and a social one (that creates conflicts with others and with social institutions) (APA, 2013). There are many categories of disorders related to personality, but in this chapter I want to highlight those that we have been highlighting in relation to the PARCUVE model (see Chapter 6).

1. Narcissistic Personality Disorder

People with narcissistic personality traits feel that they are above everything and everyone and their needs have to be met at any cost. They usually have family problems, especially with their children, because they cannot accept that no-one depends on them without this implying a constant recognition of their personality. They tend to divide and confront family members in order to remain the center of attention and perceive that they have control at all times.

They are unable to recognize that they may have a problem or make mistakes, characterizing others as incapable, ungrateful, or useless. The origin can range from children who have been overprotected in childhood (Millon, 2011) to individuals who, as children, have felt a deep sense of shame and try to protect themselves from it with fantasies of omnipotence and grandiosity (Hart, 2011).

According to the DSM-5 (2015), the traits are:

a) Has a grandiose sense of self-importance (e.g., exaggerates achievements and talents, expects to be recognized as superior without commensurate achievements);
b) Is preoccupied with fantasies of unlimited success, power, brilliance, beauty, or ideal love;
c) Believes that he is "special" and unique and can only be understood by, or should associate with, other special or high-status people (or institutions);
d) Requires excessive admiration;
e) Has a sense of entitlement, that is, unreasonable expectations of especially favorable treatment or automatic compliance with his or her expectations;
f) Is interpersonally exploitative, that is, takes advantage of others to achieve his or her own ends;
g) Lacks empathy: is unwilling to recognize or identify with the feelings and needs of others;
h) Is often envious of others or believes that others are envious of him;
i) Shows arrogant, haughty behaviors or attitudes.

2. Caregiving Personality Disorder

Adults with a caring personality are characterized by always giving priority to the needs of others, leaving aside their own. The origin is usually a process of parentification, when children learn to assume tasks and attitudes that are not in accordance with their age, for example, taking care of younger siblings, cleaning the house, behaving pathologically so as not be a burden for their parents, and so on.

They are constantly striving for their parents to be okay, sacrificing their own well-being; an example may be the child who comforts his mother but cannot talk to her about his problems with his friends or at school.

These types of personalities usually occur in situations in which the parents have problems of marriage or divorce – situations in which the child feels that he has to take sides. They also occur in situations with depressed, sick, or very busy mothers (sometimes fathers) in which the child wants to relieve the burden so that they can be a "normal" family later on.

Those who are compulsive caregivers (Crittenden, 2015) suffer many ruptures in the bond of attachment, as there is an inversion of the parent–child roles that leads to a profound rage that cannot be known or expressed. The child is exhausted in his efforts to achieve normalcy, which, when he becomes an adult, leads to anxiety, depression, and sometimes panic attacks.

According to Bourassa (2010):

> The data indicate a significant relationship between the emotional parenting of children with their mothers and fathers and a pathological style of caring in intimate relationships. Children who underwent a process of parentification

> in their childhood show insecure attachment with their partners, as well as high levels of depressive symptoms and high dissatisfaction regarding their relationships. The results indicate that the behaviors were learned during childhood in the parent-child relationship … and that this can be assessed as a transfer of the way of relating with parents to couples in adolescence.
>
> (p. 4)

3. Indolent or Schizoid Personality Disorder

Individuals with tendencies of having traits of this personality are lost without the people who are usually around them because they need a sense of security and stability. However, when their vital personal space is invaded, they feel drowned and feel the need to free themselves and be independent. They are happier when they are in relationships where the partner has few emotional or intimate demands. They use activities or substances to avoid feeling the emptiness inside, but they always try to depend on someone who meets their basic needs of closeness and intimacy.

Their personal characteristics are very similar to that of the depressives, since they do not carry out work or school activities. But, unlike these, they blame all others for their failures by not assuming any responsibility for their actions; in this they resemble people with narcissistic features.

According to the DSM-5 (2015), the traits are:

a) Neither wants nor likes close relationships, including being part of a family;
b) Consistent preference for solitary activities;
c) Little interest in having sexual experiences with another person;
d) Taking pleasure in few, if any, activities;
e) Having no close friends other than immediate relatives;
f) Indifference to either praise or criticism;
g) Emotional coldness, detachment, or reduced affect.

The origin of this disorder is in attachment relationships in which the parents have sometimes been anxious and other times avoidant, and they represent the same pattern in adult relationships: avoidant but at the same time they do not want to be alone. In adolescence, the person abandons all efforts to try to have some kind of control over events and stops trying; he blames others for his failures and avoids doing anything so as not to fail further.

4. Perfectionist Personality Disorder

Individuals with this personality trait often have obsessive characteristics. Its healthy side comprises people who achieve what they set out to do because they are quite constant and do not stop until they do things right. In its pathological aspect, the obsession with perfectionism leads them to do nothing of what they set out to do and to procrastinate, which leads to a vicious circle of intentions (sometimes grandiose and impossible) and failures. When they go to therapy, they usually do so because they have addiction problems that they can no longer control, or somatic disorders for which they cannot find an organic origin.

For Mallinger and De Wize (1993), the traits of people with this type of personality are:

- Fear of making mistakes;
- Fear of making a wrong decision or choice;
- Strong devotion to work;
- Need for order or firmly established routine;
- Need to know and follow the rules;
- Emotional guardedness;
- Tendency to be stubborn or oppositional;
- Inclination to worry, ruminate, or doubt;
- Need to be above criticism – moral, professional, or personal;
- Cautiousness;
- Chronic inner pressure to use every minute productively.

The origin of the disorder usually comes from parents with avoidance attachment (sometimes disorganized) who demand a lot from the child, who considers himself valued exclusively for his performance (mainly school). The individual feels comfortable performing tasks that avoid the feelings of discomfort and loneliness (sometimes, he can dream of great achievements when grown up). They dream of dazzling others with their achievements and, thus, can be loved and accepted. In all cases, there is low self-esteem that they try to replace by performing great acts that, due to their fear of failure, they are not able to finish.

5. Borderline Personality Disorder

People who possess these personality traits have had a disorganized attachment in their childhood and/or have suffered serious traumas that they have not been able to overcome. This causes an inability of emotional regulation of both the CNS and ANS, both with themselves and in relation to others.

The pathology is accompanied by behaviors, thoughts, and emotions that are harmful both to themselves and to others. It is often accompanied by a multitude of pathological symptoms such as self-harm, substance abuse, toxic relationships, suicide attempts, and so on. The goal of the therapy is to achieve the emotional stability that they did not have in childhood and provide them with resources to learn to regulate themselves emotionally.

According to the DSM-5 (2015) the traits are:

a) Frantic efforts to avoid real or imagined abandonment. NB: They do not include suicidal or self-mutilating behavior covered in Criterion 5;
b) A pattern of unstable and intense interpersonal relationships characterized by alternating between extremes of idealization and devaluation;
c) Identity disturbance: markedly and persistently unstable self-image or sense of self;
d) Impulsivity in at least two areas that are potentially self-damaging (e.g., spending, sex, substance abuse, reckless driving, binge eating). NB: Do not include suicidal or self-mutilating behavior covered in Criterion 5;
e) Recurrent suicidal behavior, gestures, threats, or self-mutilating behavior;
f) Affective instability due to a marked reactivity of mood (e.g., intense episodic dysphoria, irritability, or anxiety usually lasting a few hours and only rarely more than a few days);
g) Chronic feelings of emptiness;
h) Inappropriate, intense anger or difficulty controlling anger (e.g., frequent displays of temper, constant anger, recurrent physical fights);
i) Transient, stress-related paranoid ideation or severe dissociative symptoms.

Conclusions

Genetics and experiences in relation to caregivers condition the character traits that will condition how people relate to themselves and to others. When attachment is unsafe in childhood, there is a much stronger likelihood of developing pathological symptoms and personality disorders in adulthood.

Taking into account that the origin of the malaise has had a different origin in each person, the treatment must also adapt to the characteristics of the individuals who come in search of psychological treatment. In this chapter, I have proposed different approaches in the sequence of treatment based on the predominant attachment in the person; this guide is indicative and can be modified depending on the characteristics and needs of the therapy.

The PARCUVE model presents some symptoms and personality traits that will occur in individuals so that they can regulate themselves in relation to caregivers in childhood and to peers in adolescence and adulthood. Knowing the origin of the problems with which our patients come to therapy is a fundamental element to help them overcome them in a definitive way. According to the predominant attachment in the person, this guide is indicative and can be modified depending on the characteristics and needs of the therapy.

Getting to know the person, with their fears and their concerns as well as what happened that made them regulate themselves in a way that is currently pathological, allows us to make a reverse journey to the one that has been experienced. This way the patient can go back to all the situations in which he was afraid or in which he felt alone but can look at them with the eyes of the person he is today. If the therapist becomes a transient attachment figure during a certain stage, the patient becomes the attachment figure that was missing when he was a child.

References

American Psychiatric Association. (2013). *Diagnostic and statistical manual of mental disorders* (5th ed.). APA.

Bourassa, K. (2010). *Compulsive caregiving: Emotional parentification in childhood and its association with romantic relationships in late adolescence and early adulthood.* University of Arizona.

Bowlby, J. (1983). *Attachment and loss: Volume III. Loss*. Basic Books.

Bowlby, J. (1985). *Attachment and loss: Volume II. Separation.* Basic Books.

Bowlby, J. (1993). *Attachment and loss: Volume I. Attachment.* Basic Books.

Brown, D. P., & Elliott, D. S. (2016). *Attachment disturbances in adults. Treatments for comprehensive repairs*. Norton.

Crittenden, P. (2015). *Raising parents: Attachment, representation, and treatment.* Routledge.

Dozier, M., Stovall-McClough, K. C., & Albus, K. E. (2008). Attachment and psychopathology in adulthood. In J. Cassidy & P. Shaver (Eds.), *Handbook of attachment. Theory, research, and clinical applications* (pp. 718–744). Guilford.

Hart, S. (2011). *The impact of attachment*. Norton.

Hernandez, M. (2020). *Apego, disociación y trauma. Trabajo práctico con el modelo PARCUVE.* Desclee de Brouwer

Hill, D. (2015). *Affect regulation theory. A clinical model*. Norton.

Katehakis, A. (2016). *Sex adiction as affect dysregulation. A neurobiologically informed holistic treatment*. Norton.

Liotti, G. (2004). 1 trauma, dissociation, and disorganized attachment: Three strands of a single braid psychotherapy. *Theory, Research, Practice, Training, 41*, 472–486.

Mallinger, A., & De Wize, J. (1993). *Too perfect: When being in control gets out of control*. Random House Publishing.

Mikulincer, M., & Shaver, P. R. (2007). *Attachment in adulthood. Structures, dynamic and change*. Guilford Press.

Millon, T. (2011). *Personality disorders in modern life*. Wiley.

Sapolsky, R. M. (2004). *Why zebras don't get ulcers: The acclaimed guide to stress, stress-related diseases, and coping*. Holt Paperback.

Panksepp, J., & Biven, L. (2012). *The archeology of mind. Neuroevolutionary origins of humans emotions*. Norton.

Schore, A. (2001). The effects of a secure attachment relationship on roght brain development, affect regulation & infant mental health. *Infant Mental Health Journal, 22*, 7–66.

Index

For Product Safety Concerns and Information please contact our EU representative GPSR@taylorandfrancis.com
Taylor & Francis Verlag GmbH, Kaufingerstraße 24, 80331 München, Germany

www.ingramcontent.com/pod-product-compliance
Lightning Source LLC
Chambersburg PA
CBHW050629280326
41932CB00015B/2577

* 9 7 8 1 0 4 1 0 8 6 4 3 7 *